Nikon® D40/D40x Digital Field Guide

David D. Busch

1807
WILEY
2007

Wiley Publishing, Inc.

Nikon® D40/D40x Digital Field Guide

Published by
Wiley Publishing, Inc.
111 River Street
Hoboken NJ 07030-5774
www.wiley.com

Copyright © 2007 by Wiley Publishing, Inc., Indianapolis, Indiana

Published simultaneously in Canada

ISBN: 978-0-470-17148-6

Manufactured in the United States of America

10 9 8 7 6 5 4 3 2 1

For general information on our other products and services or to obtain technical support, please contact our Customer Care Department within the U.S. at (800) 762-2974, outside the U.S. at (317) 572-3993 or fax (317) 572-4002.

Wiley also publishes its books in a variety of electronic formats. Some content that appears in print may not be available in electronic books.

Library of Congress Control Number: 2007933277

WILEY

About the Author

David D. Busch was a roving photojournalist for more than 20 years, illustrating his books, magazine articles, and newspaper reports with award-winning images before he turned full time to writing and illustrating books. He has operated his own commercial studio, suffocated in formal dress while shooting weddings-for-hire, and shot sports for a daily newspaper and Upstate New York college. His photos have been published in magazines as diverse as *Scientific American* and *Petersen's PhotoGraphic*, and his articles have appeared in *Popular Photography & Imaging, The Rangefinder, The Professional Photographer*, and hundreds of other publications. He has reviewed dozens of digital cameras for CNet Networks and *Computer Shopper*.

When About.com named its top five books on Beginning Digital Photography, occupying the first two slots were Busch's *Digital Photography All-in-One Desk Reference For Dummies*, and *Mastering Digital Photography*. He has published more than 90 other books since 1983, including best-sellers *Digital SLR Cameras & Photography For Dummies*, and *Digital Photography For Dummies Quick Reference*.

Busch earned top category honors in the Computer Press Awards the first two years they were given (for *Sorry About The Explosion* and *Secrets of MacWrite, MacPaint and MacDraw*) and later served as Master of Ceremonies for the awards.

Credits

Acquisitions Editor
Courtney Allen

Project Editor
Cricket Krengel

Technical Editor
Benjamin D. Holland

Copy Editor
Lauren Kennedy

Editorial Manager
Robyn B. Siesky

Vice President & Group Executive Publisher
Richard Swadley

Vice President & Publisher
Barry Pruett

Business Manager
Amy Knies

Sr. Marketing Manager
Sandy Smith

Project Coordinator
Adrienne Martinez

Graphics and Production Specialists
Stacie Brooks
Denny Hager
Jennifer Mayberry

Quality Control Technician
John Greenough

Proofreading
Broccoli Information Management

Indexing
Sherry Massey

Special Help
Christina Wolfgang

Wiley Bicentennial Logo
Richard J. Pacifico

For Cathy.

Acknowledgments

Thanks to Courtney Allen, who is always a joy to work with, for her valuable input as this book developed; to Cricket Krengel for keeping the project on track; and to tech editor Ben Holland. Finally, thanks again to my agent, Carol McClendon, who has the amazing ability to keep both publishers and authors happy.

Contents

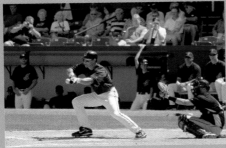

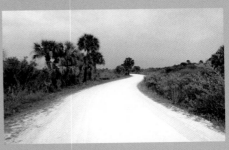

Chapter 2: Nikon D40/D40x Essentials 41

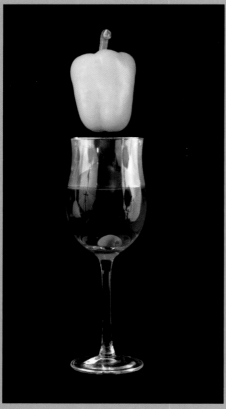

Chapter 3: Setting Up Nikon D40/D40x 51

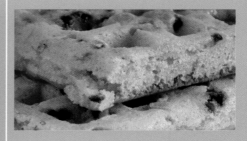

Part II: Creating Great Photos with the Nikon D40/D40x   65

Chapter 4: Exposure Essentials   67

Chapter 5: All About Lenses   79

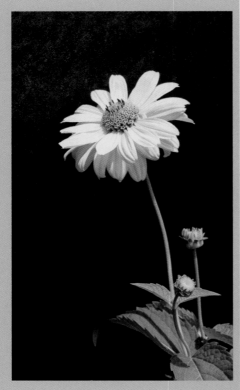

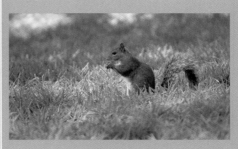

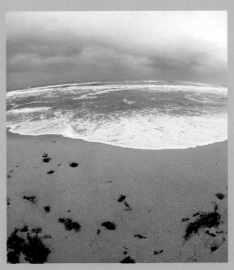

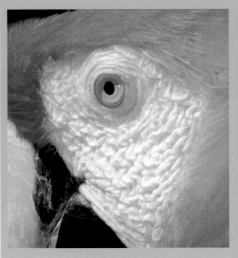

Introduction

This is my fifth Digital Field Guide devoted to a Nikon digital SLR (dSLR), and my seventh Digital Field Guide overall, and it's been one of the most enjoyable to work on. The company that we old-timers still think of as Nippon Kogaku (Japan Optical), but now goes by the moniker Nikon, has really outdone itself with its new Nikon D40 and D40X cameras. This descendant of the pioneering and wildly popular Nikon D70/D70s had a high bar to leap, but the Nikon D40 and D40X have set new standards as an ultra-compact, ultra-friendly entry-level camera for those looking for a lot of photographic prowess in a small package.

Indeed, the D40 and D40X include many of the same features found in Nikon's more upscale models, like the Nikon D80, for a lower price. If you want a flexible camera with good performance and excellent image quality, this camera is tough to beat. It's an incredible camera in its own right and can serve as a worthy companion for anyone using one of Nikon's pricier cameras.

What Nikon has done is take many of the features that were less than perfect in the D70/D70s, and upgrade them, while adopting some useful features from the D80. For example, the D40/D40X's eyelevel viewfinder is big and bright, much improved over that of Nikon's original digital SLR series, and the back panel color LCD is a huge and brilliant 2.5-inches (diagonally).

Instead of a top panel LCD with status information, Nikon has placed all the menus and shooting data on the back LCD, where it's readily accessible while shooting. The new camera is quite D80-like in its D40x version (using a similar 10.2 megapixel sensor), and includes a useful Function button that I use to switch between several different shooting modes on the fly. The D40X has a more useful ISO 100 minimum sensitivity setting, and it uses more petite memory cards. What's not to like about this pair of powerful, bargain-priced cameras?

Well, the manual that's furnished with the camera is not the best. It's thorough and complete, but doesn't explain things as clearly as it could, and you frequently must flip back and forth among two or three cross-references to find everything you need to know. That's one of the reasons I wrote this book: To provide an easy-to-understand introduction to the Nikon D40 and D40X and their features, accompanied by chapters on basic photographic concepts and techniques, and a series of recipes you can use to take great pictures in many of the most common shooting situations.

The Nikon D40/D40X's Advantages

There is a lot that's new about the D40 andD40X, but there's a great deal to like about what these cameras share with their predecessors and the other models in the Nikon line. Here are some of them:

✦ **Nikon lenses.** Nikon has a vast selection of lenses, including the 18-55mm and 18-135mm *kit* lenses, which offer lots of versatility and performance at economical prices. You can find dozens of other compatible AF-S lenses available from Nikonthat provide excellent value. Of the other digital camera vendors, very few can match Nikon's broad selection of lenses that any photographer can afford.

✦ **Full feature set.** You don't give up anything in terms of essential features when it comes to the Nikon D40/D40X. It has significant advantages over the D70/D70s it replaced, and rivals its more expensive sibling, the D80, in many ways. The D40/D40X has a large memory buffer, improved color LCD, a nifty black-and-white photography mode, and the ability to shoot both unprocessed RAW files and three quality levels of JPEG format files.

✦ **Fast operation.** The Nikon D40 and D40X operate more quickly than many other digital SLRs. It includes a memory buffer that's more than twice as large as the one found in some dSLRs, so you can shoot continuously for a longer period of time. It also writes images to the memory card rapidly. Many D40/D40X users report being able to fire off shots as almost as quickly as they can press the shutter release, for as long as their index finger (or memory card) holds out.

One popular low-end dSLR takes as long as three seconds after power-up before it can take a shot. If you don't take a picture for a while, it goes to sleep and you have to wait another three seconds to activate it each time. The D40/D40X switches on instantly and fires with virtually no shutter lag. (Actually, it uses so little juice when idle that you can leave it on for days at a time without depleting the battery much.) Performance-wise, the D40/D40X compares favorably with digital cameras costing much more. Unless you need a burst mode capable of more than two-and-a-half or three frames per second, this camera is likely to be faster than you are.

✦ **Great expandability.** There are tons of add-ons you can buy that work great with the D40/D40X. These include bellows and extension rings for close-up photography, and at least three different electronic flash units from Nikon and third parties that cooperate with the camera's through-the-lens metering system. Because Nikon dSLRs have been around for awhile, there are lots of accessories available, new or used, and Nikon cameras are always among the first to be served by new gadgets as they're developed.

Where to Go from Here

If you're brand new to digital photography and digital SLRs, you should spend a lot of time with the Quick Tour, which includes all the basic information you need to learn just enough to go out and begin taking pictures. There's no need to memorize all the controls and learn what every function is. You can learn more making a few basic settings and then going out and enjoying yourself by taking a few hundred great photographs.

Within a short period of time, you'll be eager to learn more, and you can begin reading Chapter 1 to discover the location and function of all the dials, buttons, and other controls that are on the D40/D40X. You can learn about different exposure options in Chapter 2, how to use automatic exposure, work with the retouch menu to fix red-eye defects, or do minor fix-ups of your photos.

When you're ready to customize the more advanced settings of your camera, you can find everything you need to know in Chapter 3. But I think you probably want to take a detour first into the photography basics chapters of this book. Learn about exposure in Chapter 4, discover how lenses work and how to select the lenses you need in Chapter 5, and read everything you need to know about working with electronic flash and natural light in Chapter 6.

And should you want some tips for taking pictures under a variety of photo situations, you can find discussions of photo subjects like animal and action photography, fireworks, landscapes, sunsets, and close-up photography in Chapter 7. This chapter also discusses recommended lenses, settings, accessories, and shooting techniques to get the kind of pictures you expect from your D40 or D40X.

Because this is a field guide, rather than a software manual, you won't find instructions in this book about how to use Photoshop or similar programs. In Chapter 8, you can find an introduction to Nikon Capture NX and other tools. If you're having trouble with your D40/D40X, you might find the troubleshooting tips in the Appendix helpful.

That's a lot of material to cover in a guidebook that I hope you carry along with you as you go out in the field with your D40/D40X; I hope I've given you the help you need to take the kind of pictures you expect.

Shooting Your First D40/D40x Picture

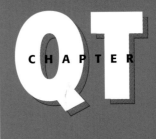

Even if you know nothing about photography, you can be taking great pictures five minutes after you slip your Nikon D40 or D40x out of that shiny gold box. The camera is smart enough to choose the correct exposure settings for you, focus a sharp, clear image, pop up the flash if there isn't enough light, and snap a winning shot at the press of a button. All you need to do is charge the battery, insert a digital memory card, and remember to take off the lens cap.

Go ahead. If you haven't already, see for yourself just how easy the D40 or D40x is to use. Rotate the lever in the upper right corner of the camera to the On position. Spin the large Mode dial on the upper right top surface of the camera to the green AUTO camera icon. Bring the camera to your eye, and when you see something you want to capture, press the shutter release button (it's located exactly where you'd expect it to be, on top of the hand grip.) You hear a comforting *click*, and the photo you just took displays on the big color LCD panel on the back of the D40/D40x. That's all there is to it.

After you've snapped a couple good photos flying solo, you can still be taking better pictures if you take the time to read through this Quick Tour. Although the D40/D40x is a digital single lens reflex (dSLR) that works very well even if you have little or no experience with photography, the camera operates better the more you know about it.

Beginners can find everything they need to know to get started on their photo journey in this chapter. But this chapter can help even more experienced photographers, too. The basics are all here, providing a perfect prep for the more detailed chapters on your Nikon's controls and features and digital photography tips you can find later in this book. There's plenty of time to learn all that. This Quick Tour is an introduction that can help you get up to speed quickly. You can learn just the basics now, so that the good-looking images you produce during your first shooting session whet your appetite to learn more.

inside a circle with a slash through it, the universal symbol for NO).

Or, you can select one of the semiautomatic or manual modes (A, S, or M) or any of the six modes that Nikon calls Digital Vari-Program (DVP) modes for specific kinds of shooting situations.

 I explain the use of DVP, P, A, S, and M modes in more detail in Chapter 1.

Selecting a Shooting Mode

If you've been able to resist activating your D40 or D40x until now, turn it on by rotating the lever that's concentric with the shutter release clockwise to the On position. Then, choose a shooting mode for the kind of pictures you want to take by using the Mode dial on the right side of the top panel of the camera (see figure QT.1). If you're willing to let the camera make all the decisions for you, rotate the Mode dial to the P (programmed exposure) or Auto (full auto exposure) settings. Either of these exposure settings work well for most picture-taking situations.

The main difference between the two is that in Auto (a sort of "fail-safe" mode) the built-in electronic flash pops up automatically when needed, and the D40/D40x locks in the settings so you can't change them. In P (programmed exposure) mode, you need to elevate the flash yourself when the "Subject is too dark" message appears on the LCD panel on the back of the camera. You can override the camera's settings to make your pictures darker or lighter if you choose.

In addition to regular Auto, an Auto "no flash" mode exists which disables the built-in flash unit (it looks like a lightning bolt

Full auto exposure

Programmed exposure

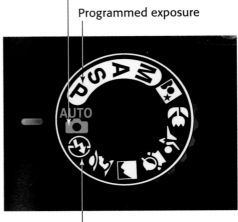

Full auto exposure
(Flash Off)

QT.1 Set the Mode dial to P (Programmed exposure), Full auto exposure, or Full auto exposure (Flash Off) if you want the D40 or D40x to make all the shooting decisions for you.

These shooting situations include portraits, landscapes, children, action pictures, close-ups, and night portraits. These modes make all the adjustments on your behalf and, at the same time, limit how much fine-tuning you can do. DVP modes give you a high percentage of good shots, but once you become more familiar with the camera, you can probably do a better job of tweaking the

Landscape

Child | Portrait

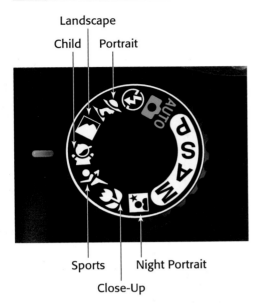

Sports | Night Portrait

Close-Up

QT.2 Automatic and Digital Vari-Program modes program all the basic settings for you.

settings yourself. That's especially true when you want to make adjustments for creative purposes, say, to make a picture lighter or darker to produce a specific mood or look. The modes are as follows:

✦ **Full Auto.** *When to Use:* When you're taking quickie shots, or when friends who aren't familiar with your D40 or D40x use it.

Don't Use: If you want absolutely consistent exposure from picture to picture. The Full Auto setting treats each shot as a new picture, and may change the exposure if you shoot from a different angle, or compose your image slightly differently. The Full Auto (Flash Off) mode is the same, but the built-in flash is disabled.

✦ **Portrait.** *When to Use:* When you're shooting a portrait of a subject close to the camera.

Don't Use: If your portrait subject is not the closest object to the camera, as the Portrait mode optimizes exposure and tones for the subjects nearest to the lens.

✦ **Landscape.** *When to Use:* When you want extra-sharp images and vivid colors of distant landscapes.

Don't Use: If you want to use flash to brighten shadows cast on human subjects who are also in the photo, as Landscape mode disables the D40 or D40x's built-in electronic flash.

✦ **Child.** *When to Use:* When you want vivid colors for clothing and background, and soft, lifelike skin tones.

Don't Use: When a more subtle look is desired, especially for photographs of older children, teens, or adults.

✦ **Sports.** *When to Use:* When you're taking any kind of action photography of moving subjects.

Don't Use: When you don't want a frozen look. Because Sports mode uses fast shutter speeds to freeze the action, avoid this DVP setting if you want to shoot subjects, such as motor sports, that often look best when a little blur remains to add a feeling of motion.

✦ **Close-Up.** *When to Use:* When you're shooting small animals, blossoms, stamps and collectibles, and other objects closer than one foot to the camera, and centered in the viewfinder.

Don't Use: If you want to place your subject somewhere other than in the center of the frame, or if you'd like to focus on one special part of the subject in order to highlight it.

Cross-Reference *These modes are discussed in much more detail in Chapter 1.*

✦ **Night Portrait.** *When to Use:* If you're shooting at night and want to illuminate the subjects in the foreground with flash while also allowing the background to be properly exposed.

Don't Use: If you are unable to hold the camera steady, or can't use a tripod or other steadying device during the long exposures this mode often produces.

If you already have some knowledge about using shutter speeds and f-stops, you might want to use one of these more advanced modes:

✦ **Program.** *When to Use:* When you want your camera to make the basic settings, with the option of switching to a different f-stop or shutter speed, or dialing in a little more or less exposure to tweak your photograph.

Don't Use: If you don't understand how these settings affect your picture.

✦ **Shutter Priority.** *When to Use:* When you'd like to use a certain shutter speed to freeze action, reduce the effects of camera shake, or allow moving objects to blur in creative ways. The D40 or D40x selects an f-stop appropriate for the shutter speed you've chosen.

Don't Use: If there is too much or too little light to produce a good exposure at the shutter speed you select.

Aperture Priority

Manual exposure

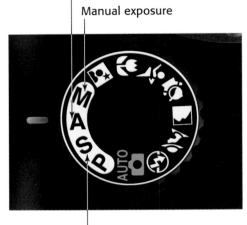

Shutter Priority

QT.3 Shutter Priority, Aperture Priority, and Manual exposure

✦ **Aperture Priority.** *When to Use:* When you want to use a certain lens opening, to control the range of sharpness of your image (*depth of field*). The D40 or D40x selects a shutter speed appropriate for the aperture you've selected.

Don't Use: If there is too much or too little light for a good exposure with the f-stop you've specified.

✦ **Manual.** *When to Use:* When you want to set the shutter speed and f-stop yourself, either for creative reasons, or because you are using an older lens that isn't compatible with the D40 or D40x's exposure metering system.

Don't Use: If you are unable to set exposure properly.

Selecting a focus mode

Your Nikon D40 or D40x can focus for you automatically if you are using an autofocus lens with the letters AF-S in its name, which signifies that the lens has an autofocus motor built into the lens itself. To activate the autofocus function, you must set the camera focus mode to one of the AF positions (AF-C, AF-S, or AF-A), rather than the Manual focus (M) setting. Some lenses, including the 18-55mm, 18-70mm, and 18-135mm, often sold as *kit* lenses with Nikon cameras, include an M/A or M/A-M switch on the barrel of the lens. You should set the focus to A or M/A on the lens. When you set the D40/D40x's lens to M/A, focus is automatic, but you can override the camera's focus setting by rotating the focus ring on the lens to manually focus.

 Note *The focus ring on your lens may be the innermost or outermost ring; it depends on the lens.*

When you set the lens autofocus/manual switch or the camera's focus mode to M, you must focus manually at all times.

When you set both the D40 or D40x and lens for automatic focus, you can initiate focusing by pressing the shutter release halfway. The area, or zone, used to calculate focus is represented in the viewfinder screen by one or more of the three brackets that are briefly illuminated in red (see figure QT.5). If you've selected a DVP mode other than Close-Up, the D40 or D40x chooses the focus zone that coincides with the subject closest to the camera. If you select the Close-Up DVP mode, the focus zone defaults to the center zone.

Lens autofocus/manual switch

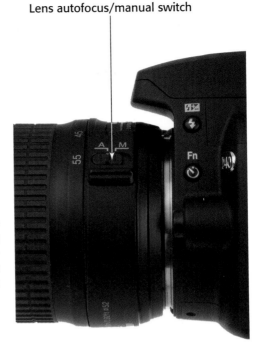

QT.4 The lens focus mode selector switch chooses autofocus or manual focus modes.

 Cross-Reference *In Sports or Close-Up DVP mode and the other non-scene shooting modes, you can set the camera so you may choose which focus zone is used, as noted in Chapter 1.*

When the autofocus mechanism locks in the correct focus point, or when you focus manually and achieve correct focus, a green light in the viewfinder glows (see figure QT.5). If you want the focus and exposure to lock at the current settings, so you can adjust the composition or take several similar photographs in succession, press and hold down the AE-L/AF-L button located to the right of the viewfinder.

Focus zone

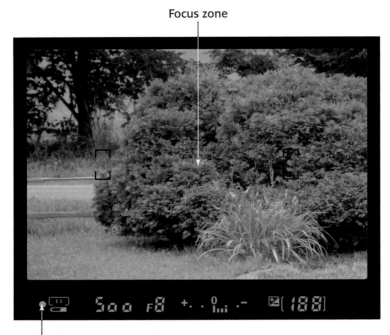

Focus Confirmation indicator

QT.5 The Focus Confirmation indicator in the lower-left corner of the viewfinder glows when correct focus is achieved.

Using the self-timer and remote controls

Perhaps you want to get into the photo yourself, or activate the D40 or D40x from a few feet away. Maybe the light is dim and you expect a long exposure and want to avoid shaking the camera when you press the shutter release. Mount the camera on a tripod and use either the D40/D40x's built-in self-timer or the optional Nikon ML-L3 infrared remote control (see figure QT.6.) Both of these features allow you to shoot shake-free pictures without the need to press the shutter release manually.

You can activate the 10-second self-timer by pressing the Fn/Self-timer button on the

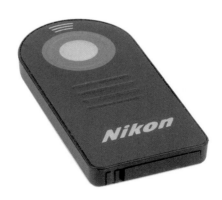

QT.6 The Nikon ML-L3 infrared remote control allows you to trigger the camera from several feet away.

left side of the lens mount (unless you've redefined this button to perform another function instead, as described in Chapter 3). You can also switch to the self-timer or activate the infrared remote control by following these steps:

1. **Press the Settings button in the lower left corner of the back panel of the camera.**

2. **Use the multi selector to navigate to the Shooting mode area (your selection is highlighted in orange), and press the center OK button.**

3. **Press the down portion of the multi selector to highlight the Self-timer icon, Quick Response, or Delayed Response Remote icons.** Press OK to make your selection.

4. **To use the self-timer to take a photo, frame your picture and press the shutter release button down all the way when you're ready to take a photo.** The self-timer starts, a white light on the front of the camera blinks, and a beep sounds. Two seconds before the camera takes the picture, the white light stops blinking and the beeping speeds up.

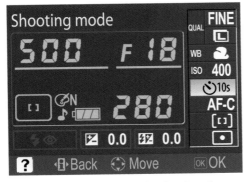

QT.7 Switch to the self-timer in Shooting Mode.

You can also take a picture by using the ML-L3 infrared remote. This inexpensive device activates the camera only from the front, because the infrared sensor is on the front of the hand grip. The range is about 16 feet. The Delayed Response Remote option produces a two second pause, while the Quick Response Remote activates the shutter immediately. Figure QT.8 shows the Quick Response Remote and Delayed Response Remote icons.

QT.8 The Quick Response Remote (left) and Delayed Response Remote (right) icons

Reviewing Your Pictures

Once you take your first picture, the image appears for review on the LCD on the back panel of the camera by default (you can turn the review display off). You can also turn on display by pressing the Playback button. If you want to delete the image, press the Delete button (located to the lower right corner of the LCD). A confirmation screen appears asking if you really want to remove the image. Press the Delete button a second time to permanently delete the photo, or press the Playback button to cancel.

To review all the pictures you've taken, press the Playback button. The most recent image appears on the LCD screen. Press the Right button on the multi-selector cursor keys to move forward from pictures taken earlier to later shots. Press the Left button to move backwards among the images stored on your memory card. You can also rotate the command dial left or right to review your images in forward or reverse order.

As you scroll through your pictures, the display wraps around so that when the last image you've taken is displayed, the first one you shot appears next. The Up and Down buttons change the type and amount of shooting information about each image that appears on the LCD.

 Cross-Reference *Learn how to use the various playback information options in Chapter 2.*

You can access other playback options by using the buttons in figure QT.9:

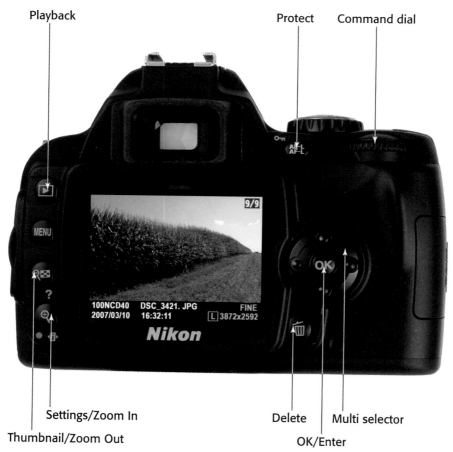

Playback

Protect   Command dial

Settings/Zoom In

Thumbnail/Zoom Out

Delete   Multi selector

OK/Enter

QT.9 Press the Playback button and use the right and left directional keys on the multi selector to scroll forward and back through the pictures you've taken on the LCD display. The up and down keys on the multi selector adjust the type of shooting information that appears and the picture.

✦ **Thumbnail/Zoom Out.** When a full-screen image appears, press the Thumbnail/Zoom Out button to change to a display of four thumbnail images. Press the button a second time to switch to a nine-thumbnail display.

✦ **Settings/Zoom In.** When viewing thumbnail images, press the Settings/Zoom In button to change from a nine-thumbnail display to a four-thumbnail display, or from four thumbnails to a full-screen image.

When viewing a full-screen image on the LCD, press the Settings/Zoom In button to zoom in on the image. Press the Thumbnail/Zoom Out button to zoom back out again. An inset miniature version of the image with a yellow highlighted box appears to show you the relative position of the zoomed area in the image. You can relocate the zoomed area by using the multi-selector buttons.

✦ **Multi selector.** You can use the multi selector pad to navigate among the thumbnail images to highlight any of them. You can use the command dial to move forward and backward among the thumbnails in numbered order.

✦ **OK/Enter.** When a thumbnail is highlighted, press the OK button to view that image full-screen.

✦ **Protect/AE-L/AF-L.** Press the Protect/AE-L/AF-L button (to the right of the viewfinder window with a key icon on the camera body) to protect the selected full-screen size image or thumbnail from accidental erasure. A key icon appears in the upper-right corner of the displayed image on the LCD to show that the image is protected.

✦ **Delete.** Press the Delete button to erase a selected image.

Correcting Exposure

If the last photograph you took is too light or too dark, you can make a correction for the next picture taken under the same lighting conditions by using the D40 or D40x's Exposure Compensation feature. Hold down the Exposure Compensation button (see figure QT.10) and rotate the command dial to the left (to reduce exposure and make the next image darker) or to the right (to increase exposure and make the next photo lighter). The LCD status display shows the amount of compensation you've dialed in, such as −0.3 or +1.0, and an exposure scale in the viewfinder (see the bottom of figure QT.10) displays the additional or reduced exposure.

Exposure compensation button

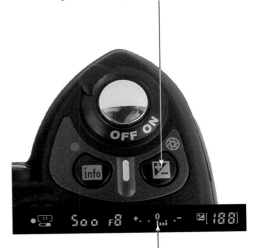

View Finder readout

QT.10 Hold down the Exposure Compensation button and spin the command dial to increase or decrease exposure.

The D40 or D40x adds or subtracts exposure compensation in one-third Exposure Value (EV) increments, with a whole EV step producing twice as much or half as much exposure. (In Chapter 2, you can learn how to change the size of the increment from one-half to one-third step, or vice versa.) When correcting exposure, it's best to increase or decrease the setting by one increment (one-third EV) to start, and then add or subtract more exposure if your first try doesn't produce the look you want.

 You can read more about setting exposure in Chapter 4.

Transferring Images to Your Computer

You can link your D40 or D40x to your computer directly by using the supplied Universal Serial Bus (USB) cable or remove the memory card from the camera and insert it into a card reader.

To connect by using the USB cable:

1. **Turn the camera off.**

2. **Open the rubber cover that protects the D40 or D40x's USB connection.** Plug the USB cable furnished with the camera into the port, as shown in figure QT.11.

3. **Plug the other end of the cable into any USB port on your computer.**

4. **Turn the camera on.**

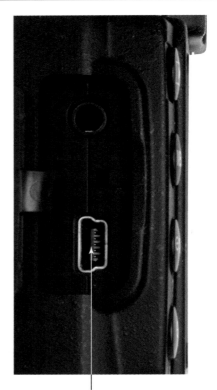

USB port

QT.11 Plug the USB cable for the camera into the USB port on the side of the D40 or D40x, and connect the other end to any USB port on your desktop or laptop computer.

5. **Your operating system (Windows or Mac OS), or software you may have installed (such as Adobe Photoshop Elements 5.0 or Nikon Picture Project), detects the camera and pops up a dialog box that offers to transfer the pictures to your computer.** Alternatively, the camera may appear on your desktop as a mass storage device, which you can open and then drag-and-drop the photos to your computer.

To connect by using a card reader:

1. **Turn the camera off.**

2. **Slide the memory card door on the right side of the camera open and press down on the memory card.** It pops up so you can remove it.

3. **Insert the memory card into the Secure Digital (SD) card slot on your memory card reader.** The reader may be an external device or a device built into your desktop or laptop computer.

4. **Your operating system (Windows or Mac OS), or software you may have installed (such as Adobe Photoshop Elements 5.0 or Nikon Picture Project), detects the memory card and produces a dialog box that offers to transfer the pictures to your computer.** Alternatively, the memory card may appear on your desktop as a mass storage device, which you can open and then drag-and-drop the photos to your computer.

Using the Nikon D40/D40x

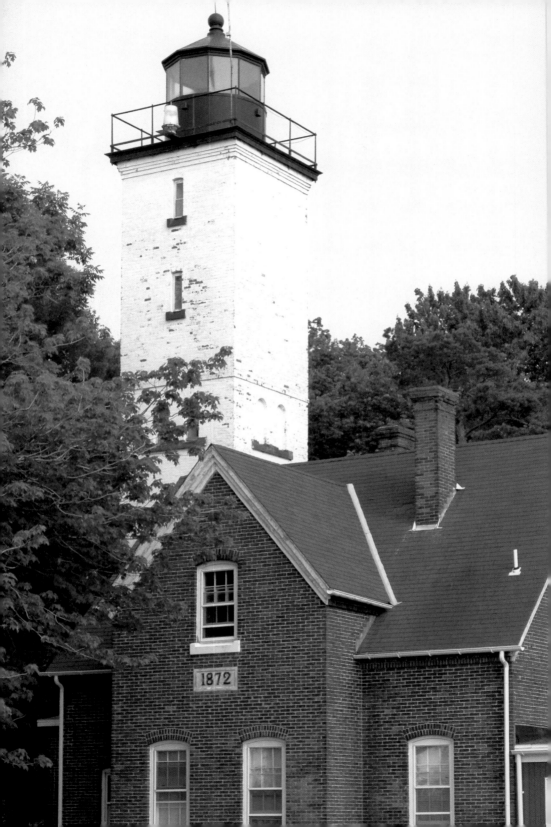

Exploring the Nikon D40/D40x

◆ ◆ ◆ ◆

I f you found the Quick Tour of your Nikon D40/D40x enlightening, you're probably ready to dive into a deeper exploration of the features of your camera, so you can master all the functions of the various buttons, dials, wheels, switches, and levers that dot the surface. There are a lot of them, but having so many dedicated controls helps you work faster. You can access the most-used functions of the D40/D40x by pressing a button and turning a command dial.

You can adjust other features through the D40/D40x's LCD display and quick-access menu interface. However, this chapter deals only with the physical controls on the camera body itself. I explain how to use the basic features, such as metering and autofocus, in Chapter 2. In Chapter 3, I provide a complete set-up guide with an explanation of the camera's thicket of menus.

Once you've taken the time to learn the functions of the D40/D40x's controls, the camera is definitely much faster to use. Unlike the official manual that comes with the D40 and D40x, this field guide provides individual full-color photographs of the camera from various views so you can quickly identify a control or component you want to locate. You should find this approach much friendlier than the original manual's tiny black-and-white line drawings, each bristling with numbered callouts that you must cross-reference against a lengthy list with two or three dozen labels.

◆ ◆ ◆ ◆

Up Front

Figure 1.1 shows the Nikon D40/D40x from the front view. To hold your camera steady and keep all the major controls at your fingertips, wrap your right hand around the handgrip and place your left hand underneath, supporting the underside of the lens with your thumb and index finger on the zoom ring.

By using this grip, you can reach the shutter release button with the index finger of your right hand and quickly turn the camera on or off with the same finger. While you keep the camera steady with your left hand (especially helpful under dim illumination for slower shutter speeds), your fingers are free to manipulate controls on that side of the D40/D40x, including the zoom ring, the focus ring (if you're adjusting focus manually), the electronic flash flip-up button, and the Function (Fn) button, which serves as a short-cut to features you specify (see Chapter 3). I explain all these controls later

in this chapter. Here you see two views of the front of the camera, from left and right angles (as seen from the photographer's position).

✦ **Autofocus assist illuminator/ self-timer lamp/red-eye reduction lamp.** This front-mounted white LED serves three different functions. When available illumination is dim, the lamp can flash to provide enough light to increase the contrast so the automatic focus mechanism can function. (You can disable this feature when it might prove obtrusive or distracting.) In self-timer mode, the lamp blinks during the delay period, serving as a countdown to the actual exposure. When you're using flash, the front panel lamp can issue a burst of light just before the exposure, which can help contract the pupils in your subjects' eyes and reduce the red-eye effect.

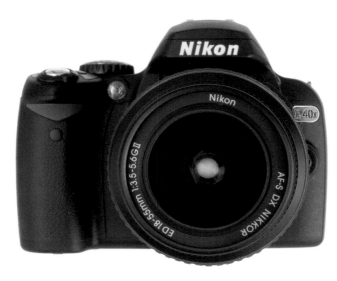

1.1 A front view of the Nikon D40/D40x

Autofocus assist illuminator/
self-timer lamp/red-eye reduction lamp

Shutter release

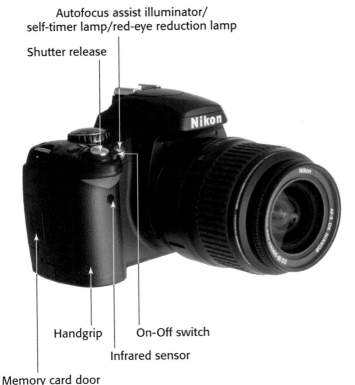

Handgrip | On-Off switch

Infrared sensor

Memory card door

1.2 The right front side of the Nikon D40/D40x

✦ **Shutter release.** Partially depress this button to lock exposure and focus settings. Press the button all the way down to take the picture. Tapping the shutter release when the camera has turned off the auto exposure and autofocus mechanisms to conserve battery power reactivates both. When a review image appears on the LCD, tapping this button removes the image from the display and reactivates the auto exposure and autofocus mechanisms.

✦ **Infrared receiver.** This dark red window receives an infrared signal from the optional ML-L3 remote control. Note that the receiver's position on the front panel of the D40/D40x means that you can't easily use it when standing behind the camera. You need to move to one side, stand in front of the camera, or reach over the camera to activate it.

✦ **On-Off switch.** Rotate this switch one notch to turn the camera on.

✦ **Memory card door.** Slide this door towards the back of the camera to reveal the camera's Secure Digital (SD) memory card.

✦ **Handgrip.** The handgrip serves as a comfortable handle for the D40/D40x that you can clasp with your fingers to support the camera. It also serves as the storage receptacle for the camera's battery.

The right side of the D40/D40x has a complement of controls, as you can see in figure 1.3. These include

✦ **Flash mode button.** Press this button to pop up the built-in electronic flash (see figure 1.4). Hold down the button while rotating the command dial on the back of the camera to change flash modes, such as Auto Flash or Red-Eye Reduction mode (see Chapter 6 for a full explanation of options). Hold

down the Flash Compensation button (located southeast of the shutter release) while holding down this button to add or subtract from the flash exposure to make your picture lighter or darker.

✦ **Function/Self-Timer button.** You can define the feature activated by this button (learn how in Chapter 3) so you can quickly access a feature of your choice, say, to change white balance or ISO sensitivity. The Fn button defaults to the self-timer function, but you can change it (as explained in Chapter 3) to another use.

✦ **Lens release button.** Hold down this button while rotating the lens to remove the lens from the camera.

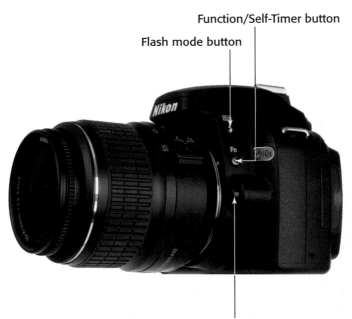

Function/Self-Timer button

Flash mode button

Lens release button

1.3 The left front side of the Nikon D40/D40x.

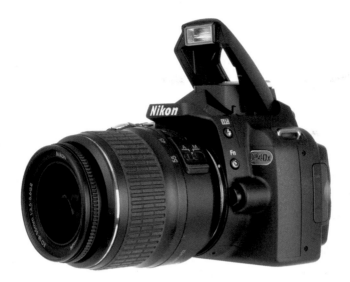

1.4 Pressing the Flash mode button pops up the built-in electronic flash, ready for use.

Sides and Bottom

The sides and bottom of the D40/D40x have only a few controls, compartments, and connectors.

Left side

On the left side of the camera you can see a rubber cover that protects the D40/D40x's primary external connectors (see figure 1.5). Underneath the top cover is an AV plug you can use to link the D40/D40x to an external monitor for viewing pictures or menus. In the middle is a reset switch button that you can press to reset all settings in the camera (including the clock). At the bottom is a port that accepts a USB cable for transferring pictures directly from the camera to your computer and also allows you to control the camera's functions by using the Nikon Camera Control Pro software (see figure 1.6).

Video connector/Reset switch/ USB port cover

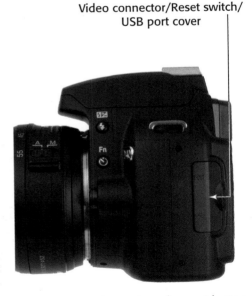

1.5 Two connector ports and a reset button hide beneath this rubber cover.

Reset switch

Video connector

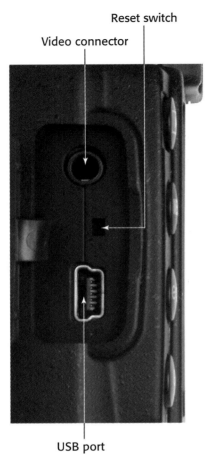

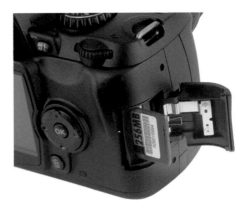

1.7 A memory card fits into the slot on the side of the camera.

Bottom

On the bottom of the Nikon D40/D40x, there is a tripod socket, and a flip-open door accepts a single EN-EL9 rechargeable lithium ion battery, as shown in figure 1.8. There is also a fold-down door to allow you to plug in the optional EH-5 AC adapter and EP-5 AC adapter connector.

USB port

1.6 Your USB and video devices plug into these connectors.

For more instructions on connecting to a computer and transferring images, see Chapter 8.

Right side

The right side of the camera has only a single door that slides back toward you and then swings open to reveal a slot for the Secure Digital (SD) memory card (see figure 1.7). Push down on the card to release the retaining catch, and it pops out for easy removal.

AC adapter access

Battery

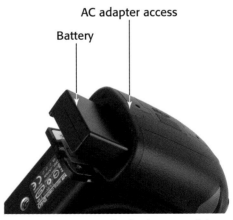

1.8 A compartment in the bottom of the D40/D40x accepts a rechargeable battery and an optional AC adapter.

On the Lens

The lenses you use with your Nikon D40/D40x each have their own set of controls. Figure 1.9 shows two lenses: the very basic 18-55mm f/3.5-5.6G ED II AF-S DX Zoom-Nikkor and the more upscale 18-200mm f/3.5-5.6G ED-IF AF-S VR DX Zoom-Nikkor vibration reduction lens. Not all lenses have all the possible controls.

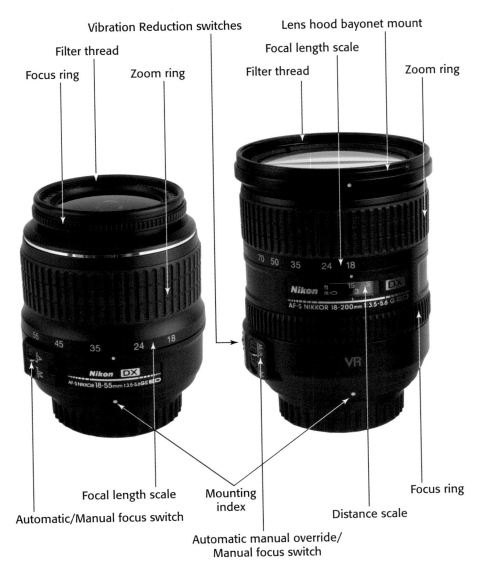

1.9 The controls found on the 18-55mm kit lens (left) and 18-200mm vibration reduction lens (right).

In fact, I'm going to have to show you a mocked-up composite lens, shown in figure 1.10, to squeeze the extra features into a single example.

By comparing the three lenses shown in figures 1.9 and 1.10, you can see that the controls may be in different locations with different lenses and can differ in size and operation. The key components shown in figure 1.9 are

✦ **Lens hood bayonet mount.** You use this lens hood bayonet mount, shown on the 18–200mm zoom for lens-specific hoods, with lenses that don't use hoods that screw into the filter ring.

✦ **Filter thread.** Most lenses have a thread on the front that you can use to attach filters and other accessories.

✦ **Focus ring.** Rotate this ring to manually focus or fine-tune focus when you set the lens or camera body focus mode switch to M. In addition, if the lens has an auto-focus/manual override position (M/A-M), you can adjust focus manually after the camera has focused automatically.

✦ **Automatic/Manual focus switch.** Changing from automatic to manual focus with the D40 or D40x is done either with an Auto/Manual focus switch on the lens, or by using a menu choice on the camera. There is no automatic/manual switch on the camera body itself. Some lenses have just a simple M-A (Manual/Automatic) switch (like the 18-55mm), while others have an M/A-M switch that indicates the

lens can be focused automatically with manual adjustment (M/A) or manually (M) as indicated in 1.9.

Note *You may notice that the 18-55mm kit lens has a much narrower focus ring than the 18-200mm lens, that the entire front element of the lens rotates during focus, and that the lens itself increases in length as you focus closer. More expensive lenses have non-rotating front elements and internal focus so the lens doesn't change in length as it focuses on nearer subjects.*

✦ **Distance scale.** This scale (shown on the 18-200mm lens, but not the 18-55 kit lens) moves in unison with the lens's focus mechanism and shows approximately the distance at which the lens has been focused. It's a useful indicator for double-checking autofocus, and for roughly setting manual focus.

✦ **Zoom ring and focal length scale.** You rotate the zoom ring to change the zoom setting. The focal length scale markings show the focal length.

✦ **Mounting index.** Match this white dot with the dot on the camera body (located at roughly 2 o'clock when you're looking at the front of the camera) to properly mount the lens.

✦ **Vibration Reduction switches.** Vibration Reduction (VR) lenses have switches that you can use to turn the vibration reduction feature on or off, or to toggle between Normal and Active mode (which makes it possible to use VR even when panning the camera).

Figure 1.10 shows a single focal length, or *prime* lens; as I explained earlier, this particular photo is a composite of more than one lens to show several features at the same time. Figure 1.10 displays some features that are not available on either of the two lenses in figure 1.9, but which you might find on some other lenses. As you might expect, this non-zooming lens doesn't have a zoom ring or zoom scale. But it does include the following:

Focus ring

Limit switch | Auto/Manual focus switch

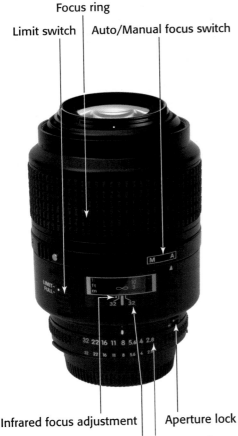

Infrared focus adjustment | Aperture lock

Depth-of-field indicator Aperture ring

1.10 This macro lens is an example of a prime (non-zoom) lens.

✦ **Limit switch.** When you use lenses that have an extensive focus range, you can see that some have a special switch that limits the range the autofocus system uses, locking out either distant subjects (when you're shooting close-up photos) or extreme macro focus distances (when you're taking photos of non-macro subjects). The limit switch can speed up focusing considerably by reducing the amount of seeking that the lens does in looking for the correct focus point.

✦ **Aperture ring.** Nikon lenses with a G suffix in their name (such as the 18-55mm f/3.5-5.6G ED II AF-S DX Zoom-Nikkor kit lens and 18-200mm f/3.5-5.6 G ED-IF AF-S VR DX Zoom-Nikkor) lack a manual aperture ring; therefore, you can only use them with cameras that are able to set the f-stop electronically from the camera body (such as all recent Nikon film and digital cameras). Lenses that retain the aperture ring, such as the lens shown in figure 1.10, have a D suffix in their names.

✦ **Depth-of-field indicator.** Some lenses have markings that show the approximate range of sharpness on the distance scale. In this case, that range is indicated only for f/32.

✦ **Infrared focus adjustment.** Infrared illumination doesn't focus at the same point as visible light. You can use the dot that appears on a few lenses to change the focus point that the lens selects or to visually focus on to the appropriate point for infrared light.

✦ **Aperture lock.** If you want to use the D40/D40x's automatic exposure system with a D-series lens, you must set the aperture ring to the smallest f-stop (in this case f/32), and lock it in that position by using the aperture lock switch. You need to unlock the aperture only if you want to use the lens with an older camera that can't set the f-stop electronically, or you are using the lens with an accessory, like an extension ring, that doesn't allow coupling with the autoexposure system.

Note *Most automatic extension rings retain full automatic exposure and focus capabilities, except when the effective maximum aperture of the lens is smaller than f/5.6. The D40/D40x needs at least that much light to operate.*

On Top

The top panel of the D40/D40x has a cluster of controls. They include

✦ **Mode dial.** You turn this knurled wheel to change among the DVP/Scene modes and Auto, Auto (Flash Off), Program, Shutter Priority, Aperture Priority, and Manual modes.

✦ **Focal plane indicator.** A few very specialized types of close-up photography require knowing precisely the plane of the camera's sensor, and the indicator, which may be hard to see, shows that plane (but not the actual location of the sensor itself).

✦ **Accessory shoe.** You can attach an external electronic flash — also known as a Speedlight, such as the Nikon SB-400, SB-600, or SB-800 — to this slide-in accessory shoe (normally covered with a piece of protective plastic), which includes multiple electrical contacts that enable two-way communication between your D40/D40x and a dedicated Speedlight (designed to work directly with compatible cameras). The communication can include exposure, distance, zoom setting, and color temperature information. You can attach other accessories as well, including radio control devices, levels, and add-on viewfinders (useful when shooting blind because an infrared filter on your lens is blocking visible light).

✦ **Shooting Information/Reset (#1) .** Press this button, marked with an Info indicator, to show the current shooting information status on the LCD. Hold down this button and the Settings/Zoom In button on the back of the camera (which has a matching green dot) to activate a reset of the camera's settings to factory default values.

✦ **Exposure Compensation/ Aperture.** Hold down this button while in Program, Shutter Priority, or Aperture Priority exposure modes and spin the command dial to add or subtract exposure from the basic setting that the auto exposure system calculates. Holding down this button in Manual mode changes the aperture. Hold down the Flash multi-button at the same time to change flash exposure compensation. Hold

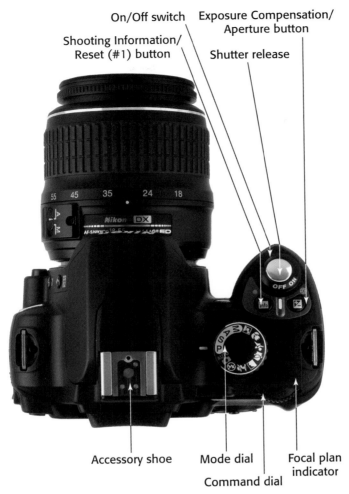

1.11 Key components on the top panel of the D40/D40x

down the Aperture button when in Manual exposure mode to adjust aperture with the command dial. (When the button is not pressed, the command dial adjusts shutter speed in Manual mode.)

✦ **On/Off switch.** Rotate this switch one notch clockwise to turn the D40/D40x on; turn it in the reverse direction to shut it off.

✦ **Shutter release.** Partially depress this button to lock exposure and focus settings. Press it all the way down to take the picture. Tapping the shutter release when the camera has turned off the auto exposure and autofocus mechanisms reactivates both. When the LCD displays a review image, tapping this button removes the image from the display and reactivates the auto exposure and autofocus mechanisms.

On the Back

The back panel of the Nikon D40 and D40x contains an array of controls, many of which do double duty. Figure 1.12 shows the back of the D40/D40x and the control center.

Upper half

The upper half of the back panel (shown in figure 1.13) has one button, a slider, and a dial. Here's what they do:

✦ **Viewfinder eyepiece and eyecup.** Peer through the viewfinder window to frame your image. The rubber eyecup shields the viewfinder from extraneous light, much like a lens hood, which is helpful because light entering the viewfinder from the rear can affect the exposure meter. The eyecup is removable and you can replace it with a cap to block that extra light when you use the camera on a tripod.

✦ **Diopter adjustment control.** Move this sliding control up or down to adjust the viewfinder's diopter correction for your eyesight if you wear glasses and would like to use the viewfinder without them, or need additional correction when using the viewfinder with your glasses.

✦ **Auto exposure/Autofocus lock/Protect image.** This button locks exposure, focus, or both, until you release the button or press the button again. A menu option, described in Chapter 3, enables you to specify the behavior of this button. In Playback mode, this button marks an image to protect it from accidental erasure.

✦ **Command dial.** Spin this dial to change settings, such as shutter speed, according to what control button you're pressed at the same time.

Lower half

The most-used buttons on the D40/D40x are located on the lower half of the camera. Most of them have more than one function, depending on the D40/D40x's current mode. If you're shooting pictures, a button may have one function, but when you're reviewing images you've already taken, the button may have another. The buttons on the left side of the camera include

✦ **Playback.** Press this button once to display the most recent photo taken. Press it again, or tap the shutter release button, to remove the image from the screen and exit Playback mode.

✦ **Menu.** Press this button to access the five levels of the Nikon D40/D40x's menus.

✦ **Thumbnail/Zoom Out/Help.** In Playback mode, when viewing a full-screen image, press the button once to change to a four-thumbnail display, and again to view nine thumbnails. To return to full-screen mode, press OK. When an image is zoomed in, press this button to zoom back out. When a menu is displayed, pressing this button activates a help screen. The Help button is a great aid when you're faced with a menu and don't know what to do next. When pressed, it brings up a brief text screen that tells you exactly what a menu or selection will do.

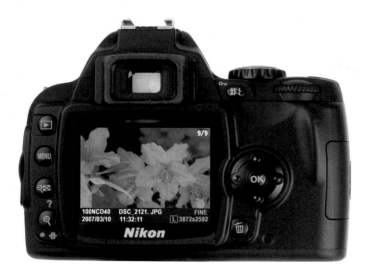

1.12 The back panel of the D40/D40x

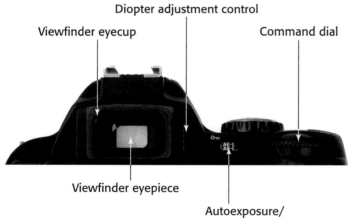

Diopter adjustment control

Viewfinder eyecup

Command dial

Viewfinder eyepiece

Autoexposure/
Autofocus lock/Protect image

1.13 Key components on the upper half of the back panel of the
D40/D40x

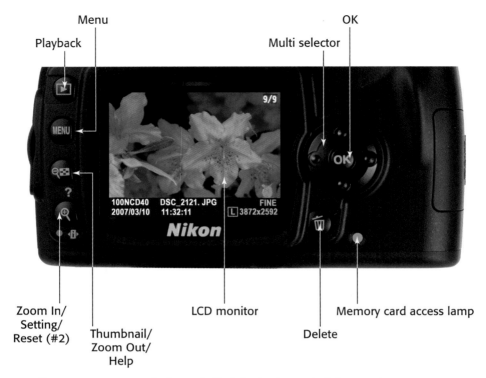

Menu   OK

Playback   Multi selector

Zoom In/   LCD monitor   Memory card access lamp
Setting/
Reset (#2)   Thumbnail/   Delete
                Zoom Out/
                Help

1.14 Key components on the lower half of the back panel of the D40/D40x

From time to time the Question Mark icon on the shooting information screen will flash. Press the Help button to receive some advice on how to fix the problem (such as "Subject is too dark").

✦ **Zoom In/Setting/Reset (#2).** In Playback mode, press this button repeatedly to zoom in several magnifications. (Use the Multi selector to move the zoomed area around in the frame.) When in a shooting mode, press this button to switch the LCD menu to setting change mode. Press this button while you hold down the Setting button on top of the camera to reset the D40 or D40x to the default settings.

In the center and right side of the lower half of the Nikon D40/D40x are the LCD monitor and several more key components:

✦ **LCD monitor.** This color LCD shows your images for review, shows the menus as you navigate through them, and has the current shooting status and settings.

✦ **Multi selector.** Press this four-way cursor button to navigate through menus, scroll through images as you review them, and change the amount of information about each image that appears on the LCD screen during picture review.

✦ **OK.** Use this button to accept setting and menu selections or to confirm choices.

✦ **Delete.** When an image appears on the LCD display, press the Delete button if you'd like to discard the image. A prompt shows up on the screen inviting you to press the Delete button again to erase the file, or the Playback button to cancel the operation.

✦ **Memory card access lamp.** This LED blinks when an image is being written to the SD memory card, and when the camera is turned on or off.

Viewfinder Display

The D40/D40x offers a great deal of information in the viewfinder. Not all of these indicators are visible at once. Here's a list of each of them, and the information they provide:

✦ **Currently selected focus area.** Shows the active focus zone.

✦ **Focus area brackets.** Displays the available focus zones.

✦ **Focus confirmation indicator.** Illuminates when an image is focused correctly.

✦ **Focus area display.** Shows the current focus area selection mode.

✦ **Auto exposure lock.** Indicates that exposure has been locked.

✦ **Battery indicator.** Displays the current power level of the battery.

✦ **Flexible program indicator.** Shows that you've adjusted the camera's calculated exposure to a different combination of shutter speed and aperture.

✦ **Shutter speed.** Displays the selected shutter speed.

✦ **Aperture.** Displays the selected lens opening.

✦ **Analog exposure display/Exposure compensation.** Shows the amount of over- or underexposure and exposure compensation (when the Exposure compensation indicator is visible).

✦ **Exposure compensation indicator.** Appears when you dial in exposure compensation.

✦ **Flash compensation indicator.** Appears when flash exposure compensation has been specified.

✦ **ISO Auto indicator.** Shows that ISO is being set automatically.

✦ **Number of exposures remaining/Other functions.** Also shows number of shots remaining before the buffer is filled, white balance present status, exposure compensation values, and the PC/USB connection status.

✦ **Flash ready indicator.** Shows when you can use electronic flash for the next shot.

✦ **Thousands of exposures.** Appears when the remaining exposures exceed 1,000.

✦ **Warning indicator.** Illuminates when an error condition exists.

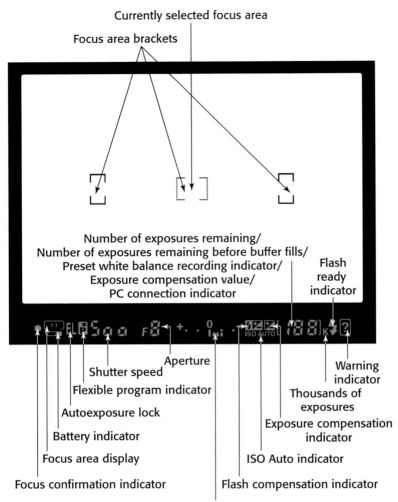

Currently selected focus area

Focus area brackets

Number of exposures remaining/
Number of exposures remaining before buffer fills/
Preset white balance recording indicator/
Exposure compensation value/
PC connection indicator

Flash ready indicator

Aperture

Shutter speed

Flexible program indicator

Autoexposure lock

Battery indicator

Focus area display

Focus confirmation indicator

Warning indicator

Thousands of exposures

Exposure compensation indicator

ISO Auto indicator

Flash compensation indicator

Analog exposure display/Exposure compensation

1.15 Viewfinder readouts and indicators

LCD Display

The color LCD display shows a broad range of current status information, including the shooting information displayed by a monochrome LCD on the top panel of other Nikon digital single lens reflex (dSLR)

cameras. This shooting information display can appear in one of three different formats, which differ both in appearance and the information the formats show.

The formats for the shooting information display are Classic, a text and icon-based format; Graphics, which uses a mixture of text, graphics, and icons; and Wallpaper, which uses a photograph you select as a background, and doesn't include shutter speed and aperture information. All illustrations in this book use the Classic format for the shooting information display, which provides the maximum amount of information with the best readability. If you'd prefer to use one of the other shooting information

displays, I show you how to do that in Chapter 3.

I have divided the screen into two figures. Figure 1.16 shows the information clustered around the center status area. Figure 1.17 shows the remaining information indicators and readouts on the shooting information display.

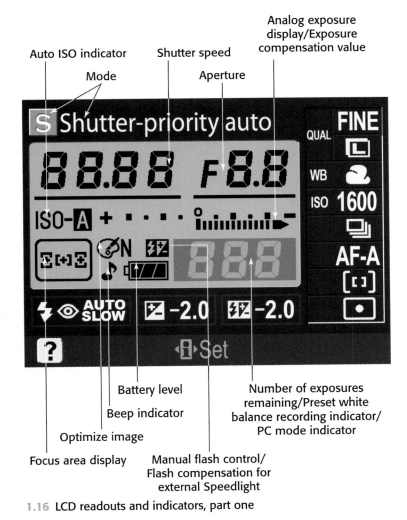

1.16 LCD readouts and indicators, part one

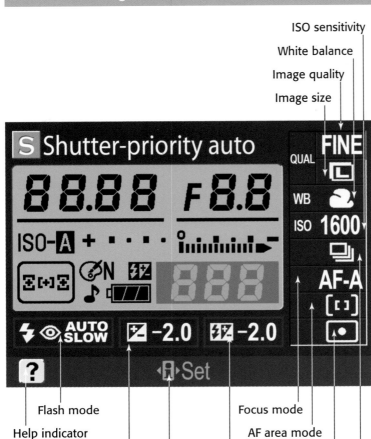

1.17 LCD readouts, continued

✦ **Shutter speed.** Displays current shutter speed setting.

✦ **Aperture.** Displays current f-stop.

✦ **Beep indicator.** Displays whether a beep sounds during certain camera functions, such as during a self-timer operation or when focus is achieved.

✦ **Focus area display.** Displays current focus area selection mode.

✦ **Number of exposures remaining/Other functions.** Displays the number of exposures left on the memory card, preset white balance recording, and the PC/USB connection mode.

✦ **Mode.** Indicates the current exposure mode.

✦ **Analog exposure display/ Exposure compensation value.** Displays the current exposure display and amount of exposure compensation being used.

✦ **Optimize image.** Displays the current optimize image setting.

✦ **Flash.** Displays when you control the flash manually or use an external flash unit.

✦ **Auto ISO indicator.** Indicates that the camera sets the ISO sensitivity automatically.

✦ **Battery level.** Displays power remaining in the D40 or D40x's battery.

✦ **Image quality.** Displays if the camera saves image files in JPEG Fine, JPEG Norm (Normal), or JPEG Basic; or in RAW format or RAW+JPEG Basic.

✦ **Image size.** Indicates the current resolution, either 10.2 megapixels (L), 5.6 megapixels (M), or 2.5 megapixels (S), for the D40x; or 6.0 megapixels (L), 3.3 megapixels (M), or 1.5 megapixels (S) for the D40.

✦ **White balance.** Displays whether the camera sets white balance automatically to one of the built-in settings, or to a manually preset value.

✦ **ISO sensitivity.** Indicates the current ISO setting.

✦ **Shooting mode.** Displays whether single shot, self-timer, continuous shot, or remote control shooting modes are active.

✦ **Focus mode.** Displays whether the camera uses AF-A, AF-S, or AF-C autofocus mode.

✦ **AF area mode.** Displays the method that selects the focus area.

✦ **Metering mode.** Indicates whether matrix, center-weighted, or spot metering is active.

✦ **Flash mode.** Displays the current flash setting.

✦ **Exposure compensation.** Indicates the exposure compensation that the camera is applying, and the amount, such as -2.0.

✦ **Flash compensation.** Indicates the flash exposure compensation that the camera is using, and shows the amount, such as -2.0.

✦ **Change settings.** Activates when you switch to settings change mode.

✦ **Help indicator.** Accesses a help screen.

Viewing and Playing Back Images

The D40 and D40x's Playback mode lets you review your images, delete the ones you don't want to keep, or jump to the Retouch menu to create a tweaked copy of images.

Follow these steps to review your images:

1. **Press the Playback button to produce the most recently taken photo on the back panel LCD.**

2. **Rotate the command dial to the right or left to switch to earlier or later photos on the memory card.**

3. **Use the Thumbnail/Zoom Out button to cycle among single-picture displays, or tiled views that show four or nine reduced size thumbnails at one time.** When viewing four or nine thumbnails, you use the Up and Down keys to navigate among the available images. Press OK to view a selected image on the LCD in full size.

4. **In single-picture display, pressing right or left on the multi selector also moves to the next or previous image.** Pressing up or down changes the type of information about the current image that appears on the screen. Your options include

   • **File Information.** Displays the image, the filename, frame number, size, quality, folder name, and so on.

   • **Shooting Data 1.** Provides you with a screen with more information, including the information in the basic File Information page, plus the camera name, date, time, metering and exposure methods, shutter speed, aperture, lens focal length, flash information, and any Exposure Value (EV) adjustment you made.

   • **Shooting Data 2.** Includes the File Information basics, plus other data such as the ISO setting, white balance, sharpening, color mode, hue, and saturation.

   • **Highlights.** The brightest areas of an image will have a flashing

border if they are overexposed so you can easily see any portions that might lack detail because of excessive exposure.

   • **Histogram.** Displays a luminance (brightness) histogram graph that displays the relationship between the dark and light tones in the image.

5. **Press the Zoom In/Setting button to enlarge the viewed image on the screen.** Press it multiple times to increase the amount of zoom. Press the Zoom Out button to reduce magnification.

6. **While zooming, use the multi selector to move the zoomed area around within the enlarged view.**

7. **Press the Protect button to keep the selected image from accidental erasure.** You can still remove the photo if you reformat the card, however. Press the Protect key while viewing a marked image to remove the protection.

 Caution *Do not reformat your memory card thinking that protected images won't be erased — they will be. All image are lost if the card is formatted.*

8. **Press Delete to erase the selected image.** When prompted, press Delete a second time to confirm removal of the photo.

9. **Press OK while reviewing an image to jump to the Retouch menu.** You can learn how to use this menu's options in Chapter 2.

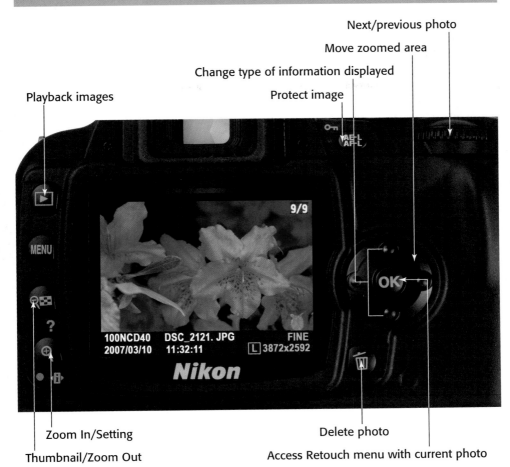

Next/previous photo

Move zoomed area

Change type of information displayed

Playback images

Protect image

Zoom In/Setting

Thumbnail/Zoom Out

Delete photo

Access Retouch menu with current photo

1.18 Review your photos using the color LCD

Activating the onboard flash

You can set the built-in electronic flash to pop up automatically when the D40/D40x detects low light levels while you're using Auto, Portrait, Child, Close-Up, or Night Portrait modes. You can manually pop up the flash by pressing the Flash button on the left side of the camera when in Programmed Auto, Shutter Priority, Aperture Priority, or Manual modes. Once the flash is in place,

you can choose from the options that follow by holding down the Flash button and spinning the command dial. Note that not all flash options are available in every shooting mode.

 Cross-Reference *You can find a detailed explanation of which options are available in each mode in Chapter 6.*

If you're using Programmed Auto or Aperture Priority modes, you can choose

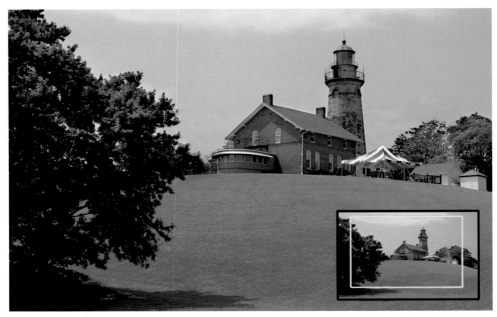

1.19 Moving the zoomed area

✦ **Front Curtain Sync (default/no indicator).** The flash fires as soon as the shutter opens. The Nikon D40 sets the shutter speed between 1/60 and 1/500 second (1/60 to 1/200 second with the D40x).

✦ **Red-Eye Reduction.** This flash mode triggers the front-panel lamp (also used for focus assist) one second prior to exposure to reduce red-eye effect.

✦ **Slow Sync.** This option uses slow shutter speeds (as long as 30 seconds) to add background illumination to the flash exposure. Not available with Shutter Priority or Manual modes.

✦ **Slow Sync + Red-Eye Reduction.** This option adds red-eye reduction to Slow Sync mode.

✦ **Curtain + Slow Sync.** This option delays flash when using longer shutter speeds until just before the shutter closes, to add background illumination to the flash exposure. Not available with Shutter Priority or Manual modes.

If you're using Shutter Priority or Manual modes, you can choose

✦ **Front Curtain Sync (default/no indicator).** The flash fires as soon as the shutter opens. Set the shutter speed of your choice (generally up to 1/500 or 1/200 second for the D40 and D40x, respectively).

✦ **Red-Eye Reduction.** This option triggers the front-panel lamp (also used for focus assist) one second prior to exposure to reduce the red-eye effect.

✦ **Rear Curtain Sync.** The camera delays the flash until just before the shutter closes. This puts any ghost images from the ambient light caused by moving objects behind the flash image.

If you're using Auto, Portrait, or Close-Up modes, hold down the Flash button and spin the command dial to switch among

✦ **Auto Front Curtain Sync.** This option is similar to Front Curtain Sync, but the flash pops up automatically.

✦ **Auto + Red-Eye Reduction.** This option is the same as Auto Front Curtain Sync, with red-eye reduction.

✦ **Off.** The flash does not fire.

If you're using the Night Portrait mode, hold down the Flash button and spin the command dial to choose

✦ **Auto + Slow Sync.** This option is similar to Slow Sync, but the flash pops up automatically.

✦ **Auto + Slow Sync + Red-Eye Reduction.** This option is the same as Auto Slow Sync, but with red-eye reduction.

✦ **Off.** The flash does not fire.

Choosing Metering Modes

The D40 or D40x can use any of three different exposure metering methods when it is set to Program, Shutter Priority, Aperture Priority, or Manual mode. Select the mode by pressing the Info button, followed by the Setting button. Then scroll to the metering

mode section of the LCD display, press OK, and choose the metering mode you want from among

✦ **Matrix.** The camera examines 420 segments in the frame and chooses the exposure according to that information. With Type G and D lenses the camera also incorporates distance range data.

✦ **Center-Weighted.** The camera collects exposure information over the entire frame, but when it makes the calculations, the camera emphasizes the center area of the viewfinder.

✦ **Spot.** The camera calculates exposure entirely from the area indicated by the active focus bracket. (In other words, you can spot-meter off-center subjects.)

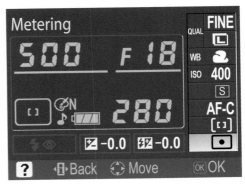

1.20 Metering modes appear on the LCD.

Adjusting ISO Sensitivity

The D40/D40x can choose the sensitivity setting (ISO) for you automatically, or you can manually select an ISO setting. Press the Info button, followed by the Setting button. Then scroll to the ISO section of the LCD display, press OK, and choose from the available settings (200, 400, 800, 1600, and H1) on the D40; the D40x also has ISO 100.

Setting White Balance

To more closely match the D40/D40x's color rendition to the color of the illumination used to expose an image, you can set the white balance. To use a value already programmed into the camera, just press the Info button, followed by the Setting button. Then scroll to the White Balance section of the LCD display, press OK, and choose from among Auto, incandescent, fluorescent, direct sunlight, flash, cloudy, shade, and preset.

You can also set the white balance by using the menu system, with additional options for fine-tuning or defining a preset value. You can learn how to use these options in Chapter 3.

Programmed Exposure Modes

The D40/D40x has six Digital Vari-Program modes (see figure 1.21) that make some of the setting decisions for you. You can choose any of these modes from the Mode dial. They include

✦ **Auto and Auto (Flash Off).** In these modes, the D40 or D40x takes care of most of the settings, according to the kind of shot

you've framed in the viewfinder. For example, the camera knows how far away the subject is and the color of the light, and it can make some pretty good guesses about the kind of subject matter from exposure data and other information. After comparing your shot to the 30,000-picture database, the D40 or D40x decides on the best settings to use when you press the shutter release. For example, Auto is the mode to use when you hand your camera to the waiter and ask him to take a quick picture of your group. Don't use this mode if you want every picture in a series to be exposed exactly the same way. If you change shooting angles or reframe your image, the camera might match your shot with a different image in its database and produce a slightly different look. Use the Auto (Flash Off) mode when you want to suppress use of the built-in Speedlight.

✦ **Portrait.** Use this mode when taking a picture of a person or two posing relatively close to the camera. The D40/D40x automatically focuses on the nearest subject and uses a wider lens opening to blur the background. The camera's sharpening effects are not used, which creates a less-detailed picture with smoother skin tones. This exposure also tends to favor smooth tonal gradations that flatter your subjects. Flash (if used) reduces red-eye effects. Don't use this mode if your portrait subject is not the closest object to the camera.

Portrait Auto (Flash Off)

Landscape Auto

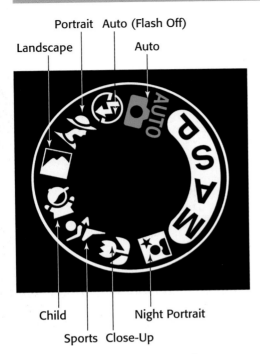

Child Night Portrait

Sports Close-Up

1.21 Six Digital Vari-Program, or Scene, modes are available, plus Auto and Auto (Flash Off).

✦ **Landscape.** Even though many landscape pictures are taken of distant objects, the D40 and D40x are smart enough to know you might have important subject matter closer to the camera, too, and they use a nearest subject focus. This mode locks out the flash, because the Speedlight isn't much good for objects more than about 20 feet from the camera. At the same time, this mode increases sharpness and enriches colors to improve the appearance of foliage. Don't use this mode if you need to use flash as a fill-in to illuminate shadows in subjects who are relatively close to the camera and posing in front of vistas.

✦ **Child.** This mode optimizes your camera's settings for active, lively children and their colorful attire and playthings. You probably don't want to use this mode for older children or adults, who might not look their best with such vibrant colors and such high contrast.

✦ **Sports.** In this mode, the D40/D40x switches into AF-C (Continuous Autofocus) mode so it can better track moving subjects and keep them sharp. The camera also favors higher shutter speeds to freeze action, and disables the flash.

✦ **Close-Up.** If you're shooting flowers or other close-up subjects, use this mode, which concentrates the D40 and D40x's automatic focusing efforts on the center of the frame, where most close-up subjects are positioned.

✦ **Night Portrait.** This mode balances flash exposure with the background illumination by using front curtain slow synchronization to provide an evenly lit photo of both your main subjects in the foreground and the area behind them.

Semiautomatic and Manual Exposure Modes

The Nikon D40 and D40x have three semi-automatic modes that enable you to specify shutter speed, aperture, or combinations of the two. If an appropriate exposure cannot be set, HI or LO messages appear in the viewfinder, and Subject is too dark or Subject is too light messages appear on the LCD. There is also a Manual mode that enables you to set shutter speed and aperture independently. You set these four modes (see figure 1.22) using the Mode dial:

✦ **Manual.** Select both the shutter speed and aperture by using the command dial (shutter speed) and command dial plus Exposure Compensation/Aperture button (f-stop). When you specify the exposure, the indicator in the exposure scale in the viewfinder and on the LCD display is centered between the + and – indicators.

✦ **Aperture Priority.** Use the command dial to choose the aperture, and the D40/D40x chooses the correct shutter speed for the right exposure.

✦ **Shutter Priority.** Turn the command dial to choose the shutter speed. The D40/ D40x selects an appropriate aperture to provide the correct exposure.

✦ **Programmed Auto.** The D40/D40x selects a shutter speed and aperture for you. You can override the camera's calculated exposure by holding down the EV button and rotating the command dial left (to add exposure) or right (to subtract exposure). If you feel

the exposure is satisfactory, but you'd like to use a different shutter speed or f-stop, rotate the command dial to the right to select a higher shutter speed and larger aperture or to the left to change to a slower shutter speed and smaller aperture combination.

Aperture Priority

Manual

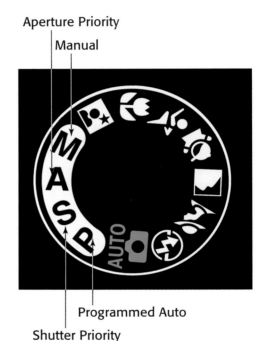

Programmed Auto

Shutter Priority

1.22 Manual, Aperture Priority, Shutter Priority, and Programmed Auto Exposure modes are also available.

Nikon D40/D40x Essentials

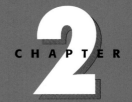

In This Chapter

Choosing metering modes

Adjusting exposures with EV

Adjusting ISO sensitivity

Using noise reduction

Working with the Retouch menu

You've learned the basic layout of the Nikon D40 and D40x, and how to activate their primary controls. Now there are two more tasks to complete to gain total mastery over your digital SLR (dSLR). First, you need to learn how to apply the D40/D40x's exposure, ISO, and noise reduction controls. Then, you'll be ready to tackle the camera's other playback, shooting, setup, and custom menu settings to define the default values for other parameters, which I explain in Chapter 3.

As you work through these next two chapters, you'll see that the D40 and D40x have a rich array of options and choices you can make. The ability to fine-tune the way your camera operates gives you the greatest possible control over your results.

Choosing Metering Modes

The Nikon D40 and D40x's three metering modes determine the method used to collect exposure information from a 420-pixel RGB (red, green, blue) array in the viewfinder screen. In each of these modes, the camera applies a different set of exposure meter pixels to the calculations. The exposure sensor reads both brightness information as well as color information, enabling the camera to analyze your scene in much more detail.

You can choose the mode by pressing the Info button (if the shooting information display is not visible), followed by the Setting button. Then use the multi selector keys to navigate to the metering mode choice and press OK (see figure 2.1). Use the multi selector to choose the metering mode and press OK a final time. Choose from the following metering modes

✦ Matrix

✦ Center-weighted

✦ Spot

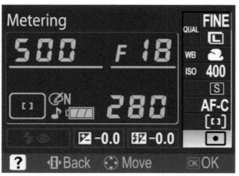

2.1 Use the D40 or D40x's LCD settings menu to change metering mode.

Matrix metering

Matrix metering is usually your best choice for most situations. In this mode, the 420-pixel exposure sensor covers roughly 60 percent of the image frame (all but strips of the image area at the top, bottom, and sides). A representation of the sensor grid appears in figure 2.3.

Because the sensor measures both intensity and color of the individual points in the image, the scheme is called *Color Matrix II* metering. If you're using a D- or G-type lens

(which have a built-in computer chip to enable them to convey additional information), the metering system also takes into account the focus distance of your subject with the *3D Color Matrix II.*

This exposure information is processed by a set of algorithms that compares your scene with an internal database of 30,000 different sample images to make a guess about the kind of photo you're taking. For example, a picture with a centered image and the subject about 6 to 8 feet from the camera is probably a portrait; a similar image with the subject closer than 12 inches is likely to be a close-up of a flower or similar object. If the lens focuses at or near infinity and the top half of the frame is much brighter than the bottom half, the algorithms might assume you're taking a scenic photo and try to balance the detail in the sky and foreground as much as possible. These guesses enable the D40 and D40x to vary the exposure to tailor the settings for the kind of photo you're shooting.

The system can spot images that are high in contrast and choose whether to expose for the highlights and shadows, or, perhaps, to underexpose slightly to preserve detail in

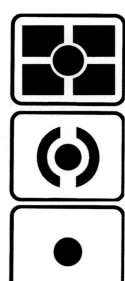

2.2 Select from matrix (top), center-weighted (middle), or spot (bottom) metering patterns.

darker areas. The capability to discern color information, and thus spot an image that has light yellows or dark greens, is much more useful than measuring intensity (on a black-and-white scale) alone.

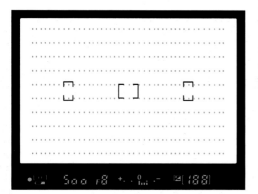

2.3 Matrix metering collects exposure information from a 420-cell sensor array (which isn't visible in actual use).

 Cross-Reference *You can find more about exposure in Chapter 4.*

Center-weighted metering

Center-weighted metering is a good choice if your main subject is in the middle of the frame, and outside the center are areas that are very bright or very dark and might confuse even the matrix metering system. Portraits and close-up photography often are exposed more accurately when you use center-weighting.

This mode emphasizes an invisible 8mm circle in the center of the frame (some other Nikon dSLRs display an actual circle in the viewfinder), assigning a 75 percent weight to that area, but also taking into account a fuzzy area outside that circle within the 420-pixel sensor grid; this gives it a 25 percent weight, as you can see in figure 2.4.

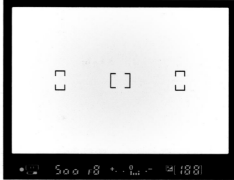

2.4 Center-weighted metering gives a 75 percent priority to the center of the frame.

Spot metering

Spot metering may be your best choice if there is a dramatic difference in illumination between your subject and the surroundings, particularly if the subject isn't moving rapidly. An actor delivering a soliloquy on a spot-lit stage is the kind of image that can be exposed successfully using spot metering.

In this mode, the Nikon D40 and D40x measure exposure solely from a 3.5mm circle positioned at the currently active focus area, roughly 2.5 percent of the entire frame. The spot does not have to be located dead center; the camera uses the focus area that the camera selects or you select manually.

You can use spot metering successfully for off-center subjects. When user-selectable focus areas are available (Chapter 5 explains how to activate that option and manipulate focus zones), use the multi selector to move the red-highlighted focus zone to the area you want to use for spot metering, as shown in figure 2.5.

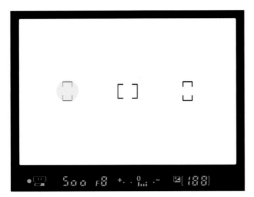

2.5 Spot metering reads only a small, moveable circle centered around an autofocus zone.

Adjusting Exposures with EV

You can add or subtract exposure from the settings calculated by the D40 or D40x's meter in Programmed Auto, Shutter Priority, or Aperture Priority modes by using Exposure Value (EV) corrections. Each 1/3 EV increment represents 1/3 stops' worth of exposure. To add or subtract exposure compensation, hold down the Exposure Compensation/Aperture button on top of the camera (located just southeast of the shutter release) and rotate the command dial to the left (to add exposure) or right (to subtract exposure).

An icon appears in the viewfinder at lower right (see Chapter 1 for the exact location) to alert you that you've selected an exposure other than the metered value. An indicator on the LCD (outlined in yellow in figure 2.7) shows the exact amount of EV you've dialed in, and the exposure scale in the viewfinder provides a graphical representation of how much compensation — from +5.0 to −5.0 EV — you've applied. Use the histogram display available for the last picture taken (Chapter 4 shows you how to do this) to decide how much of an adjustment to make for your next shot.

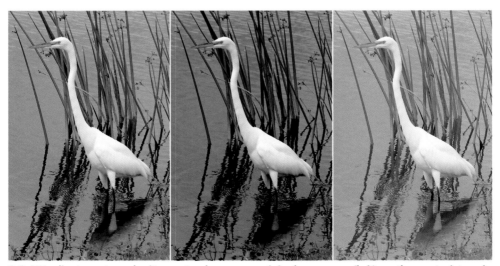

2.6 EV adjustments make it easy to change an original exposure (left) so the next picture is darker (center) or lighter (right).

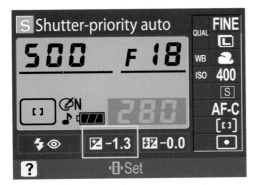

2.7 Use the LCD settings menu to change EV settings.

Your EV adjustment doesn't change after you've taken a photo, so be sure to change back to 0 EV when you want to return to using the actual metered value. If you don't change the EV back to 0 and begin shooting a different subject, you can end up with photos that are underexposed or overexposed.

Cross-Reference *Flash exposures can also be increased or decreased by using Flash EV changes. You can find directions for increasing or decreasing flash exposures in Chapter 6.*

Adjusting ISO Sensitivity

ISO is a numeric representation of a digital camera sensor's relative sensitivity to light. The basic sensitivity setting of the D40 is ISO 200; for the D40x, the lowest ISO setting available is ISO 100, which is roughly equivalent to the speed of an ISO 200 or ISO 100 photographic film. Your camera has the capability to amplify the incoming signal, producing higher settings up to the equivalent

of ISO 3200, but with an increase in the graininess, called image *noise*, with each sensitivity boost.

Lower sensitivity settings provide better overall image quality, but require you to use longer shutter speeds or larger lens apertures, which themselves can reduce the sharpness of the image. Higher ISO settings call for faster shutter speeds and/or smaller f-stops. Selecting the right ISO is a matter of deciding on the sensitivity that provides the right combination of image noise, shutter speed, and aperture.

Note *ISO isn't an acronym for anything with a particular photographic relevance. It simply represents an international standards body that establishes benchmarks for thousands of different standard yardsticks or measurements used in many different industries, including the photographic arena.*

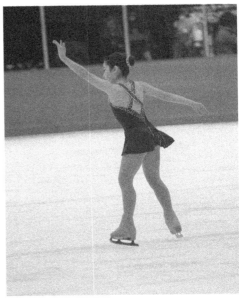

2.8 Higher ISO settings add noisy grain to your photos.

Setting the ISO on the D40 or D40x is easy. If the LCD shooting information display isn't visible, press the Info button, and then press the Setting button and use the multi selector to navigate to the ISO settings option on the right side of the screen. Press OK, and then use the multi selector up/down buttons to choose the ISO you want, from 200, 400, 800, 1600, or H1 (equivalent to ISO 3200). Press OK a final time to lock in your choice. You can also specify ISO with the ISO sensitivity setting in the Shooting menu, as described in Chapter 3.

The D40 and D40x also include an automatic ISO sensitivity option (available when you use one of the DVP (scene) modes or either of the Auto modes. This setting increases the ISO setting to a maximum of ISO 1600 when there isn't enough illumination at the current ISO setting to take an optimally exposed photograph. Although this option is useful, you should use it with care, because it can switch you from a relatively grain-free ISO 400 setting to a far noisier ISO 1600 setting unexpectedly. Although an ISO Auto alert exists in the viewfinder and on the LCD, it's easy to overlook.

When you use the ISO Auto feature, the D40/D40x increase the ISO setting from 100 (or 200) to as high as ISO 1600 whenever the exposure mode in use indicates a shutter speed of 1/30 second or slower. Unfortunately, that's not always your best option. If, for example, the camera is mounted on a tripod, you could probably keep the ISO at a much lower setting and use longer shutter speeds to get the right exposure.

Conversely, you might want to boost the ISO even when using a higher shutter speed; for example, when you're using a telephoto lens that magnifies camera shake even at shutter speeds of 1/125 or 1/250 second. In those situations, you might want to increase the ISO setting so you could use 1/500 second or faster at the same lens aperture.

Because the ISO Auto feature might not make an ISO change that's the same as the one you might make yourself, you can turn the feature off entirely in Custom Settings menu CSM 10; either do this, or tell the camera to go ahead and use the ISO Auto option, but do use a shutter speed guideline you specify and a maximum ISO setting that you indicate. I show you how to set up your camera for these custom adjustments in Chapter 3.

Using Noise Reduction

Several things can cause noisy grain. Increase the ISO sensitivity and your D40/D40x amplifies the signal produced by incoming illumination so that a reduced number of photons are needed to produce an image in dark areas of your photograph. Unfortunately, random background pixels in the image, caused by electrical interference between adjacent pixels, are amplified and register in your image as noise. The higher you boost the ISO setting, the more noise you're likely to have in your image.

Longer exposure can also introduce noise, regardless of the ISO setting you're using. As the exposure time stretches out, the sensor begins to heat, and some of that heat produces spurious image artifacts that can be seen as noise, even at a low sensitivity setting such as ISO 100 or ISO 200.

Your D40/D40x automatically eliminates some noise, but even stronger, more aggressive noise reduction processing is available. Unfortunately, over-enthusiastic noise reduction can rob an image of detail, so you can turn this feature on and off in the Shooting menu (as described in Chapter 3).

If you don't want to use the D40 or D40x's noise reduction facilities or want to customize the amount of noise reduction you apply, you can also perform noise reduction tasks with image editors like Adobe Photoshop; cut noise when importing RAW files using Adobe Camera Raw, Nikon Capture NX, and other RAW utilities.

Working with the Retouch Menu

Adjusting an image after the picture is already taken is commonly referred to as *post processing*. Of course, you usually perform that step using a personal computer. If you can't wait to make some quick adjustments to your photos (say, you want to upload a few and share them via e-mail), you can do a surprising amount of image manipulation right in your Nikon D40 or D40x.

You can brighten shadows, minimize red-eye, crop photos, change color pictures into black-and-white renditions, add some filter effects, combine several photos into a double exposure, and then squeeze the finished shot down to a smaller size suitable for e-mailing. Best of all, your original shot remains unmodified. The Retouch menu, which is available only when you have images on your memory card and enough room to store a revised version, creates a duplicate image with all the changes you specify, and saves it onto your memory card along with the original picture.

In this section, I show you how to use these retouching tools. You can access these tools by pressing the Menu button, scrolling down to the Retouch menu, selecting a tool, and then activating that tool by pressing the right directional key on the multi selector, or by pressing OK. You can also access the Retouch options by pressing OK when in Playback mode.

For the D-Lighting, Red-Eye Correction, Trim, and Image Overlay tools, you are immediately presented with a set of thumbnails of the images on your memory card. For the Monochrome, Filter Effects, and Small Picture tools you first need to choose an option within the submenu before selecting an image from the thumbnails. Press the multi selector left or right to scroll around among the available images, press OK to select the image, and then work with the tool as follows.

D-Lighting

This option brightens dark shadows. Even with the best exposure techniques, you still end up with an occasional picture in which backlit subjects are too dark. There may be lots of detail in the light areas of the photo, but the darker areas—which may be the most important parts of the picture—are murky and the details are hidden. D-Lighting is a perfect solution for those pictures, particularly when you don't mind if the lighter areas, such as sky or windows in the background, become brighter and lose some detail during the process (see figure 2.9).

Select the image you want to modify. You are shown a pair of side-by-side images, with Normal highlighted under the version on the right side. Press the multi selector up to choose High lightening (to dramatically lighten the photo), or the down directional key to select Low lightening.

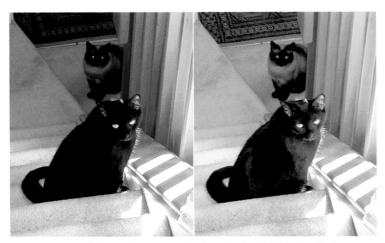

2.9 You can brighten dark areas (left) with the D-Lighting feature (right).

Hold down the Zoom button to briefly view the image on the LCD display in full size. When you've evaluated the modified image, press OK to save a tweaked version of the photo on your memory card. To go to the menu instead, press the Menu button.

Red-Eye Correction

If red-eye reduction efforts deployed when you took the picture didn't completely tame red eyes, this tool can often provide an additional measure of correction.

Choose your image. If the camera is unable to detect the red-eye effect in the photo you select, the camera tells you so and refuses to select the picture. Use the Zoom In and Zoom Out buttons to magnify or reduce the picture. You can use the multi selector's directional keys to move the zoomed area around within the full image. Press OK to activate the red-eye correction function. To reiterate, note that the D40 or D40x modifies only images in which it is able to detect red eye effects, and does not create a modified copy if it is unable to find any red eyes.

Trim

To use this tool, view your image on the LCD by using the Zoom In and Zoom Out buttons, along with the multi selector's directional keys to crop the image down to the area you'd like to appear in the finished picture. Press OK, and the visible area on the LCD saves as a new, separate file on your memory card.

Monochrome

Choose Black-and-white, Sepia, or Cyanotype monochrome effects. If you choose Sepia or Cyanotype, you see brownish or bluish versions (respectively) of your original image in a preview. Press the multi selector button up to increase the color saturation, or down to decrease the color saturation. The monochrome copy of your image is created when you press OK.

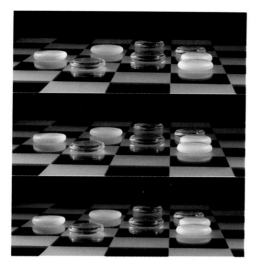

2.10 The Monochrome tool can convert your color image into a black-and-white (top), sepia (middle), or cyanotype (bottom) version.

Filter Effects

This tool has three options: Sky light (which adds a cooler, blue cast to the image), Warm filter (which adds a red cast), and Color balance (which enables you to change the color bias of the photo).

To adjust color balance, press the multi selector up to add green; down to increase the magenta tone; left to add blue; and right to increase the red. A small thumbnail of the image appears, flanked by red, green, and blue histograms that show the levels of the tones in each of the primary colors as you make your adjustments. Press OK to create a copy of the image with the filter effects you choose.

Small Picture

The Small Picture tool enables you to create smaller versions of your images, suitable for

display on a television screen, on a Web page, or for e-mailing. Nikon's recommendations for an appropriate size are:

Display on television	640 × 480
Display on Web pages	320 × 240
Sending by e-mail	320 × 240

In practice, you're not locked into those applications for any particular image size. Indeed, you might want to send slightly higher resolution versions of your images via e-mail. Or, you might want to use an image in a size other than 320 x 240 for Web display.

To use this tool, select Small Picture from the Retouch menu. Then select Choose Size and specify one of the three small picture sizes available. Press the multi selector right directional button or press OK to return to the Small Picture menu. Then choose Select Picture and choose one or more images you want to convert. Use the left or right directional buttons to move among the available thumbnails, and press the up or down directional buttons to mark the shots you want to convert, or to unmark them if you change your mind.

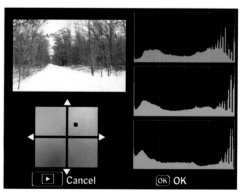

2.11 With the Retouch menu, you can add filter effects, including a Color balance option.

When you've made your selection, press OK, and select Yes from the confirmation screen that appears to create your copies.

Image Overlay

This tool enables you to combine two RAW-format images on your memory card into a new, single shot. When you select the tool, a dialog box appears with spaces for Image 1, Image 2, and a preview of the combined version. The overlay feature works best when your two pictures have background areas that are plain so the image pair can merge seamlessly (see figure 2.12).

1. **Highlight the Image 1 choice on the screen and press OK.**

2. **Select the image you want to use from the selection window (only RAW files can be selected) by scrolling among the available shots with the left or right directional buttons.** Press OK to select your first image.

3. **To select the second image, highlight Image 2 on the screen and press OK.**

4. **Select the image you want to use for Image 2 from the selection window (only RAW files can be selected) by scrolling among the available shots with the left or right directional buttons.** Press OK to select your second image.

5. **Decrease or increase the transparency of the images in relation to each other.** Highlight the image you want to adjust by pressing the multiselector left or right, and press the up or down directional buttons to increase or decrease the relative transparency.

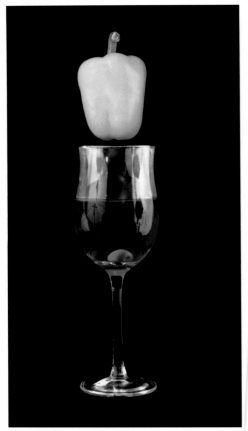

2.12 Plain backgrounds allow two images to merge almost seamlessly.

6. **Highlight the Preview thumbnail and choose Overlay to preview the combined image.**

7. **Press OK to save the merged shots, or press the Zoom Out button to make other adjustments, including selecting different pictures to combine.** You can also choose Save and press OK to save a copy of the merged pictures without previewing them first.

Setting Up the Nikon D40/D40x

If you used a point-and-shoot camera prior to the Nikon D40/D40x, you'll find that there are many more settings and options available with your new dSLR than you might have used with your previous camera. Even so, you can get even better photos by fine-tuning various adjustments from time to time.

Many of the basic settings on your D40/D40x are available through buttons on the camera itself or through the quick-access shooting information menu on the LCD display.

You still need to visit the camera's menu system from time to time. You can find lots of things to do to adjust the behavior of your D40/D40x so that it performs in the way you want. You can define the Function button to perform the action you prefer, (such as activating the self-timer) turn the camera's beep sound on or off, or adjust the brightness of the LCD display.

As with all my Digital Field Guides, this book is not intended to provide a rehash of the manual furnished with the D40/D40x, nor does it aim to replace that manual entirely. Instead, I want to provide you with fast access to the key information you need with, where appropriate, longer explanations of some of the less intuitive features. You'll find some repetition of what appears in the official manual, but I hope you find the information here easier to understand and more fully explained.

To get started, you simply need to know that the settings selected for each operation appear to the right of each menu listing, and that individual menus may have submenus with indicator bars that show you where you are within the menu list. Most of the menus are similar in appearance, with some

allows you to determine whether the camera marks all hard copies with a data imprint and/or date imprint by the printer appears. The DPOF is used, so your memory card can be interpreted by a retail print kiosk, as well as digital minilabs and some desktop printers.

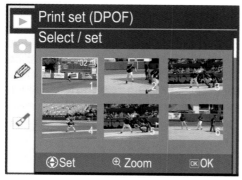

3.2 The picture selection screen specifies images for printing.

Shooting Menu Preferences

You can find picture-taking preferences within the Shooting menu, represented by a green camera symbol. Here are the options available in the submenus (shown in figure 3.3):

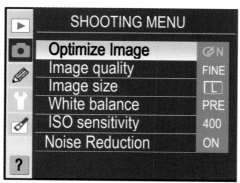

3.3 The Shooting menu.

Optimize Image

This submenu offers options for fine-tuning the color, contrast, sharpness, saturation, and hue of your photos. Your choices include

✦ **Normal.** This setting provides the best overall combination of sharpness, contrast, and colors.

✦ **Softer.** This setting reduces harsh detail in images by softening outlines for a smoother look. This setting is often good for portraits.

✦ **Vivid.** This setting enriches the color saturation, boosts sharpness, and increases contrast to produce vibrant images. This setting is a good choice on overcast days.

✦ **More vivid.** This setting provides even more color saturation, exaggerated sharpness, and snappy contrast. Use this setting for dull days or to provide an almost flamboyant look.

✦ **Portrait.** This setting reduces contrast to produce an effect that can be flattering in portraits.

✦ **Black-and-White.** This choice converts your JPEG image to black-and-white. RAW images are black-and-white as their default, but contain color information if you choose to override this RAW setting.

✦ **Custom.** This setting enables you to select image sharpening (auto, normal, low, medium low, medium high, or high); tone compensation (auto; or from normal contrast to less contrast, medium low contrast, medium high contrast, or more contrast; or a custom contrast curve you upload to your camera using Nikon Capture NX); color mode, including two variations of sRGB plus Adobe RGB; saturation (auto, normal, moderate, or enhanced), and hue adjustment.

More on custom image optimization

Most of the optimization choices are self-explanatory. The Custom option can benefit from a little more detail.

When you choose Custom, you can set sharpening and saturation yourself, and have the option of choosing tone compensation adjustments by using Nikon's choices that range from 0 (Normal) to −1 or −2 (lower contrast) or +1 and +2 (higher contrast).

With the Custom option's Color Mode choice, you can choose from three different *color spaces* or *gamuts*, which each contain a slightly different palette of colors best suited for particular types of output, such as computer display screens, personal printers, or professional printing. In theory, all three color modes reproduce the exact same *number* of colors, specifically 16.8 million hues in a 24-bit image. However, the actual colors within their gamuts differ. Color spaces Ia and IIIa (both based on the sRGB model) are intended for Web display or output to an inkjet printer, with Ia producing better results for portraits because it has more colors corresponding to skin tones, while IIIa is preferable for scenic photography because it contains a wider selection of greens. If you can imagine a box of crayons with 16.8 million different colors, the Ia box is heavily stocked with many different variations of flesh-toned crayons, while the IIIa box emphasizes a huge variety of colors that can easily represent foliage and other subject matter that appears in landscapes.

The Mode II color space is based on the Adobe RGB color gamut. It, too, contains 16.8 million colors, but they are spread over a larger *area*, producing what is called a *wider gamut*. Use Mode II if you print your images professionally, or if you do a lot of post-processing.

The other option available is Hue Adjustment, which involves moving all the colors in your image 9 degrees around the color wheel either clockwise or counterclockwise. Rotation in the plus direction makes reds more orange, greens more blue, and blues more purple. Rotation in the other direction makes reds more purple, blues more green, and greens more yellowish (see figure 3.4).

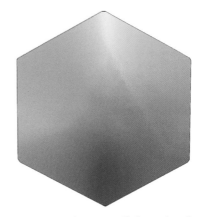

3.4 Hue controls move all the colors in an image clockwise or counterclockwise around the color wheel.

Image quality

This submenu duplicates the file format selection functions (RAW, JPEG, RAW+JPEG) of the shooting information display. You can choose to capture images in RAW format, JPEG Fine, JPEG Normal, JPEG Basic, or RAW+JPEG Basic.

Image size

This submenu duplicates the resolution selection functions of the shooting information display, as explained in Chapter 1. You can select L, M, and S (large, medium, and small) resolutions.

White balance

This submenu enables you to set white balance, duplicating the functions of the white balance (WB) settings in the Shooting information menu. In addition, you can create new white balance presets, or choose existing presets. The section that follows explains these functions in more detail.

White balance quick start

As I cover in Chapter 6, white balance is the relative color of the light source, measured in terms of *color temperature*. Indoor, incandescent illumination has a relatively low (warm) color temperature in the 3,000K (degrees Kelvin) range; outdoors in sunlight, the color temperature is higher (colder), from about 5,000K to 8,000K. Electronic flash units have a color temperature of about 5,400K, but this can vary with the length of the exposure. The flash built into the D40 and D40x, and Nikon-dedicated flash units like the SB-600 and SB-800, can actually report the color temperature they use to the camera for automatic adjustment.

Your camera can make some pretty good guesses about the color temperature of its environment by measuring the color of the image using the 420-cell exposure sensor in the viewfinder. In addition, you can specify white balance when working in P, S, A, and M modes:

✦ **Use the shooting information screen to change white balance.** Press the Info button if the menu is not visible on the LCD display. Then press the Setting button, scroll to the WB section in the right column and press OK. Choose one of the built-in color balance settings, including automatic (A), incandescent, fluorescent, direct sunlight, flash, cloudy conditions, shade and preset.

✦ **Use the White Balance menu option in the Shooting menu to specify a white balance and to fine-tune white balance.** Scroll to White Balance and press OK; then select from automatic (A), incandescent, fluorescent, direct sunlight, flash, cloudy conditions, shade, and preset. When you choose any selection other than preset, you can fine-tune the balance by using the up directional key to make the color balance slightly redder or yellowier or the down directional key to make the color balance bluer.

Creating white balance presets

You can create your own white balance presets, or use the white balance of an existing photo. To create a white balance preset from an existing photo, follow these steps:

1. **In the Shooting menu choose White balance ⇨ White balance preset.**

2. **Select Use Photo.** The most recent image taken appears. You can use that photo by selecting This Image and pressing OK, or can select a different image by choosing Select Image.

3. **Next, select the folder on your memory card in which the image you want to use appears.** Work with the D40/D40x's standard image selection screen to find the image you want. Scroll among the images by pressing the left or right multi selector directional keys. When you find the image you want, press OK.

To create a new white balance preset, follow these steps:

1. **In the Shooting menu choose White balance ⇨ White balance preset.**

2. **Select Measure.** If you have previously created a preset, a message appears that reads "Overwrite existing preset data?" Select Yes.

3. **While looking through the viewfinder, fill the frame with a neutral white or gray object, and then press the shutter release completely.** The camera measures the white balance of your subject. The viewfinder and LCD display show a PrE message if the camera successfully captured the white balance, and Data acquired appears on the top row of the LCD display. Otherwise, the following message appears: Unable to measure preset white balance. Please try again.

ISO sensitivity

This submenu duplicates the functions of the ISO settings on the shooting information menu, as explained in Chapter 2.

Noise Reduction

You can activate noise reduction in any exposure mode, including the seven DVP (scene) modes. In this menu, you have the option to turn on or off noise reduction applied by the camera to exposures taken at ISOs higher than ISO 800 or at shutter speeds of 1 second or slower on the D40 or at ISOs higher than ISO 400 and shutter speeds of 8 seconds on the D40x. If you turn noise reduction off, the camera applies some noise reduction to exposures at the HI 1 setting (equivalent to ISO 3200) on the D40 and ISOs higher than ISO 800 on the D40x.

When the feature is turned on, the camera applies noise reduction to any exposure taken using an ISO setting of ISO 800 (D40) or ISO 400 (D40x) or greater and a shutter speed of one second on the D40 (eight seconds on the D40x) or longer. Note that the long exposure noise reduction works by taking a second, blank frame following the actual exposure, effectively doubling the time needed to take a picture. An indicator that reads Job nr appears in the viewfinder during the post-shot processing. You might switch off this option if you don't want to wait for the long exposure noise reduction to be applied. Noise reduction can also reduce the frame rate top speed if you use it during continuous shooting.

Custom Settings

The full Nikon D40/D40x has 17 customizable parameters in the Custom Setting menu (CSM), represented by a red pencil symbol. In the next section, I provide explanations of each of the parameters.

Note *If you see only six entries in the Custom Setting menu, it is set for Simple display; you can learn how to change to the full menus in the CSM/Setup Menu choice in the next section.*

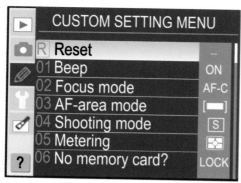

3.5 The Custom Setting menu, part one.

R Reset

Use this option to restore all your Custom Settings to their factory-default values, including those not restored with the D40/D40x's two-button reset. (You do this by holding down the Info and Zoom In/Settings buttons simultaneously.) Use this menu item when you've made extensive changes to your D40/D40x's custom settings, may not remember what they all are or what they do, or want to start over.

CSM 01: Beep

Your D40/D40x can chirp at you during a self-timer countdown, when the camera locks in focus, and in other situations. If you're taking pictures in a museum, library, lecture, house of worship, or another quiet location, you can turn the beep off here.

CSM 02: Focus mode

This choice duplicates the focus mode selection option in the Shooting information menu. You can select AF-C (Continuous servo Autofocus), AF-S (Single servo Autofocus), AF-A (Automatic Autofocus), or M (Manual focus).

CSM 03: AF-area mode

This setting duplicates the Shooting information menu option for setting the autofocus area. It determines the method the D40/D40x uses to choose an autofocus zone. Choose Single Area to focus only on subjects within the active focus area that you select. Dynamic Area uses the focus area you select, but if a moving subject leaves that area, the camera uses information from other focus areas instead. This setting is a good choice for sports, and is used by the Sports DVP mode. AF-area mode tells the camera to select the appropriate focus zone itself. Auto, Portrait, Landscape, Night Scene, and Night Portrait modes use this setting by default.

CSM 04: Shooting mode

You can choose the shooting mode here, just as you can in the Shooting information screen. Choose from single frame, continuous, self-timer, and either delayed remote or quick response remote, as described in Chapter 2.

CSM 05: Metering

This is the Custom Setting menu equivalent of the metering mode selection in the Shooting information screen. When the camera is in Program, Shutter Priority, Aperture Priority, or Manual modes, you can choose Matrix, Center-weighted, or Spot metering, as described in Chapter 2.

CSM 06: No memory card?

You can lock the shutter release when no memory card is inserted in the D40/D40x or, you can allow the camera to operate normally and display the images you "take," but the pictures will not be stored, of course. Choose either Release Locked or Enable Release.

▶	CUSTOM SETTING MENU	
⬛	07 Image Review	ON
✎	08 Flash Level	0.0
	09 AF-Assist	ON
🔧	10 ISO Auto	OFF
✄	11 ◔/Fn button	ISO
	12 AE-L/AF-L	AF
?	13 AE lock	OFF

3.6 The Custom Settings menu (continued).

CSM 07: Image Review

When you switch this option on, images appear on the LCD display immediately after they are taken, for the length of time specified in CSM 15 (Auto off timers; from 4 seconds to 20 seconds, or a custom time you select). You can turn image review off to save battery power, or when the bright LCD display might be distracting or obtrusive to others (at a concert, for example). You can still review your images by pressing the Playback button.

CSM 08: Flash Level

In Program, Shutter Priority, Aperture Priority, or Manual modes, this setting applies Flash Exposure Compensation level, from −3.0 to +1.0 stops, in one-third stop increments. This duplicates the procedure of holding down the Flash button and Exposure Compensation/Aperture button while spinning the command dial.

CSM 09: AF-Assist

This option enables or disables the Autofocus Assist lamp; this provides additional illumination to aid the autofocus system under dim lighting conditions in AF-S mode (or the AF-S mode of the AF-A setting). The AF-Assist lamp is most effective only at distances of a few feet, and may be distracting in some venues, so you can turn it off here. AF-Assist is not available in Landscape and Sports DVP/Scene modes.

CSM 10: ISO Auto

You can set this tricky option, which you can use in Program, Shutter Priority, Aperture Priority, and Manual modes only, here. The ISO auto option determines whether the camera boosts ISO automatically to achieve proper exposure, and the parameters used to make the adjustments. Your choices with this setting include

✦ **Off.** With this default setting, ISO remains at the value set in the Shooting information screen, or by using the ISO menu choice in the Shooting menu. Automatic adjustment of ISO is disabled.

✦ **On.** ISO is automatically adjusted by using the Max. sensitivity and Min. shutter speed parameters you enter.

✦ **Max. sensitivity.** Here you can set the highest ISO setting that ISO Auto uses when making the adjustment. If you want to avoid the noise levels that can result from higher ISO settings, but are willing to accept a moderate boost, set the maximum sensitivity to a low value, such as ISO 400. The D40/D40x then uses only ISO 100 (on the D40x), 200, or 400.

If you're willing to accept more noise, use a higher value, such as ISO 800 or ISO 1600. (The boosted value HI 1 cannot be specified as a maximum, nor does ISO Auto shift sensitivity into those lofty levels.)

✦ **Min. shutter speed.** Use this value to indicate the slowest shutter speed before ISO Auto kicks in. You can choose from 1/125 second to 1 second. If you're using a short telephoto lens, you might want to activate ISO Auto any time you need a shutter speed slower than 1/125; conversely, with the camera mounted on a tripod, you might feel that you do not need an ISO boost until shutter speeds exceed 1 second.

CSM 11: Self-Timer/Fn button

The Function (Fn) button is on the front of the Nikon D40/D40x just below the Flash button, which you can easily reach with your left index finger as you grip the camera. You can assign any of five different functions to this button. The default function is to make the self-timer active. You can also set the function button so you can change the shooting mode (single shot, continuous, self-timer, or remote), Image Quality/Image Size, ISO sensitivity, or white balance (P, S, A, and M modes only) while holding the button and spinning the command dial.

CSM 12: AE-L/AF-L

Use this feature to determine the behavior of the AE-L/AF-L button. You can choose to have this button lock both the exposure and focus; lock either the exposure or focus, or lock the exposure (this is not an option for the focus) when the button is pressed, and keep it locked until the button is pressed again (to take several consecutive photos using the same exposure); or to activate autofocus. You have five options to choose from, as show in Table 3.1.

CSM 13: AE lock

This option specifies which controls you can use to lock the exposure at the current value. When it is switched to On, both the focus and the exposure are locked when the shutter release button is pressed halfway. When it set to Off, the camera continues to meter when you press the shutter release halfway; only the focus is locked.

Table 3.1
AE-L/AF-L Functions

Option	Description
AE/AF Lock	The exposure and focus are locked when the button is pressed.
AE Lock only	Only the exposure is locked when the button is pressed.
AF Lock only	Only the focus is locked when the button is pressed.
AE Lock Hold	The exposure is locked when the button is pressed, and remains locked until you press the button again or the exposure meters turn off.
AF-ON	Pressing the button activates autofocus instead of partially depressing the shutter release.

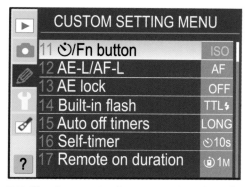

CUSTOM SETTING MENU

11	⏱/Fn button	ISO
12	AE-L/AF-L	AF
13	AE lock	OFF
14	Built-in flash	TTL⚡
15	Auto off timers	LONG
16	Self-timer	⏱10s
17	Remote on duration	⏱1M

3.7 The Custom Settings menu (continued).

✦ **TTL (through-the-lens metering).** The D40/D40X's flash metering system automatically sets the flash level for you.

✦ **Manual flash setting.** You can choose a fixed power level from full power to 1/64 power.

If the SB-400 Speedlight is attached, this custom setting is used to select flash control for the SB-400 instead, and the menu choice changes to Optional Speedlight.

CSM 14: Built-in flash

This is a multilevel menu with several options for the D40/D40x's built-in flash unit when you are using Program, Shutter Priority, Aperture Priority, or Manual modes. You can choose the following

CSM 15: Auto off timers

Use this option to determine how long the LCD screen, Menu display, exposure meters, and picture review screen remain active. Shorter timers preserve battery power, but provide less time to view or measure exposure. Your choices are listed in Table 3.2.

Table 3.2
Timer Increments

Feature	Time(s) Available
Short	
Playback/menus	4 seconds
Image review (if active)	4 seconds
Auto meter-off	4 seconds
Normal	
Playback/menus	8 seconds
Image review (if active)	4 seconds
Auto meter-off	8 seconds
Long	
Playback/menus	20 seconds
Image review (if active)	20 seconds
Auto meter-off	1 minutes

Continued

Table 3.2 (continued)

Feature	Time(s) Available
Custom	
Playback/menus	4, 8, 20, or 60 seconds, or 10 minutes
Image review (if active)	4, 8, 20, or 60 seconds, or 10 minutes
Auto meter-off	4, 8, 20, or 60 seconds, or 30 minutes

CSM 16: Self-timer

You can set the self-timer to delays of 2, 5, 10, or 20 seconds.

CSM 17: Remote on duration

This setting tells the D40/D40x how long the camera should wait for a signal from the optional infrared remote control before deactivating. Your choices are 1, 5, 10, or 15 minutes.

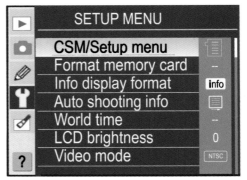

3.8 The Setup Menu.

Setup Menu Options

In this menu, represented by a yellow wrench symbol, you can find options that you set and forget about — such as the current time or your language preferences, plus a few, including memory card formatting, that you use more often.

CSM/Setup menu

If you find the number of the menu options intimidating, you can limit the number of choices available using this option. You can select Simple, which causes the D40/D40x to display only the first six options in the Custom Settings menu; Full, which shows all available menu options; and My Menu,

which enables you to choose exactly which menu items appear in the Playback, Shooting, Custom Settings, Setup, and Retouch menus. If you select My Menu, you can choose any of these menus individually, and mark or unmark boxes next to each menu choice to make that option visible or invisible.

Format memory card

Use this feature to format a new memory card for use, and to reformat existing cards to remove all the photos on them and return them to a fresh, clean condition. Formatting your card often is a good idea; it can avoid potential problems by locking out bad portions of the card before they have a chance to corrupt your data.

Info display format

Use this feature to select what type of shooting information menu displays will be used for DVP/Scene modes and Program, Shutter Priority, Aperture Priority, and Manual modes. You can choose from Classic mode text display; Graphic mode with mixed text and graphics, or Wallpaper, which uses a photo of your choice as the background.

Auto shooting info

You can use this option to select whether to display shooting information on the LCD screen in DVP/Scene modes and/or in Programmed Auto, Shutter Priority, Aperture Priority, and Manual modes. Turn the display on to automatically show shooting information after the shutter release button is released. If Image Review is turned off in CSM 07), shooting information will be displayed after a photograph is taken.

World time

Set the D40/D40x's internal clock to your time zone, choose the current date and time and a date format, and whether daylight saving time should be observed. This information is written to the image file along with the exposure and other camera settings, so you can tell when the image was taken when you review it in your image editor, or need to organize and archive your photos by date, or want to imprint the date the picture was taken on your photos.

LCD brightness

When this option is selected, a grayscale brightness chart is displayed that you can use to increase the brightness of the LCD (to

make it more viewable in bright light) or decrease the brightness (which may help cut glare when using the D40/D40x indoors in dim light).

Video mode

Use this option to toggle the AV port still image output of the D40/D40x from NTSC, or the National Television Standards Committee (used in the United States, Japan, and some other countries) to PAL, or Phase Alternating Line (used in much of Europe and other regions) for television display.

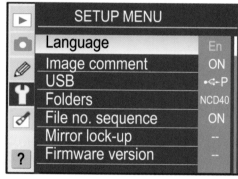

3.9 The Setup menu (continued).

Language

Choose the language you want your D40/D40x to use.

Image comment

If you elect to use this feature, the camera appends a comment to each image file. You can enter the comment by using the text entry screen, or can type the comment on your computer by using Nikon Capture NX and upload the comment to the camera.

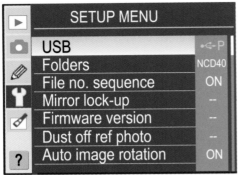

3.10 The Setup menu (continued).

USB

Use this option to tell your D40/D40x to operate in either a PTP (Picture Transfer Protocol) or Mass Storage device mode. You can use both for transferring pictures. In Mass Storage mode, the camera behaves like a card reader and your memory card is the equivalent of a floppy disk or hard drive that can be accessed by the computer. In PTP mode, the camera and software can communicate more completely in both directions, giving the software (such as Nikon Capture Control Pro) the capability of controlling the camera.

Folders

Use this option to create, rename, or delete folders. You can name folders by using the same text entry screen as with the Image Comment feature.

File no. sequence

This option determines how sequential numbers are created for your file names on the memory card. If you choose Off, the D40/D40x resets the file number to 0001 each time you create a new folder or you use a new or reformatted memory card. When the option is switched to On, file numbers increase up to 9,999 and then start

over. Choose Reset, and the numbers start over again at 0001. If you insert a memory card with images numbered higher than the current image number in the D40/D40x's memory, the camera starts with that number instead, to avoid duplicate file numbers.

Mirror lock-up

This mirror lock-up option is not a picture-taking feature but rather a means of getting the mirror out of the way and the shutter open so you can clean your sensor. This option is only available when the D40/D40x's batteries are fully charged, or when the camera is connected to the optional EH-5 AC adapter with the EP-5 AC adapter connector. For more information about cleaning your sensor, see Appendix A.

Firmware version

This display shows the current camera firmware version.

Dust off ref photo

With this option, you can take a dust reference photo that images any dust or other particles clinging to your sensor, so that Nikon Capture NX can use the information to filter out the dust from your images.

Auto Image Rotation

This option tells the D40/D40x to embed in the image file information about the camera's orientation — either horizontal or vertical — when the picture was taken. Many software programs can use this information to display the image in the proper orientation; the D40/D40x's Rotate Tall playback option can also use this data to present images shot in a vertical format on the LCD in their proper rotation.

Creating Great Photos with the Nikon D40/D40x

Exposure Essentials

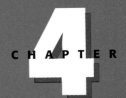

As a new owner of a Nikon D40/D40x, it's possible that you've never had to give much thought to proper exposure. That's especially true if you're just graduating from a fully automated point-and-shoot camera. Snapshot models with fewer options and capabilities than Nikon dSLRs often make all the exposure decisions for you. Most of the time, your pictures come out reasonably exposed, but you also probably end up with more than a few that look a little murky or a bit too bright. With the Nikon D40/D40x, you no longer have to settle for exposures that are "just OK."

Indeed, you can fine-tune your exposure, as you shoot, actually *improving* the settings your camera makes for you automatically. If you want your photos to be a little lighter for a high-key effect, or a little darker to create a moody look, you can do that easily. Even though the camera does a great job of determining exposure on its own, it includes features that let you tweak the settings, if you want, to get even better pictures.

In this chapter, I introduce the essentials of exposure. In Chapter 5, I provide a refresher course on choosing and using lenses and working with the range of sharpness called *depth of field.* Then I explain how to use various types of illumination (including electronic flash) in Chapter 6.

Understanding Exposure

With the Nikon D40/D40x, you always have the safety net of the camera's built-in exposure features. You can choose to let the camera select an exposure by using the Auto mode. Or, you can tell your Nikon camera what kind of picture you're taking by dialing in one of the pre-programmed Digital Vari-Program (DVP) scene modes for situations like portraits, sports, or landscapes.

You might prefer the D40/D40x's intelligent autopilot, the P (Programmed Auto) mode, which has manual override features that allow you to perfect your images on the spot. In P mode the camera sets the basic exposure but still enables you to add to or subtract from the amount of exposure, or to choose a different shutter speed/lens opening combination at the same exposure if you want a faster or slower shutter speed to freeze action or allow artistic blur effects, or if you want to use a particular f-stop to change the amount of sharp focus in creative ways.

If you know you want to use a particular shutter speed or lens aperture, you can mandate either value with the D40/D40x's Shutter Priority or Aperture Priority modes. You select the shutter speed or f-stop you want, and your camera chooses the other setting to match and provide the best exposure. As you gain experience, you can still use your judgment to modify the camera's exposure selection if you choose to make your photos a little darker or a little lighter for a special effect.

The D40/D40x even gives you the flexibility of switching to Manual mode and setting exposure entirely yourself. Even in Manual mode, you're not working without a net. A helpful scale in the viewfinder provides a reminder of the exposure the camera *would have* selected if you'd been using one of the automated or semiautomated modes. You can use that scale to set your manual exposure, or choose to ignore it entirely.

The common factor in these options (aside from the full-auto DVP [scene] modes and Auto) is that your understanding of how exposure works gives you the power to accept the camera's recommendations, or modify them to suit the needs of a particular

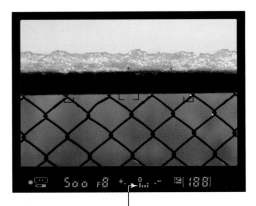

Exposure scale

4.1 Even when you're using Manual mode, the exposure scale in the viewfinder shows you whether your settings are providing more or less than the metered exposure.

image. In the next section, I provide an overview of exposure, which can serve as a reminder to photographic veterans and as an introduction for newer users.

The term *exposure* can have multiple meanings. An *exposure* can mean the image itself (or, more than one image in the case of a *double exposure*), as in "I took twelve exposures in a row." It can mean a way of producing an image, as in "At night, I sometimes use lengthy shutter speeds to make time exposures." But, most of the time, *exposure* refers to the amount of light required to create the optimum visible image (as in the *correct exposure*).

In photography, exposure involves four concepts: the amount of light present in a scene; the light levels that make their way through the lens into the camera; the length of time that light is allowed to fall on the sensor/film; and how much of that illumination is actually captured. The photographer has at least some control over each of these factors.

The important thing to remember is that in digital photography the elements of exposure are reciprocal and proportional. That is, you can double the amount of light as long as you reduce the length of time the sensor is exposed to that light by half. The relationship is a little like cooking something in your microwave: You can nuke a baked potato at full power for five minutes, or cook it at half power for ten minutes, and get more or less the same results.

In photography, this relationship exists in an interdependent way for all four of the factors that figure into correct exposure. You can increase or decrease the amount of light in a scene, vary the light that actually passes through the lens, control the length of time that illumination falls on the sensor, and alter the sensitivity of the sensor to adjust the exposure. Increase one of these elements while decreasing another by an equal value, and the exposure stays the same. To produce more or less exposure, increase or decrease any of the four elements by the same amount and your results should be equivalent.

Light produced by a scene

The first element of exposure is the *amount* of light produced by a scene. Outdoors in daylight, *reflected* light originates with the sun, but a lot can happen to it before it reaches the camera lens. Daylight may be diffused and softened by clouds, filtered by trees and other forms of shade, and bounced off bright walls (or reflectors you use) before being reflected off your subjects toward the camera. Indoors, such continuous reflected light might come from lamps and other artificial forms of illumination, or perhaps from sunlight streaming through windows. Reflected light can be absorbed or

blocked before it reaches your subject, too. Figure 4.2 shows a mixture of direct light — the brightly-lit background — and softer light that suffuses through the canopy overhead.

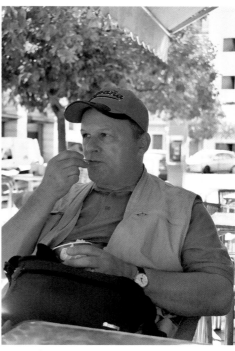

4.2 Light in a scene can be direct and bright, or soft and diffused, as the mixed illumination in this image demonstrates.

In addition to reflected light, some illumination can come from *transmitted light*, which passes through translucent objects that are lit from behind. A Tiffany lamp or an advertising transparency in a store window are subjects that you can photograph successfully with transmitted light.

Images can be captured by the light that objects emit. Campfires, for example, provide their own illumination. It's possible to photograph subjects that include more than one of these forms of illumination, too, such as a building photographed late in the afternoon with the lights in the office switched on. In exposure terms, you can influence the amount of light produced by a scene by increasing or decreasing the light levels in some way. That may involve adding or removing existing lights, pumping a little extra illumination into the scene by using an electronic flash, or redirecting the light that's already there with a reflector. If you're working with a human or another moveable subject, you can relocate to an area that's better illuminated or one that has less light, depending on the mood or intent you want the image to take.

In practice, you change the nature of the light in a scene for one of three reasons: either there is too little or too much overall illumination; or, the *balance* of the light is wrong: some areas are too bright, while others are too dim; or the *quality* of the light is wrong: it may be too harsh or too soft. For the current discussion on exposure, I'm concerned only about the *quantity* of light. If you imagine the light in a scene traveling from the subject to the sensor within the confines of a garden hose (an odd analogy that works better as you continue in this chapter), the illumination can consist of a trickle, a gushing flow, or something in between.

> **Cross-Reference** *You can learn more about manipulating light in Chapter 6.*

Light transmitted by the lens

Once reflected, transmitted, or emitted light reaches the camera, the light must pass through the lens as it wends its way to the sensor. Not all of that illumination makes it all the way through. Filters on the lens can block some light, while the rest of the light has to pass through a variable-sized diaphragm called the *aperture*, which resides within the barrel of the lens.

This aperture is used to modify the amount of light passing through the lens. You can think of the diaphragm as a garden hose of differing diameters, ranging from a large tube that admits all the available water (or light, in this case), to a smaller pipe that can allow only a small amount through at one time. You and your camera's exposure system can change the size of the aperture to allow more or less light to reach the sensor.

Filters are most often mounted on the front of the lens, but can be located elsewhere in the optical path. In all cases, though, filters are designed to remove light, blocking some of that flow through the pipe. Some filters remove specific colors to make an image appear to be more blue, orange, or some other hue. Others (called *neutral density* filters) remove all colors equally to reduce the total amount of light so exposures can intentionally be longer. There are even *split* filters with different types of filtering material in their upper and lower halves, designed to, for example, balance an overly-bright sky with a foreground that is less generously illuminated.

Polarizing filters remove light bouncing at certain angles to reduce the amount of glare from reflective surfaces, or to darken the sky. Any time you use a filter of any sort, you're cutting down on the amount of light that reaches the sensor.

You may never use a filter or use one only rarely. The lens diaphragm, on the other hand, is called into play every time you take a picture. This mechanism consists of an arrangement of (usually) five to nine blades that create what is called an *iris aperture* (or just *aperture*) that dilates and contracts to admit more or less light to enter the lens. The relative size of the aperture is called the *f-stop*.

- ✦ f/1.4
- ✦ f/2.0
- ✦ f/2.8
- ✦ f/4
- ✦ f/5.6
- ✦ f/8
- ✦ f/11
- ✦ f/16
- ✦ f/22
- ✦ f/32

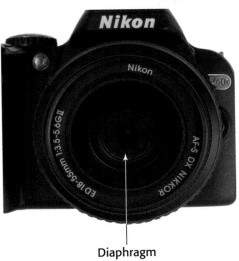

Diaphragm

4.3 The diaphragm dilates and contracts to change the size of the lens opening.

Note *The larger the number, the smaller the aperture. So, the minimum f-stop of a particular lens is a larger number, such as f/22; its maximum f-stop is a smaller number, such as f/2.8. When you stop down the lens, you're changing to a smaller f-stop, with a larger number. When you open up the lens, you're switching to a larger f-stop, with a smaller number.*

These f-stops are numbered in a confusing way: the larger the number, the less light admitted. So, f/11 allows half as much light as f/8, but twice as much as f/16. Think of f-stops as the denominators of fractions: 1/8 is larger than 1/11, which is larger than 1/16, and so forth. A second point of confusion comes in the numbers themselves. They are calculated from the square root of 2 (1.414), so f/8 is not twice as large as f/16 — it's *four times* as large. To double (or halve) the exposure, you have to use an "in between" f-stop; in this case, f/11. The actual common progression of f-stops, from larger opening to smaller opening in *one stop* increments (each allowing half as much light as the last), is

There are also "fractional" f-stops between those numbers in increments of 1/3 or 1/2 f-stop. They'll appear in your D40/D40x's indicators as figures like f/4.2, and so forth, as you or the camera adjusts the aperture. As you work with lenses and f-stops, you find yourself (or the camera's exposure system) increasing the amount of light passing through the lens by changing to a larger f-stop (a smaller number) or decreasing the amount of light by changing to a smaller f-stop (a larger number).

Tip *Lenses are generally marketed by the maximum f-stop they provide at a particular focal length, such as an 18-55mm f/3.5-5.6 lens, which has a maximum aperture of f/3.5 at its 18mm zoom position and f/5.6 at its 55mm zoom position.*

Changing the size of the lens opening has other effects on your photography in addition to exposure. Using a larger or smaller f-stop can affect the sharpness of the lens (many lenses produce better images at an intermediate f-stop than at the largest or smallest openings); and the range of sharpness (depth of field).

To adjust the f-stop directly when using your Nikon D40/D40x, you need to work in either M (Manual) or A (Aperture Priority) modes. When using Aperture Priority mode, spin the command dial on the back of the camera and the aperture changes. When the meter is active, you see the current f-stop displayed on the LCD and in the viewfinder. If you're using Manual mode, press the Exposure Compensation/Aperture button (located southeast of the shutter release on top of the camera), while spinning the command dial.

 You can find an explanation of the factors related to lens apertures in Chapter 5.

Light admitted by the shutter

Think of the shutter as a valve that opens and closes, allowing the flow of light for only a specific period of time. When you adjust the shutter speed, you change the exposure by reducing or increasing the amount of time the light is allowed to fall on the sensor. With the Nikon D40/D40x, the shutter speed can vary automatically from 30 seconds (or even longer in Manual mode using the Bulb exposure setting) to 1/4000 second.

In addition to its effects on exposure, the shutter speed controls the amount of blur (or lack thereof) in your images. Slow shutter speeds allow moving objects to blur and camera motion to affect image sharpness. Higher shutter speeds freeze action and counter any camera shake. The exact shutter speed required to reduce or allow blur varies according to the speed of movement of your subject, the amount of camera shake, and the relative magnification of the image: Fast-moving objects, shaky photographers, and highly magnified subjects photographed

close-up or with a telephoto lens all call for higher shutter speeds.

 You can learn how to choose a shutter speed to stop action in Chapter 6.

To adjust the shutter speed directly when using your Nikon D40/D40x, you need to be working in either M (Manual) or S (Shutter Priority) modes. Spin the command dial on the back of the camera and the shutter speed changes. When the meter is active, you see the shutter speed displayed on the LCD and in the viewfinder.

Light captured by the sensor

The fourth element that affects exposure is the sensitivity of the sensor. The Nikon D40x has a basic sensitivity setting of ISO 100, and the D40 has a minimum sensitivity of ISO 200, which is roughly equivalent to the sensitivity of an ISO 100 and ISO 200 film, respectively, as determined by the body that governs such things, the International Organization for Standardization.

You can change your camera's ISO from its basic ISO 100/200 value all the way up to ISO 1600 in one-stop increments (that is, ISO 100, 200, 400, 800, and 1600), and from there, up to the equivalent of ISO 3200 with the HI 1 setting.

So, if you want to double the amount of exposure for a particular image, you can produce the same effect by doubling the ISO: use a shutter speed that's twice as long or select an f-stop that's twice as large. Of course, there's a catch: Just as changing the shutter speed affects blur and adjusting the f-stop affects the range of sharpness, increasing the ISO setting has an effect. The higher the ISO, the more random grain, called *noise*, appears in your photographs. Noise artifacts are those multicolored speckles that are most easily discerned in shadow areas of your images, but can be bothersome in the lighter areas, too.

The amount of noise increases as ISO is boosted, because the D40 and D40x achieve their higher sensitivity ratings by amplifying the light captured by the sensor. The amplification also multiplies random, non-image information. Fortunately, the D40 and D40x do an excellent job of suppressing this noise, and you're unlikely to even notice it at settings between ISO 100 and ISO 400. Noise begins to become objectionable at ISO 800 to ISO 1600, and probably will provide a thick background texture for any photographs taken at HI 1.

You can change the ISO setting when you are using any of the D40/D40x's modes, from the DVP (scene) modes to Auto, M, A, S, or P modes. There are two ways to change the ISO setting. Press the Menu button and navigate to the Shooting menu, and then choose the ISO sensitivity setting. You can select a value from ISO 100/200 to ISO 1600, plus HI 1. If you're using Auto exposure mode or one of the DVP (scene) modes, you can also choose Auto ISO, which directs the camera to choose an ISO setting for you. Or, press the Setting button (the bottom button to the left of the LCD screen), use the directional keys to navigate to the ISO setting, and press OK. Then select the ISO you want to use.

 You can find more about setting ISO in Chapter 2.

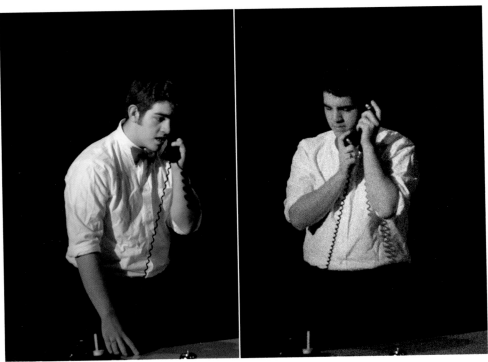

4.4 At ISO 400 (left) noise is not much of a problem. At the HI 1 setting (ISO 3200 equivalent; right), the noise is horrendous.

Getting the Right Exposure

Given the sophisticated electronics in your Nikon camera, why aren't exposures always right on the money? Why is it possible to get images that are too light, too dark, or contain highlight or shadow areas with no detail?

Unfortunately, no sensor can capture all the details possible in an image at every possible light level. Some details are too dim to capture them, and others overload the photosites in the sensor, so you end up with dark or light areas that should contain detail, but don't. Because a digital sensor can't handle the largest variations between light and dark areas, the best exposure for a given picture is likely to be one that preserves the detail at one end of the scale, while sacrificing detail at the other end.

Because you are in the best position to determine which tones in an image should be preserved, that makes you smarter than your D40 or D40x's exposure meter. You're the one who needs to make the exposure adjustments that might be required to give you the kind of image and range of tones that you want.

Keep in mind that the camera makes the basic exposure setting according to the assumption that your subject is reflecting about the same amount of light as a neutral gray card with a reflectance of 18 percent. It makes that assumption because different subjects reflect different amounts of light. In a photo containing a white cat, a dark gray cat, and a black cat, the white cat might reflect five times as much light as the gray cat, and ten times as much light as the black cat.

An exposure based on the white cat causes the gray cat to appear to be black, and the black cat to be an inky, dark blob. An exposure based only on the black cat makes the white cat seem washed out and the gray cat seem somewhat darker than usual. If the gray cat happened to reflect about 18 percent of the light bouncing off it, it's actually possible that all three cats would be rendered realistically, assuming that the white cat isn't too white, and the black cat isn't too black. In that case, the tonal range of the scene would be too broad to be captured by the sensor. It's these troublesome black and white cats that force photographers to make exposure adjustments.

Figure 4.5 shows a black cat with the exposure optimized (at left) for the cat's surroundings, causing the cat to become a black blob. At right, the exposure was set for the cat itself, providing lots of detail in the fur, but overexposing the cat's environment.

Enter the histogram

The tonal range is the distribution of light and dark shades in your image. You can view that distribution using the histogram feature. View the histogram chart for any image by pressing the Playback button to the left of the LCD, scrolling to the image you want by pressing left or right on the multi selector, and then pressing up or down until the histogram information display appears, as shown in figure 4.6.

A brightness, or *luminance*, chart overlaps the bottom of the image display. The brightness histogram is a simplified bar graph that shows the number of pixels at each of the 256 brightness levels. Each vertical line in the graph represents the number of pixels in the image for each brightness value, from 0 (black) on the left to 255 (white) on the right. The vertical axis measures the number of pixels at each particular level; the taller the bar, the more pixels of that brightness.

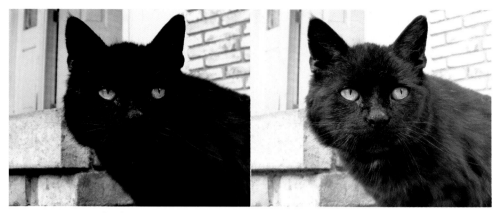

4.5 Exposing for the background (left) causes the cat to render completely black; exposing for the cat only (right) makes the background detail too light.

The typical histogram in figure 4.6 shows most of the pixels concentrated roughly in the center of the graph, trailing off to fewer pixels at the dark end (on the left) and light end (on the right) of the scale. Ideally, there should be some pixels across the full scale, but none clipped off at either side (showing that dark or light pixels weren't properly recorded), and relatively few very dark pixels (on the left) or very few light pixels (on the right). A suitable histogram would have the toes of the curve touch both the left and right ends of the scale.

If the exposure is not perfect, a histogram shows that. With an underexposed image, some of the dark tones are clipped off at the left end of the scale, and highlight tones appear toward the center of the graph rather than the far right, leaving an area of unused tones in the gap (see figure 4.7). Increasing the exposure moves all the tones toward the right, so the dark tones aren't clipped off and the lighter ones appear at the right side of the histogram.

With an overexposed image, some highlight tones extend beyond the right side of the scale (see figure 4.8), and the dark tones move toward the middle. In this case, reducing the exposure produces a better image.

Adjusting exposure

If you're using M, A, S, or P modes, you can adjust the exposure in several different ways, depending on which of these modes you're using. In Manual mode you can simply use the command dial to change the shutter speed, press the Exposure Compensation/Aperture button and the command dial to adjust the aperture, and set the ISO to modify the sensitivity setting.

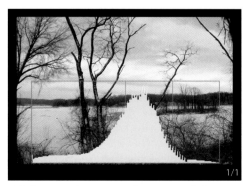

4.6 A normal exposure has most of the tones in the middle, with dark and light tones trailing off to the left and right ends of the graph.

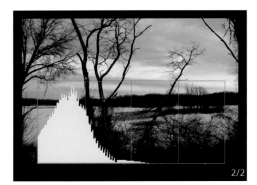

4.7 In an underexposed image, the dark tones are clipped off at the left side of the histogram.

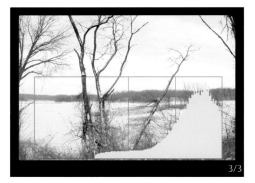

4.8 In an overexposed image, the light tones are clipped off at the right side of the histogram.

In Programmed Auto, Shutter Priority, or Aperture-Priority modes, you have a little more flexibility.

Exposure value compensation

You can set the D40/D40x to automatically add or subtract a certain amount of exposure from the value that it calculates by applying EV (Exposure Value) compensation. You can specify up to plus or minus five full stops worth of compensation in 1/3 stop increments. Once you've activated EV compensation, the camera adds or subtracts this amount of exposure from every shot you take until you change to another EV setting, or turn the feature off by setting the EV back to zero.

It's important to keep that in mind, because you can easily dial in some EV changes that suit a particular shooting environment, and then forget that you've made the setting when you begin taking pictures of a different scene. The camera is nice enough to include an indicator in the viewfinder, and on the back panel color information display, that shows you've departed from the recommended exposure with an EV change, but both are easy to overlook in the heat of a shooting session.

 Caution *Remember to check your EV settings from time to time!*

To apply EV settings, hold down the Exposure Compensation/Aperture button (located southeast of the shutter release on top of the camera), and spin the command dial to the right to add exposure, and to the left to subtract exposure from the D40/D40x's default meter reading. In S mode, the camera uses the aperture to make the adjustment; in A mode, it uses the shutter speed; and if you're working in P mode, the D40/D40x uses internal programming to determine which value to change. The new shutter speed or f-stop appears in the viewfinder and in the LCD, along with the amount of exposure compensation you've selected (see figure 4.9).

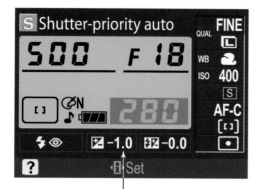

Amount of exposure compensation

4.9 As you dial in more or less exposure using EV compensation, the amount you've added or subtracted appears in the LCD display.

| Tip | In Programmed Auto mode, if you want to use the metered exposure, but would prefer a different shutter speed or f-stop combination for that exposure, just rotate the command dial without pressing the EV button. The exposure remains the same, but the D40/D40x switches to a different f-stop/shutter speed combination. Use this facility to change from, for example, 1/125 second at f/16 to 1/500 second at f/8 when you want a faster shutter speed to stop action. Both pairs of settings are exactly the same from an exposure standpoint. |

Tone compensation

The final exposure tweak you can make is called *tone compensation*, which is a method for controlling how the D40/D40x handles exposure of the darkest and lightest areas of your image. You can use tone compensation to adjust the contrast of the image as you make the picture, which is usually a better solution than trying to fix faulty contrast later on in your image editor. The drawback to using tone compensation in the camera is that a custom change you make applies to all the shots you take until you switch back to one of the non-custom modes.

Even so, some more experienced D40/D40x users prefer a different default contrast range for all the pictures they shoot, and dial in a custom tone compensation setting, as explained in Chapter 3.

You can access tone compensation in the Shooting menu. Select Optimize Image ➪ Custom ➪ Tone Compensation. Then you can choose from Normal, Less Contrast, Medium Low, Medium High, More Contrast, or Custom (which applies a tonal curve you've uploaded by using an optional program called Nikon Camera Control Pro).

More advanced photographers can upload to the camera curve created with Nikon Camera Control Pro (see figure 4.10). If you search Nikon-oriented forums on the Internet, you locate curve settings with various properties such as improved shadow detail, better preservation of tones in the highlights, or a snappier, more contrasty appearance.

Most D40/D40x photographers probably won't need to use custom curves; using this feature requires a lot of experience with sophisticated image editors like Adobe Photoshop. (The Curves feature isn't even available in Adobe Photoshop Elements, for example.) Many of you will get along just fine with the Optimize Image menu's range of contrast selections.

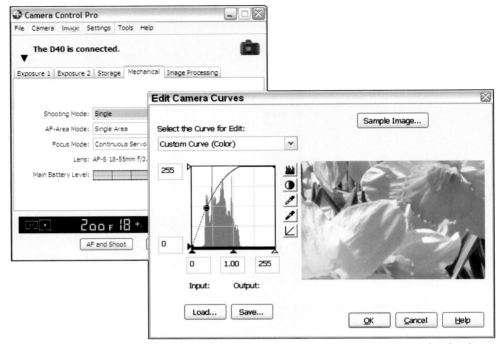

4.10 Nikon Camera Control Pro enables you to edit custom contrast curves and upload them to the D40/D40x.

All About Lenses

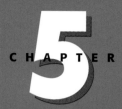
If you're like most new Nikon D40 or D40x owners, purchasing a new lens isn't at the top of your agenda right now. You're probably excited about all the different kinds of photos you can take using the lens that came with your camera. Studies have shown that budding photographers working with their first-ever single lens reflex (SLR) want to master the other sophisticated and exciting features of their camera before expanding their optical arsenal.

But if you're honest, you'll probably admit that even now you're taking a peek at the future and the nifty add-on lenses you might get for your Nikon D40 or D40x. If you happen to have some SLR experience under your belt already, that future may not be very far away. After all, one of the key advantages of an SLR like the Nikon D40 and D40x is the ability to remove one lens and replace it with another.

This flexibility enables you to achieve a longer reach with the added magnification of telephoto lenses, the broader perspective that comes from using wide-angle lenses, and the power to focus closer using macro lenses or take pictures with lenses that have a faster f-stop in lower light levels than you could with any single, fixed lens permanently mounted on your camera.

Digital SLRs are winning the hearts of avid photographers even with stiff competition from super-zoom fixed-lens non-SLR cameras. The non-SLR models have lenses with 12X to 18X zoom ratios that include just about every focal length you might think you'd need in a single lens, from moderate wide-angle to ultra-telephoto. But these monster zooms are not a panacea: For each image you can produce with such a camera, you can find others that are possible only with a model like the D40 or D40x, using lenses that are wider, longer, more sensitive to light, or able to focus closer.

In fact, after the glow of simply owning a sophisticated dSLR has waned, add-on lenses still shine as a leading accessory option for D40 and D40x photographers who want to stretch the capabilities of what is already a multitalented picture-taker. In this chapter, I cover all the bases of selecting and using lenses for the Nikon D40 or D40x dSLRs. I'll show you how to choose your initial lens for your basic camera body/lens kit, and how to select the best lenses for expanding your optical collection.

Evaluating Your Basic Lens Options

When Nikon introduced the original D40 in November 2006, it offered the camera in a single configuration that included the new 18-55mm f/3.5-5.6G II ED AF-S DX Zoom-Nikkor. In March 2007, when the D40x was added to the product line, it first became available with either the 18-55mm *kit* lens, or as a body alone for about $70 less.

You can also outfit your camera with a zoom lens with more "reach." For example, for about $300 more, you might prefer the 18-135mm f/3.5-5.6G ED-IF AF-S DX Zoom-Nikkor. This is a more expensive lens that has the same wide-angle perspective as the 18-55mm zoom, but has a more useful 135mm telephoto maximum focal length. There is also the amazing 18-200mm f/3.5-5.6 G ED-IF AF-S VR DX Zoom-Nikkor, for about $750 separately. It has built-in vibration reduction, which, when active, automatically counters camera shake (but not subject motion) and allows you to hand-hold your camera at much slower shutter speeds.

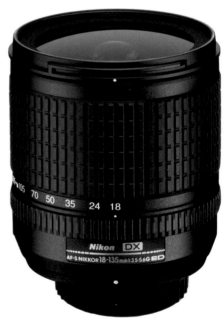

5.2 This 18-135mm lens is an upgrade to the basic kit lens.

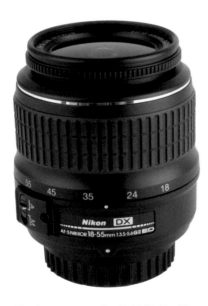

5.1 The least expensive D40/D40x kit includes this 18-55mm zoom lens.

Finally, if your D40 or D40x is not your first Nikon dSLR, you might already own an older lens that was introduced with the Nikon D70, the 18-70mm f/3.5-4.5G ED-IF AF-S DX

Zoom-Nikkor. It's noted for being an extremely sharp lens, and covers a useful range of focal lengths in a compact package.

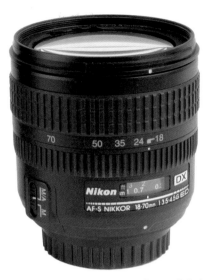

5.4 The 18-70mm lens provides a slightly longer zoom range than the basic D40/D40x kit lens, at a moderate increase in cost.

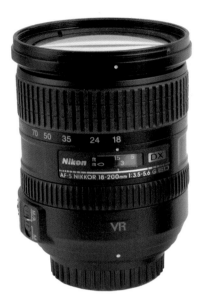

5.3 The 18-200mm f/3.5-5.6 G ED-IF AF-S VR DX Zoom-Nikkor, with vibration reduction, is probably the ultimate "walking around" lens.

Advantages of the kit lenses

The four lenses I just named as often referred to as "kit" lenses, because they are often furnished as part of the basic package with current models like the Nikon D40/D40x, D80, D200, and older models such as the D70/D70s and D50. Any of these four make good starter lenses for the Nikon D40 or D40x, and any of them can perform flexibly in a wide range of picture-taking situations. If you choose to work with one lens only, a kit lens will do a good job for you. Here is what you can expect from all of the basic lenses available for the D40 and D40x.

✦ **Minimal cost.** At about $70 when you purchase it in the kit, the 18-55mm zoom is a remarkable bargain. It offers the equivalent of a moderate wide-angle to short-telephoto lens in a compact package. The extra $300 for the 18-135mm zooms is well worth it for the extra telephoto range you get. The 18-200mm Vibration Reduction (VR) lens is not inexpensive, but it does provide you with a lot of versatility and plenty of different focal lengths to choose from for the price.

✦ **Useful zoom range.** These four lenses have 3X, 3.8X, 7.5X, and 11X zoom ranges (for the 18-55mm, 18-70mm, 18-135mm, and 18-200mm models). As I've mentioned before, the D40/D40x's sensor, because it is smaller than a full 24 x 36mm film frame, crops the field of view of all lenses (when compared to a full-frame digital or film camera). All of them begin at 18mm, which is the full-frame equivalent of 27mm, and reach out to the equivalent of 82.5mm, 105mm, 202mm, and 300mm (respectively). Depending on how much sports or wildlife photography you do (which tend to require longer telephoto focal lengths), any of these lenses may be suitable.

✦ **Adequate aperture speed.** All four lenses have a maximum aperture of f/3.5 at the wide-angle position, which shrinks to f/5.6 at the telephoto end (except for the 18-70mm kit lens, which has an f/4.5 maximum aperture at the 70mm setting). You may find this aperture range limiting for available light shooting (particularly sports when in telephoto mode), but remember that faster lenses are much more expensive. Nikon's 17-55mm lens, with a fixed (non-changing) f/2.8 maximum aperture tops $1,300. Also keep in mind that if your subject is not moving rapidly, you can often use the 18-200mm VR lens at a slower shutter speed because of its anti-shake properties, which affords you about two to three extra f-stops , although Nikon claims up to a four-stop improvement.

✦ **Good image quality.** All four of these lenses include extra-low dispersion glass and aspherical elements, which are optical components that minimize distortion and chromatic aberration (color "ghost" images), and produce sharp pictures. Considering the low (or reasonable) price tags on these optics, they are image-quality bargains suitable for all but the most demanding photographic applications.

✦ **Compact size.** At a mere 7.2 ounces (for the 18-55mm zoom) to 19.8 ounces (for the 18-200mm VR lens), any of these four are light enough and small enough in size to take with you when you want to leave the camera bag at home and venture out with your D40 or D40x and just one lens.

✦ **Fast, close focusing.** These lenses all focus quickly and silently, and, while none of them is a macro lens, they do let you focus as close as a foot or two. They are all AF-S model lenses, which include the internal focusing motor which is a requirement for the D40 and D40x. Your camera cannot focus automatically with lenses that don't have the AF-S or AF-I designation. (More on that later in this chapter.)

Figures 5.5 and 5.6 show just how much zoom you can get from the four basic starter lenses for the D40 or D40x. Figure 5.5 shows the full view you might get from any of these lenses at the 18mm zoom position, with inset frames illustrating the field of view at each of the maximum zoom settings of the respective lenses. Figure 5.6 is an enlarged view of all four maximum zoom views, showing 55mm, 70mm, 135mm, and 200mm perspectives.

Upgrading your capabilities

You may take lots of great pictures using nothing but your basic lens, but, sooner or later, you may find an image you want to capture that calls for capabilities that just aren't built into the lens you have. That's

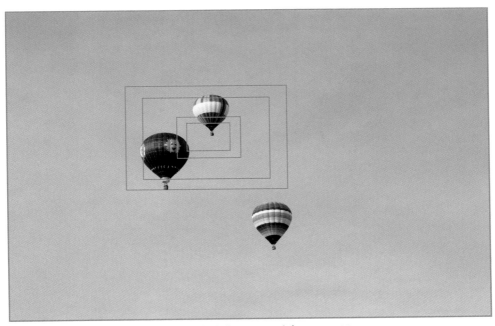

5.5 The entire image shows the field of view you might get at 18mm.

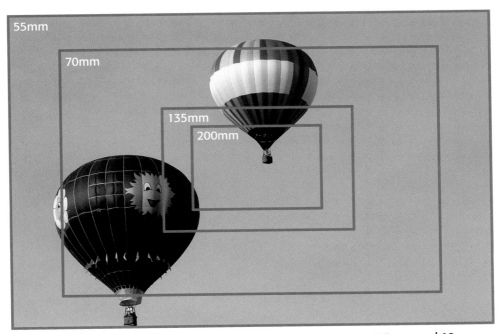

5.6 At the maximum zoom settings of the 18-55mm, 18-70mm, 18-135mm, and 18-200mm lenses, you would see these perspectives.

when you want to consider adding an add-on lens or two to your stable of interchangeable optics. The chief limitations to overcome include

✦ **The need to bring your subject closer.** Telephoto lenses and tele-zooms bring distant objects closer to your camera, so necessary physical distance from your subject doesn't have to be a huge obstacle. You can frame a tightly cropped close-up of a V-formation of geese against a blue sky, a shy tiger at the zoo, or the fierce action on the opposite side of the rugby pitch. Such lenses can also help you isolate subjects and reduce the apparent distance between objects. For the D40 or D40x, telephoto focal lengths encompass everything from around 55mm to 500mm, or even more if you can afford a super-telephoto lens.

✦ **The desire for a wider view.** Wide-angle lenses and wide-angle zooms enable you to photograph expansive landscapes or capture everything in a room when there is nowhere to back up, while emphasizing the foreground. Wide angle lenses for the D40 and D40x range from about 20mm down to 10mm.

✦ **The urge to get closer.** Macro/micro lenses are special optics with close-focusing capabilities that may bring you to subjects only an inch or two from the front of the lens. These lenses are available as fixed-focal-length (non-zooming) prime lenses, such as the 60mm and 105mm Micro-Nikkors, as well as in macro-zoom configurations. As I write this, the current 60mm f/2.8 Micro-Nikkor is an AF model (not AF-S), and doesn't auto-focus with the D40/D40x, but

that's not much of a handicap, as, most of the time, you'll probably want to focus your close-ups manually, anyway. On the other hand, the latest 105mm f/2.8G ED-IF AF-S VR Micro-Nikkor does provide autofocus capabilities, but an older, similar lens does not. (You have to watch out for the AF-S in the lens name whenever you consider buying a new lens.)

✦ **The necessity of shooting in lower light, or with faster shutter speeds.** In dim lighting, an f/4.5 maximum aperture may not allow you to use a shutter speed that's fast enough for handholding the camera. You can break out your tripod, switch to a lens with vibration reduction, boost the ISO of your camera to noise-inducing levels, or attach a lens with a faster maximum aperture (from f/1.2 to f/2.8) to your D40 or D40x. If you're shooting sports and need a fast shutter speed, you might find a faster lens useful even when there is plenty of light. The action-stopping capability of an f/2.8 lens at 1/500 second is much better than, say, that of an f/4.5 lens at 1/180 second.

✦ **The quest for a sharper image.** Some lenses are simply sharper than others. When you're taking pictures that are likely to be cropped significantly or enlarged for display, such as an 11-x 14-inch or larger print, you most likely want a a sharp lens. Some are better than others when used at large apertures; others perform more capably for macro photography; and some zooms do a better job at certain focal lengths than others. When sharpness is important to you, having a suitable lens available can save the day.

✦ **The lure of special features.** When the job at hand is specialized, a special lens might be available to do the job right. I've already mentioned the superior performance of macro lenses in close-up photography, and fast, large-aperture lenses in low light or when higher shutter speeds are desirable. Vibration reduction, which compensates for camera and photographer shake by shifting elements inside the lens as the picture is taken, is another special feature that's becoming relatively commonplace. Some lenses provide specialized capabilities you can't get with the most common lenses. These include optics with shifting elements that provide a certain amount of perspective control; and lenses like the Nikon DC (defocus control) series (all non-AF-S, unfortunately) that let you adjust how the out-of-focus portions of an image appear (especially useful in portraiture). Other special lenses include fish-eye lenses, and ultraviolet lenses for scientific applications. If you need one of these unusual features, nothing else will do the job.

Choosing Between Zoom and Fixed Focal Length

Zoom lenses used to be cumbersome, expensive, not very sharp, and they didn't have large maximum apertures. Today you can still find zooms that are big and expensive, but, by and large, they are much sharper than their predecessors, and are accompanied by other, more practical zooms that are small, light, and relatively inexpensive (but still slow in the maximum aperture department).

The chief limitation of zoom lenses is maximum aperture and, with some of the longer zoom ranges, weight. These limitations are worse at one end of the zoom scale than at the other. For example, the 70-300mm f/4.5-5.6G ED-IF AF-S VR Zoom-Nikkor makes a pretty good 300mm f/5.6 lens. Its Vibration Reduction feature can be especially useful for wildlife photography when you don't want to set up a tripod. But, when you're using this lens at the short end of its zoom range, it makes a rather large 26-ounce 70mm f/4.5 lens. You can make similar comparisons with other zooms that tend to compromise maximum aperture and size to give you a useful zoom range.

That's where fixed-focal-length (also known as *prime*) lenses come in. They are built to be used at only one focal length, and therefore can be more compact, have larger maximum apertures, and boast a little extra sharpness. They are a good choice when you have enough freedom of movement to move closer to or farther away from your subject as is required to fill the frame.

In recent years Nikon has offered f/1.4 lenses in fixed 28mm, 50mm, and 85mm focal lengths that are unmatched for speed and resolution, but none of them is an AF-S lens suitable for autofocus with the D40 or D40x. (I actually don't mind using manual focus when using an extra-fast lens at its maximum aperture, because I want to focus very, very carefully anyway.)

If you have deep pockets, you can buy 300mm and 400mm Nikkors with f/2.8 maximum apertures, and 500mm or 600mm f/4 super-telephotos, all with AF-S internal focusing motors. Even wide-angle and short telephoto zoom lenses from Nikon with f/2.8 maximum apertures tend to be very expensive.

Assessing Lens Compatibility

Until fairly recently, lens compatibility was almost a nonissue for Nikon users. You could mount any autofocus lens on any Nikon SLR camera — film or digital — and use it with full functionality. You could use manual focus lenses, too, with manual focusing, of course, and with the proviso that very old lenses (those made before 1977) needed to have a small adjustment made to ensure compatibility with newer cameras (those made in the last 30 years).

Until late 2006, the only real compatibility issue was with older, non-electronic cameras that had to be used with lenses that included a real aperture ring. Modern G-type lenses (they include a G in their model name) don't have an aperture ring, and the camera must set the f-stop. All Nikon dSLRs set the aperture electronically and can do this with both G-type lenses and other autofocus lenses that do have an aperture ring, as long as the ring is locked at the smallest f-stop, thanks to the electronic coupling on the lens (shown in figure 5.7). So, prior to the unveiling of the D40 and D40x, if you owned any Nikon dSLR, you could use virtually any autofocus lens with all of that lens's features and functions.

Surprise! The introduction of the D40 and then, a few months later, the D40x introduced a whole new ballgame. As I've mentioned, the new cameras' autofocus feature operates *only* with lenses that include an internal motor to handle focus. The Nikon version of these lenses is labeled AF-S or

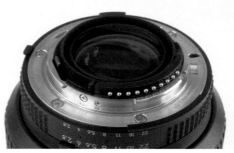

5.7 With all autofocus lenses, the camera communicates the lens opening required to the camera through these electrical contacts on the edge of the lens mount.

AF-I. Nikon dSLRs other than the D40 also have their own motor built into the body that turns a screw in the lens through a magnetic coupling, which supplies the focusing action for lenses without their own built-in autofocus motor.

So, with the D40, Nikon rather unexpectedly introduced the element of lens incompatibility between the D40/D40x and some fairly recent lenses, including those produced by a number of third-party lens vendors. If you do decide to purchase a lens from Tokina, Tamron, or Sigma, you need to do some research to see if the lens you're contemplating has a built-in autofocus motor, because the third-party vendors don't use the AF-S and AF-I designations.

The problem I'm describing may be less of an issue than you might think. As a new owner of a D40 or D40x camera, you probably don't already own a ton of lenses (with potential incompatibilities), in all probability won't be buying a large number of new lenses (a few select optics can cover most typical shooting situations), and when you do purchase new lenses, you will likely select from the newer models, which *are* AF-S models.

There's one small bonus that I should mention. Unlike all other Nikon dSLRs to date, both the D40 and D40x can be used with older manual focus/manual exposure lenses made prior to 1977 without modification. You must focus manually with these lenses, of course, and can't rely on the D40/D40x's built-in metering for exposure. (Instead, check a histogram and add or subtract exposure after a test shot, if you must.) With every other Nikon dSLR, these ancient lenses must be physically modified to fit on the camera without damaging that autofocus pin that the D40 and D40x lack.

This is a small benefit, it's true (unless you inherited some older lenses from a relative or friend), but can come in handy. For example, I often have friends asking to try out their antique lenses on my D40x to see if the optical quality is worth having that lens modified for use on their newer digital cameras. I personally use an old 55mm f/3.5 Micro-Nikkor lens dating back to the 1960s for close-up photography. I manually focus macro images anyway, and it's no big deal to review an image on the LCD and then make an exposure adjustment if necessary. You can find many great old lenses on eBay or from other sources for less than $100.

Deciphering Nikon's Lens-Naming Scheme

Before the electronic age, just about everything you wanted to know about a Nikon lens was readily discernable from its name. Most lenses were Auto-Nikkors (meaning the lens had an automatic diaphragm that stopped down to the taking aperture during the exposure). There were Micro-Nikkors for close-up work, and a few Zoom-Nikkors

with variable focal lengths. Many lenses had a letter appended that indicated how many elements the lens had. If you knew Latin, you understood that a Nikkor-P lens had five elements (penta), a Nikkor-H lens had six (hexa), and a Nikkor-S had seven (septa), and so forth.

Today, we have a virtual alphabet soup of designations, and you almost need a program to know what Roman number II is doing in the name of the latest 18-55mm f/3.5-5.6G II ED AF-S DX Zoom-Nikkor. (It means that it's the second lens in a series that otherwise has the same specifications.) The list that follows explains what various parts of the lens names signify:

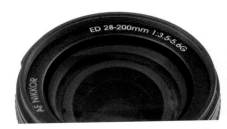

5.8 Many lenses have their vital statistics imprinted on the ring surrounding the front element, or on the lens barrel itself.

✦ **AI, AI-S.** Nikkor lenses produced after 1977 have an *Automatic Indexing* (AI) feature and *Automatic Indexing-Shutter* (AI-S) feature that eliminates the need to manually align the aperture ring on the camera. Nikon first included the letters AI or AI-S in the lens name to indicate that the lens had this feature, but eventually dropped the designation. In practice, *all* lenses introduced after 1977 are AI/AI-S compatible and include automatic aperture indexing, except for G-type lenses, which have no aperture ring at all.

✦ **E.** Nikon's E Series lenses are bargain-priced lenses with aluminum or plastic parts, which makes them a little less rugged than more expensive optics that use brass parts. However, the image quality is generally pretty good.

✦ **D.** The D Series lenses can relay focus distance information to the camera, used with 3D Matrix metering and flash exposure calculation.

✦ **G.** G-type lenses have no aperture ring, and you can use them at other than the maximum aperture only with electronic cameras like the D40/D40x that set the aperture automatically or by using the command dial while the Exposure Compensation/Aperture button is depressed.

✦ **AF, AF-D, AF-I, AF-S.** If you find AF in the lens name, the lens is a type of autofocus lens. The additional letter provides more information: D (it's a D-type lens), I (focus through an internal motor is "integrated," which means it can be manually adjusted even with the autofocus turned on), or S (internal focus with a *silent wave* motor; you can focus or fine-tune focus manually even with AF engaged). Remember, only AF-I or AF-S lenses autofocus on the D40 and D40x.

✦ **DX.** The DX lenses are designed exclusively for use with digital cameras using the APS-C-sized sensor having the 1.5X crop factor, which at this writing includes every model from the D2Xs to D40/D40x. The image circle they produce isn't large enough to fill up a full 35mm frame at all focal lengths. The digital-only design means that these lenses can be smaller and lighter

than their full-frame counterparts. If Nikon comes out with a full-frame digital camera in the future, I'd expect it to have an automatic crop mode that would crop the image to include only the APS-C-sized image area when a DX lens is mounted.

✦ **VR.** Nikon's expanding line of VR (Vibration Reduction) lenses, including the very affordable 70-300mm, 55-200mm, and 18-200mm VR zooms, includes vibration reduction technology, which shifts lens elements to counteract camera shake or movement (but not subject motion) and enables you to take photos without a tripod at slower shutter speeds.

✦ **ED.** The ED designation indicates that the lens has elements made of extra-low dispersion glass, which tends to reduce chromatic aberration (those color "ghosting" effects I mentioned) and other image quality defects.

✦ **Micro.** The term *micro* is Nikon's designation for a lens that focuses to produce a life-size image (or larger) on the sensor. Other vendors call their close-up optics *macro* lenses, but they may or may not focus to life-size.

✦ **IF.** The IF code signifies that the lens has internal focusing, so the length of the lens doesn't increase or decrease as the lens is focused. Internal focusing also makes it possible to use filters that depend on a particular orientation, such as polarizing filters, split-density/color filters, and some special effects filters.

✦ **IX.** These lenses were produced for Nikon's Pronea APS film cameras. While you can use many standard

VR: Very Rewarding

Nikon's Vibration Reduction (VR) feature counters camera shake with lens elements that are shifted internally in response to the motion of the lens during handheld photography, offsetting the shakiness the camera and photographer produce and telephoto lenses magnify. (Although VR works well with wide-angle focal lengths, such as those found in Nikon's 18-200mm and 24-120mm VR lenses.)

VR provides the equivalent camera steadiness of at least two shutter speed increments (Nikon claims four increments with its latest vibration reduction implementation), letting you shoot telephoto pictures at 1/250 second that might have required 1/1000 second without VR; or wide-angle photos at 1/15 second that would have mandated a 1/60 second shutter speed without VR. In some cases, VR can eliminate the need for a tripod. However, keep in mind that VR doesn't freeze action: You may still need that 1/1000 second shutter speed to stop sports action. Nikon's exceptional 105mm f/2.8G ED-IF AF-S VR Micro-Nikkor may enable you to shoot macro photos handheld — but it won't help you photograph outdoor blossoms that are wavering in the breeze. Nor does VR always work well when you're panning the camera. There are still many situations where a steady hand, monopod, or tripod does the best job for you.

Nikkor lenses on the Pronea 6i and Pronea S, the reverse is not true. You can't use these IX lenses on the D40 or D40x. I include this designation only for the sake of completeness, and as a caveat for anyone who happens to spot an old IX Nikkor and wonders if it can be used with his camera.

✦ **DC.** The DC stands for *defocus control*, which is a way of changing the appearance of the out-of-focus portions of an image; this is especially useful for portraits or close-ups. No Nikon DC lens offers autofocus with the D40/D40x.

Understanding Automatic Focus

To take advantage of your Nikon D40 or D40x's autofocus features, you must be using an AF-S or AF-I autofocus lens, of course. Nikon autofocus lenses include an AF designation in their name. The company still has a limited number of manual focus lenses in its product line, all with the AI-S code in the lens name.

To activate autofocus, make sure you've selected Auto-servo AF (AF-A), Single-servo AF (AF-S), or Continuous-servo AF (AF-C) and not MF (Manual focus) in the Custom Setting menu (CSM) using option CSM 02. You can also set the autofocus mode by pressing the Info button (left of the LCD at the bottom), scrolling to the autofocus setting on the right side of the LCD display, pressing OK, and then choosing the focus mode you want from the menu that pops up.

If your lens has its own A-M switch, it must be set to AF, too. The M setting in the camera or lens always takes precedence: If you've selected Manual focus in either case, then you must focus manually, regardless of whether AF is set or not on the camera or lens. Some lenses include an M/A-M switch. In the M/A position, autofocus is active, but you can override the camera's focus setting manually if you want.

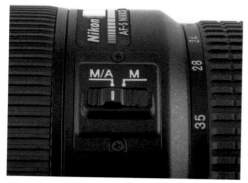

5.9 Some lenses have their own autofocus/manual switches.

If you do want to focus manually, just twist the focus ring on the lens, which is usually narrower than the lens's zoom ring. The focus ring may be either the innermost or outermost ring, depending on the design of the lens itself. When you rotate the focus ring, you see the image pop in and out of focus as you peer through the viewfinder. If you press the shutter release down halfway, the information display at the bottom of the viewfinder appears, and the D40/D40x's green focus confirmation indicator at the bottom left lights up when correct focus is achieved.

In autofocus mode, partially depressing the shutter release button activates the focus mechanism. If your lens has an f/5.6 or larger maximum aperture, one or more of the three brackets visible in the viewfinder illuminates in red to show you which areas of the image are calculating correct focus. When the lens has locked in autofocus, the green focus confirmation indicator glows.

Current autofocus area

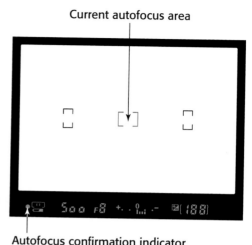

Autofocus confirmation indicator

5.10 The current focus area and an in-focus LED appear in the viewfinder.

The autofocus system works best under bright lighting conditions, with subjects that have lots of contrast. Some patterns and fine details, or areas with no details at all (such as the sky), can confuse the autofocus mechanism. If there are objects at widely different distances within the same focus zone (Nikon cites shooting through chain link fences as an example), the focus system may be unable to lock onto a specific subject.

When the light is dim or your subject's contrast is low, the D40/D40x's focus assist lamp (see figure 5.11) illuminates. The lamp, which also flashes when the self-timer is used, is located on the front of the camera between the shutter release button and lens mount. External Nikon electronic flash units, such as the SB-800 Speedlight and the Nikon SC-29 flash extension cable (which clips onto the flash accessory shoe on top of the camera), also have focus assist lights. If you find the focus assist feature distracting, you can disable it in the Custom Setting menu (CSM) using CSM 09.

Although the D40/D40x's autofocus system is smart enough to achieve sharp focus under most conditions, you can customize its operation, including specifying when and how the camera locks in focus, or which areas of the frame should be used to calculate focus.

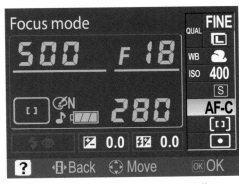

5.12 Press the Info button, then scroll to Focus mode, and press the OK button to set autofocus mode.

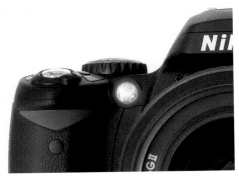

5.11 The focus assist lamp illuminates to provide additional light for the autofocus system.

Autofocus modes

The D40/D40x has three autofocus modes to choose from, each suitable to a particular type of shooting situation. As described earlier, the fastest way to choose the focus mode is to press the Info button, using the multi selector to scroll down to the Focus Mode choice, press OK, and then select the focus mode you want on the screen that pops up (see figure 5.12). Note that AF-S and AF-C are available only in Program (P), S (Shutter Priority), A (Aperture Priority) and M (Manual exposure) modes. The D40 and D40x use AF-A mode by default in Auto or any of the DVP (scene) modes, but you can also choose Manual focus.

Here's an explanation of how each of these focus modes works:

✦ **Single-servo autofocus (AF-S).** In this mode, the D40/D40x locks in a focus point when you press the shutter release button down halfway, and the focus confirmation light glows in the viewfinder. A beep sounds when sharp focus is achieved. (You can disable the beep sound in the Custom Setting menu with CSM 01.) The focus remains locked until you release the button or take the picture, and the shutter can only be released when the subject is in focus. (The D40/D40x prevents you from taking an ill-focused photo.) If the camera is unable to achieve sharp focus, the focus confirmation light blinks. This mode is best when your subject is relatively motionless.

✦ **Continuous-servo autofocus (AF-C).** In this mode, the D40/D40x sets focus when you partially depress the shutter button, but it continues to monitor the frame and refocuses if the camera or subject moves. This is a useful mode for photographing sports and other subjects in motion.

✦ **Auto-servo autofocus (AF-S).** In this mode, which is the D40/D40x's default autofocus setting, the camera switches between AF-S and AF-C as appropriate. That is, it locks in a focus point when you partially depress the shutter button (AF-S), but switches automatically to AF-C if the subject begins to move. This mode is handy when photographing a subject, such as a child at play, who might move unexpectedly. As with the other focus modes, the shutter releases only when the image is in focus.

While you can set the camera to use AF-A in P, A, S, and M exposure modes, it is the only autofocus setting available for Auto and all DVP/Scene modes – even Sports, which can benefit from the AF-C setting. So, if you want to use AF-C for action photography, change from the Sports scene mode to another mode (such as Shutter Priority) and select AF-C manually.

Setting focus zones

The Nikon D40/D40x uses three different focus areas to calculate correct focus, and has three AF-Area modes:

✦ **Closest Subject.** The camera selects one of the three focus areas containing the subject closest to the camera. Use this option when your area of interest is always the nearest object to the camera.

✦ **Dynamic Area.** The camera uses the focus area you select, but will use the other two focus areas instead if the subject moves outside the original zone. This option is a good choice if your subject is moving (and it's always selected when you use the Sports DVP/Scene mode.)

✦ **Single Area.** You select the focus area, and the camera focuses on subjects in that area only. This choice is best if your subject is not moving, and may be located somewhere other than closest to the camera. This mode is chosen automatically when you use the Close-Up DVP/Scene mode.

To recap these sometimes confusing focus options: If you're using the default AF-area mode (Closest Subject) with P, S, A, and M exposure modes, plus Auto, Flash Off, Portrait, Landscape, Child, Night Portrait DVP/Scene modes (but not Sports or Close-Up), the camera selects one of the three focus zones automatically. You have no control over the focus area selected when Closest Subject is active.

You can also chose Dynamic Area or Single Area modes for P, S, A, and M exposure modes, plus all DVP/Scene modes (except for Sports and Close-Up, which use only Dynamic Area and Single Area, respectively.) There are two ways to choose from among Closest Subject, Dynamic Area, or Single Area autofocus modes. You can use Custom Setting Menu option CSM 03, or, simply press the Info button, scroll to the AF-area mode selection, press OK, and choose either of the three autofocus modes (in addition to Manual focus) from the screen that pops up.

Then, if you haven't selected Closest Subject, you can choose the focus zone yourself:

1. **While framing your image in the viewfinder, press the shutter release halfway to activate the autofocus system.**

2. **Use the directional buttons of the multi-controller to choose the focus area you want to use.** The selected focus area is highlighted in red.

3. **To lock in the focus area for the current picture only, hold down the AE-L/AF-L button located to the right of the viewfinder window.** The focus is now fixed as long as you keep holding the button down, so you can reframe the photo if you want and retain the same focus setting (see figure 5.13).

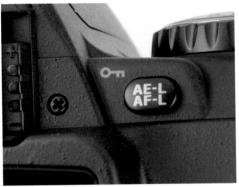

5.13 Hold down the AE-L/AF-L button to lock the current focus.

 You can learn how to change the behavior of the AE-L/AF-L button in Chapter 3 to lock only exposure or only focus, instead of both.

Working with Depth of Field

Depth of field is an important concept that you must understand to use the focusing capabilities of your D40 or D40x effectively. Broadly speaking, *depth of field* (DOF) is the distance range in a photograph in which all the included portions of the image are acceptably sharp. That sounds like a simple enough definition, except for the *acceptably*

sharp qualification. What's acceptable and what is not acceptable in terms of sharpness can vary significantly depending on the viewing distance, amount of enlargement of an image, and even the person doing the viewing. Depth of field that looks fine in a 4-x-6-inch print viewed from 10 inches away might be intolerable in a 16-x-20-inch print viewed at a distance of 2 feet. And, what I think is acceptably sharp may not be acceptable to you.

In theory, only one plane of an image is actually in sharp focus for any given image (see figure 5.14). Everything else in the picture is, at the very least, a little bit out of focus. However, in practice, a much larger distance range of the image may be acceptably sharp, because the difference between

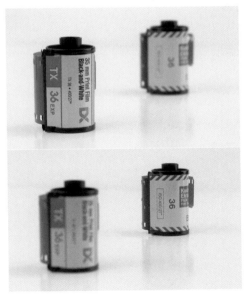

5.14 Because depth of field is limited to a single plane at wide apertures, when the lens is focused on the object at left (top image), the object at right is out of focus. Focusing on the farther object (bottom image), causes the closer object to be out of focus.

perfect focus and almost-perfect focus is difficult for the eye to detect. Because our eyes have a poor memory for sharpness, good focus can be confusing.

In fact, the term *circle of confusion* is applied to the slightly defocused points in an image that are large enough to appear to our eyes as fuzzy discs rather than points and, therefore, seem to be out of focus. The exact size of the circle of confusion varies, as I've noted, by the amount of enlargement, viewing distance (all of which make the circles seem larger to our eyes), and the discernment (or fussiness) of the viewer. Points that are smaller than the circle of confusion for a given image appear to be in sharp focus. Points that are larger make up the out-of-focus portions of the image. The range in which the apparently sharp points reside is that image's depth of field.

The approximate DOF range extends one third in front of the plane of sharpest focus, and two thirds behind it. So, assuming your depth of field at a particular aperture, focal length, and subject distance is 3 feet, everything 1 foot in front of the focus plane and objects 2 feet behind it should appear to be sharp.

Some of the out-of-focus discs in an image are more noticeable than others because of the way they blend (or don't blend) together. This property, named for a variation of the Japanese word for blur, is *bokeh.* (It rhymes with *mocha.*) A lens's bokeh depends on things like the shape of its diaphragm (the more leaves in the diaphragm, the rounder and more pleasing the disc shapes it produces) and the evenness of the illumination of the blurry shapes created (see figure 5.15).

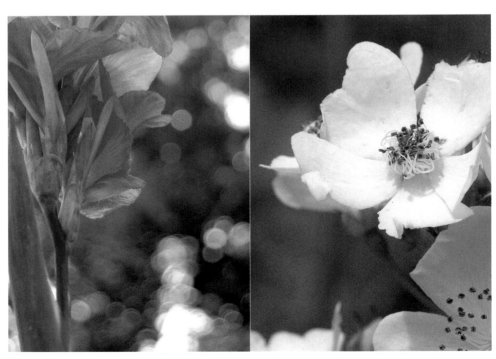

5.15 When the out-of-focus discs in the background are as obvious as the shapes in the shot at left, bokeh is said to be bad. Lenses with good bokeh provide a smooth background.

Lenses with good bokeh produce out-of-focus discs that fade at their edges, in some cases so smoothly that they don't produce circles at all. Lenses with intermediate bokeh qualities generate discs that are evenly shaded, or perhaps have some fade to darkness at their edges. The worst lenses from a bokeh standpoint create discs that are darker in the center and lighter on their edges.

F-Stop Foibles

Here are some things to understand about the lens aperture and its effect on focus and other aspects of your photographs:

✦ **Depth of field.** Larger openings (smaller numbers, such as f/2.8 or f/3.5) provide less depth of field at a given focal length. Smaller openings (larger numbers, such as f/16 or f/22) offer more depth of field. When you change exposure using the aperture, you also modify the range of your image that is in sharp focus, which you can use creatively to isolate a subject (with shallow depth of field) or capture a broad subject area (with extensive depth of field).

✦ **Sharpness.** Most lenses produce their sharpest image approximately two stops less than wide open. For example, if you're using a zoom lens with an f/4 maximum aperture, it probably has its best resolution and least distortion at roughly f/8.

✦ **Diffraction.** Stopping down further from the "optimum" aperture may create extra depth of field, but you also lose some sharpness due to a phenomenon known as *diffraction*, which is caused by interference with the light by the edges of the diaphragm. You want to avoid f-stops like f/22 unless you must have the extra depth of field, or need the smaller f-stop so you can use a preferred shutter speed.

✦ **Focal length.** The effective f-stop of a zoom lens can vary depending on the focal length you use. That's why the D40 and D40x's 18-55mm kit lens is described as an f/3.5-5.6 optic. At the 18mm position, the widest lens opening is equivalent to f/3.5; at 55mm, that same size opening passes 1.5 stops less light, producing an effective f/5.6 aperture. At intermediate zoom settings, an intermediate effective f-value applies. Your camera's metering system compensates for these changes automatically, and as a practical matter, this factor affects your photography only when you need that widest opening.

✦ **Focus distance.** It's a minor point, but the effective f-stop of a lens can also vary depending on the focus distance. This is really a factor only when you're shooting close-ups. A close-focusing macro lens can lose a full effective f-stop when you double the magnification by moving the lens twice as far from the sensor. The selected aperture then "looks" half as large to the sensor, which accounts for the light loss. Your D40 or D40x's exposure meter compensates for this, unless you're using gadgets like extension tubes, bellows, or other add-ons that preclude automatic exposure.

Using Wide-Angle and Telephoto Lenses

From a theoretical photographic standpoint, the chief difference between wide-angle and telephoto lenses is their angle of view and how much they magnify the image. On a practical basis, there is a lot more to consider. Wide-angle and telephoto lenses are constructed differently, and are commonly plagued by different kinds of optical problems, or *aberrations*, as well as various real or apparent types of distortion. These two classifications of lenses also offer very different perspectives on a subject, and, because of the relationship between the subject and distance, even on the amount of depth of field you have available. Close-up, or *macro*, lenses and teleconverters (see figure 5.16) are special beasts, too, with characteristics of their own. This section explains some of those key differences.

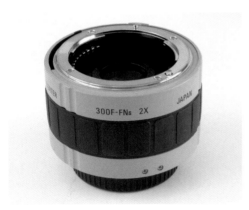

5.16 Teleconverters increase the magnification of compatible lenses.

Working with wide-angles

There are six basic reasons for using wide-angle lenses/wide zoom settings, although there is no reason why you must choose just one of them for a particular image. Often, you want to use more than one of the special properties of a wide lens setting as a compositional or creative tool in your images.

To give you more room to shoot

A wide-angle lens lets you shoot in tight surroundings, where you might not have room to back up in order to take in everything you want to include in the frame. Indoors, you might find yourself with your back up against a wall, and the alternative of going outside and shooting through an open window is either impractical or silly. For outdoor photos, you may find that you can't back up any farther because of obstacles behind you, such as a crowd of people, or walls, trees, or other natural features, or that taking a few steps back ruins your composition.

In all of these cases, a wide-angle lens enables you to stand your ground and shoot without the need to step back. When quarters are tight, the wider the lens you have available, the better.

To broaden your field of view

A wide-angle lens can increase your field of view when you're taking distant shots. Certainly, you could capture a sweeping panorama by taking multiple pictures and stitching them together in your image editor. But you might find it easier and faster to use a wider lens to grab that wide-angle view in a single shot, and then snip off the top and/or bottom of the frame to produce the wide-screen look you want.

To increase apparent depth of field

As a practical matter, wide-angle lenses offer more depth of field at a given aperture than a telephoto lens. Of course, the fields of view and perspective differ sharply, but if lots of depth of field is what you need, a wide-angle lens gives it to you.

Of course, strictly speaking, for the same *subject size*, depth of field is identical for both wide-angle and telephoto lenses. That is, if you took a photo of a friend standing 100 feet away with both a wide-angle and a telephoto lens, and then enlarged and cropped the wide-angle picture so your friend appeared to be the same size as in the telephoto shot, the depth of field would be identical (and your friend would seem a lot fuzzier in the extreme enlargement). But who would be crazy enough to do that? For real-world photography, it's enough to apply the increased depth of field that results from taking a picture with a wide-angle lens.

To emphasize the foreground

The sweeping perspective of wide-angle lenses emphasizes the subjects that are closest to the camera (in the foreground) and makes subjects farther away appear to be much smaller in proportion. You can put that effect to good use when you *want* to place emphasis on the foreground. A picturesque lake, a bed of flowers, or some other attractive element in the foreground can be emphasized by using a wider focal length.

You can use this emphasis on the foreground as a creative tool, but you must also keep the emphasis in mind when shooting subjects that don't have an attractive foreground. In such cases, use a slightly less wide lens or zoom setting, step back (if you can), and shoot. The field of view can end up the same, but there is less emphasis on the foreground in the shot taken with the slightly longer focal length.

To add creative distortion

Foreground emphasis, carried to the extreme, can result in outright distortion, where the objects closest to the camera are extraordinarily enlarged compared to subjects farther away. This distorted perspective can work for you if you use it intentionally. A type of wide-angle lens called a *fish-eye* uses exaggerated distortion to create a unique look (see figure 5.17)

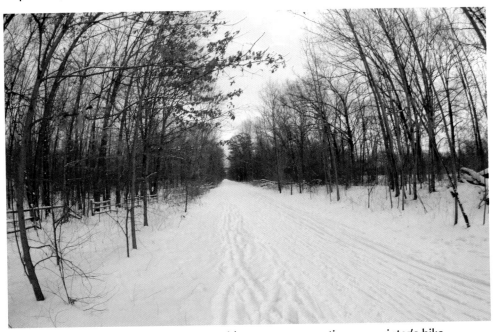

5.17 A wide-angle semifish-eye lens provides a new perspective on a winter's hike.

To provide an interesting angle

Wide-angle lenses produce significantly different viewpoints when you use them at angles that are higher or lower than normal. Eye-level shooting tends to be the default for most photographers, but if you get down low and shoot up at your subject, or elevate yourself and shoot downward, you can find interesting new angles. Wide-angle lenses only emphasize those new perspectives.

Similarly, you see familiar subjects in a new light when you get up higher than normal and shoot down. Once you've explored these angles with a wide lens, you may find yourself reluctant to shoot from eye-level ever again.

Working with telephotos

There are six key reasons for using telephoto lenses and telephoto zoom settings, too. Not all of them involve sports or wildlife photography either. The important thing to remember about using telephoto lenses is that they tend to provide a flat perspective that isn't as varied as the one you get with wide-angle lenses. You can use that creatively or work extra hard to keep your flat viewpoint from becoming boring. Here are the key reasons for using a telephoto lens.

To decrease distance

If getting closer to a distant subject isn't practical, a telephoto lens or telephoto zoom can help. Some subjects, such as the moon, are impossibly distant. Others, like erupting volcanoes, are impossibly dangerous. Frequently, it's just impractical to get closer to your subject. A telephoto lens can magnify distant objects so you can photograph them as if you were not so far away at all.

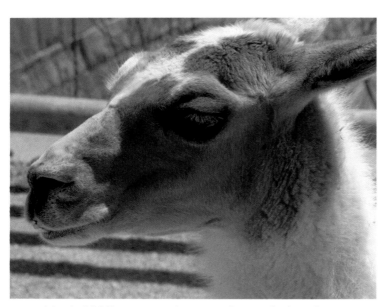

5.18 This placid fellow was 30 feet away, but a telephoto lens brought him almost nose-to-nose with the photographer.

Wide-Angle Pitfalls

For each reason that you might want to use a wide-angle lens, a potential pitfall that you might want to avoid exists. As with everything, there can be too much of a good thing, and even the best tool can be misused.

✦ **Tilting lines.** Wide-angle lenses tend to make horizontal and vertical lines more prominent. Avoid tilting or rotating the camera to produce off-kilter lines in your subject. If you lean back to take in the top of a tall building, you end up with a structure that appears to be falling backwards.

✦ **Perspective distortion.** Wide-angles exaggerate the relative size of objects close to the camera, compared to those farther away. Although this property is a good creative tool, it can also be misused, particularly when you photograph people up close. Human subjects rarely are improved by making their noses (which are closest to the camera) appear huge in proportion to the rest of their faces.

✦ **Lens aberrations.** Wide angles may suffer from outwardly-curving lines at the edges of the frame (*barrel distortion*), or dark corners (*vignetting*). Sometimes you can improve these defects by using a smaller f-stop. In any case, you may want to keep important subject matter away from the edges and corners of your images.

✦ **Flash follies.** Electronic flash units, including the Speedlight built into your D40/D40x, often provide coverage for wide-angle settings no wider than the 18mm position of the basic kit lenses. At wider angles, the flash might not cover the edges of the frame, or might cast shadows of the lens or lens hood on your subject. An external flash unit equipped with a diffusing panel can solve both problems by elevating the illumination high enough not to cast a shadow, and by providing broader flash coverage.

To isolate your subject

Because telephoto lenses tend to reduce the amount of depth of field in a given image, you can use them to isolate your subject through the magic of selective focus. Just focus carefully on the subject you want to separate from the foreground and background, and use a large enough f-stop to throw the rest of the image out of focus. Indeed, depth of field with longer lenses is so shallow that you may be able to accomplish this feat even at smaller apertures, such as f/11 or f/16.

To grab sports action

Even indoor sports may be difficult to photograph up close. Certainly, you might be able to stand along the baseline at a high school basketball game, but other indoor sports, such as pro basketball, arena football, or indoor tennis may have you shooting from the stands where a telephoto lens comes in handy. Most outdoor sports are even more suitable for long lens photography, because even from the sidelines a lot of the action on a soccer field, baseball diamond, or football arena is 50 or more yards away.

Telephoto lenses — particularly telephoto zooms that let you zoom in and out as the action unfolds — can help you grab sports action without racing from place to place to keep pace with the players.

To capture wildlife in its native habitat

Wildlife may be wary of an approaching photographer. Instead, you often need to quietly stalk your photo prey, get as close as you can, and capture your photo from a distance of 10 to 20 yards — frequently, much farther. Even zoo animals are difficult to photograph up close.

A telephoto lens can reach out and grab the photos you want without spooking the wild animals. Sometimes the distances aren't even all that great. You can photograph a skittish tree frog or squirrel from 10 feet with a telephoto, when a closer approach would send the creature running.

To create flattering portraits

Perhaps your family and friends aren't terrified of your camera and are willing to sit for an informal portrait or two. Still, a short telephoto lens (with an actual focal length of about 50-85mm) could serve you well. Human beings photograph in a more flattering way with a slightly longer lens, as a wide-angle tends to make noses look huge and ears tiny in a frame-filling shot. A little extra telephoto distance also gives you room to arrange the lighting that illuminates your portrait subject, adding to the improved look that even a semiformal portrait session often has over a grin-and-grab candid snapshot.

To get up close — from afar

Macro photography is a third way of using the telephoto lens or telephoto zoom's magnification. The capability to focus close in isn't the only attribute of a macro lens that you need to pay attention to. The working distance can be even more important. Nikon's popular 60mm Micro-Nikkor lens brings you to within an inch or two of a tiny object, but

Teleconverters

Teleconverters are magical devices that multiply the magnification of your lenses by 1.4X, 1.7X, 2X, or 3X, but at a price. Fit between your prime or zoom lens and the camera body, teleconverters include optics that magnify the image, changing a lens with a true focal length of 200mm into a 280mm, 340mm, 400mm, or 600mm lens. They also rob you of a little sharpness (with expensive Nikon converters) or a lot of sharpness (with some inexpensive third-party models). You also lose a half f-stop of illumination with a 1.4X model, and up to three full stops with a 3X converter. That's a double whammy, exacting a cost in the maximum aperture department (converting an f/2.8 lens into an f/8 lens with a 3X adapter), especially when you must use an even smaller aperture to regain some of the sharpness you lose. Because the D40 or D40x's autofocus system requires the equivalent of at least f/5.6 worth of light, (and an AF-S or AF-I compatible lens) you can lose autofocus capabilities, too. Teleconverters are priced between $100 and $400, and work best when you use them with the vendor's own recommended lenses. Stick with the 1.4X and 1.7X models if possible. The "price" may be too high otherwise.

that might be so close that the camera or lens itself casts a shadow on your subject. For that reason, telephoto macro lenses, like Nikon's 105mm f/2.8 VR Micro-Nikkor come in very handy. Armed with one of these, you can back up and still shoot close-up images.

Telephoto Pitfalls

Telephoto lenses involve some special considerations of their own, some of which are the flip side of the concerns pertinent to using wide-angle lenses. Here's a summary:

✦ **Faster shutter speeds needed.** Because telephoto lenses magnify photographer and camera shake when the camera isn't mounted on a tripod, monopod, or other support, higher shutter speeds are mandated. There is a fairly useless rule of thumb that suggests using the reciprocal of the focal length of the lens (that is, 1/200 second with a 200mm lens) as the minimum shutter speed to be used with a handheld telephoto lens. This "rule" should be used as an absolute *minimum*, because it doesn't take into account the size and weight distribution of the lens, the ability of the photographer to hold the lens steady, and how much the image will be enlarged. In my own case, I find I must use at least 1/2000 second to successfully handhold a favorite zoom lens at 500mm; the suggested 1/500 second setting invariably produces blurred photos. If you can't use a sufficiently fast shutter speed with a telephoto lens, you really should consider a tripod or monopod (or springing for one of Nikon's cool VR lenses). It's too easy to lose a critical amount of sharpness through camera motion.

✦ **Reduced depth of field.** The reduced depth of field that results from longer focal lengths isn't imaginary. If you're using selective focus to isolate a subject in your photo, the shallow depth of field is a good thing. But, most of the time you want enough depth of field to allow all the important elements of your photo to remain in sharp focus simultaneously. Use a smaller f-stop as required.

✦ **Atmospheric haze and fog.** Unless you live in Southern California or a typical big-city area plagued with haze and smog, the diffusing effects of the atmosphere may not be part of your everyday life. Even so, haze and fog are present everywhere to some extent, even when you're hundreds of miles from civilization shooting that placid mountain vista. Dirt or moisture in the air reduces contrast and mutes colors, and the effect worsens as the focal length of your lens increases. Sometimes a haze filter on the front of your lens can theoretically help, but you still need to be prepared to increase the contrast and color saturation of your images, either using the D40 or D40x's Optimize Image controls, or with your image editor.

✦ **Contrast-robbing flare.** Stray light bouncing around inside your lens reduces the contrast of your photos and can provide unattractive bright spots and flares. Because telephoto lenses often produce low-contrast images to begin with (see "Atmospheric haze and fog" above), you don't want any further contrast loss. Use the lens hood that came with your lens (or purchase one if a hood wasn't included).

Continued

Continued

✦ **Flash coverage (*redux*).** While wide-angle lenses sometimes cover more visual real estate than flash units can illuminate, with telephoto lenses the problem is more one of distance. That subject 50 feet from your camera may appear close at hand, but to your electronic flash, it's still 16-plus yards away. Your D40/D40x's built-in flash usually finds its limit at about 20 feet; for greater distances (say for nighttime wildlife photography or night sports), you need a more powerful flash. I recommend the Nikon SB-800 Speedlight, which has several times the power of the D40/D40x's built-in unit.

✦ **Squeeze plays.** Telephoto lenses compress the apparent distance between objects, making a row of columns that are separated by 20 to 30 feet appear to be only a few feet apart when you photograph them with a 500mm lens. Human faces tend to look flatter when you photograph them with longer telephoto lenses, too. You can use the telephoto's compression effect as a creative tool if you want, but you should be aware of possible unwanted squeeze plays when you're not looking for a flattened look.

Working with Light

Light is the magic tool we use to create our images, affecting virtually every aspect of the photo. The direction of light shows the shape and contour of our subjects, and emphasizes or mutes the texture. The intensity of the light and the proportions of multiple sources of illumination help establish the contrast of an image. Colors present or absent in the light and the balance between the hues can tint our view. Effective lighting can produce a flattering portrait of someone with less-than-perfect features, while illumination that's poorly arranged can turn a portrait masterpiece into a monsterpiece. The quantity and duration of the light you use can affect motion and camera blur (or lack thereof) and, indirectly, the range of sharpness (or *depth of field*) in an image.

Light comes in many forms. It bounces off opaque or semi-transparent objects, is filtered through translucent subjects, and emitted by things that produce light of their own. The light you use to shape your images may be *continuous* like daylight, moonlight, or electric lamps, or exist only as a brief *burst* from an electronic flash.

Mastering light in all its permutations is one of the keys to raising the bar on the quality of your photographs. In this chapter, I introduce you to what you need to know to work with existing light and electronic flash, especially the Nikon D40/D40x's built-in, pop-up Speedlight.

Choosing Between Continuous and Flash Illumination

There are two types of illumination that you work with: continuous light, such as daylight, moonlight, or the light provided by incandescent or fluorescent sources; and the burst of light produced by electronic flash units, including the built-in, pop-up flash in your D40/D40x as well as external supplementary flash units.

Your creative choices include whether to work with the continuous light as it is present in your scene, or whether you need to supplement it with additional or repositioned continuous lights, redirect it with reflectors that bounce light in new directions, or completely (or partially) override the existing light with electronic flash. More advanced photographers can even modify lighting by *subtracting* illumination to produce shadows where none existed before. You can see that the use of continuous and electronic flash lighting can be a powerful creative tool.

But at the most basic level, you need to decide whether to go with continuous lighting of daylight or artificial light sources, or to use electronic flash. There are some advantages and disadvantages related to each type of illumination:

Ability to preview the lighting effect

Continuous lighting wins on this point. With constant illumination, the lighting effect you will end up with is visible at all times as you compose your shot and take the picture (see figure 6.1). You know when you peer through the viewfinder whether the light will be soft or harsh. You can spot any undesirable shadows. If there are multiple light sources (such as several table lamps in an indoor scene), you can tell how they interact, and whether the additional light sufficiently brightens the shadows cast by the main light, or whether you might need a little extra illumination on the background to separate your subject from its surroundings.

Previewing can be less certain with electronic flash. Indeed, the general effect you're going to get may be a total mystery. Some types of external flash units have what is called a *modeling lamp* that shows what the lighting effect will be, but most of the time you'll need to rely on your experience in shooting similar photos in the past, reinforced by reviewing a test image on the D40/D40x's LCD. After reviewing your shot, you can then make some adjustments and shoot another test image until you get exactly the lighting look you want. After all, that's exactly what studio photographers did with their Polaroid test shots in the olden days.

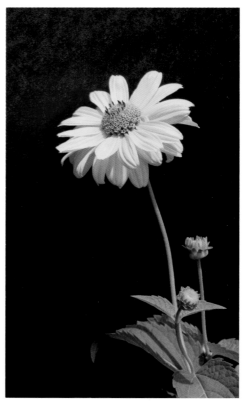

6.1 Continuous illumination lets you see the exact lighting effect you will get through the viewfinder before you take the photo.

If you're planning on using subtle lighting effects, particularly those where the placement of shadows or highlights is important, continuous lighting is probably your best bet. Shiny objects, those with irregular surfaces that cast shadows, and other types of tricky subjects can be photographed more simply with continuous illumination.

Ease of exposure calculation

Calculating the exposure of continuous light sources is simple, because the illumination remains constant and can be easily measured by the exposure system of your D40 or D40x. Measuring electronic flash exposure is theoretically a little trickier, because the light source that provides the illumination may exist for only 1/1000 second, at the moment the picture is taken.

The solution is to use a burst of flash illumination released a fraction of a second before the picture is taken. That preflash, not used for the exposure itself, is measured by the camera and used to calculate the correct exposure. Nikon's through-the-lens (iTTL) flash metering technology allows the D40 and D40x to measure the amount of illumination that bounces off the subject and determine the exposure using that information (plus camera-to-subject distance data supplied to the camera by a D-type lens). The iTTL system is sophisticated enough that it even works when you're using multiple Nikon electronic flashes, such as the SB-600, and SB-800, which can be mounted on the camera or used off-camera and fired remotely, and the Nikon SB-400, which must be used mounted to the camera.

You can also calculate flash exposure manually using a handheld electronic flash meter,

although such an accessory is generally considered a "pro" tool that most D40 or D40x owners will not need or use. Such a meter can be particularly useful in multiple flash situations, because it's easy to measure the amount of light each of the strobes produces in a particular setup. Flash meters, although they can cost several hundred dollars, are worth the expense for those who need them, and are available in models that can read both flash and continuous illumination.

Continuous illumination should be theoretically easier and more convenient to meter, but the technology built into your camera makes exposure with flash comparably fast and accurate.

Portability of add-on illumination

For those who don't want to tote around additional gear, portability can be an important consideration. Both continuous and electronic flash illumination in their most basic forms are eminently portable. Daylight and other forms of existing illumination are always there for you, and your D40 or D40x's built-in flash can be flipped up and used anytime it's needed.

But continuous lighting may not be bright enough for the picture you want to take, and supplementary artificial light sources almost always involve AC-powered lamps, which can be bulky and, of course, require an external source of electricity. While your camera's electronic flash has some extra pop, it, too, may not be bright enough, particularly for subjects more than 15 to 20 feet from the camera. However, if you need more flash power, external flash units that can fit in your camera bag are battery powered and easy to tote. Electronic flash is a clear winner in the portability department for most applications.

Evenness of illumination

Some types of continuous light sources, particularly daylight, offer illumination that fills a scene, with lots of light for the foreground, background, and your subject. If there are shadows, you can use reflectors or fill-in light sources to even out the illumination further. Outdoor illumination and indoor lighting in a well-lit interior can be quite even, without serious hot spots or dingy shadows. There are exceptions, of course, both outdoors and indoors.

You're most likely to be concerned about evenness of illumination when you're using electronic flash units. As with all types of highly directional illumination, the uneven lighting is caused by something called the *inverse square law*, which dictates that as a light source's position increases from the subject, the amount of light reaching the subject falls off proportionately to the square of the distance. In plain English, that means that a flash or lamp that's 4 feet away from a subject provides only one-quarter as much illumination as a source that's 2 feet away (rather than half as much). This translates into relatively shallow "depth of light." (Figure 6.5, later in this chapter, illustrates this concept.)

So, if you're using an electronic flash to photograph a group that includes members who are 12 feet from the camera, a few standing just 6 feet away, and some distant participants milling about 18 feet or more from your shooting position, you may have problems. If the correct exposure for the main group is f/11, the subjects closer to the camera will be two stops overexposed (f/22 might be a better setting for those

nearby subjects alone), while the stragglers at the periphery of the scene will be at least one stop *under*exposed. In terms of evenness of illumination, daylight and other forms of ambient illumination are clear winners. (Studio lamps also suffer the inverse square penalty, but a D40 or D40x owner is much more likely to be using electronic flash.)

Action-stopping ability

When it comes to the ability to freeze moving objects in their tracks, the advantage frequently goes to electronic flash. When the electronic flash is the main or only source of illumination, the "shutter speed" is determined by the duration of the flash itself. Your D40/D40x's shutter speed may be set for 1/200 second (or some other speed) during a flash exposure, but if the flash illumination predominates, the *effective* exposure time is 1/1000 second or even shorter, depending on the duration of the flash's burst of light.

This variation in flash duration occurs because the flash adjusts the amount of light it produces by reducing the length of the burst. If the full power of the flash unit is required, all the energy stored in the Speedlight's capacitor "holding tank" is released at once, within about 1/1000 second. If less light is required, the flash can "dump" the excess during the actual exposure (by-passing the flash tube that produces the burst of light), creating a flash that may last 1/2000 second, 1/4000 second, or even briefer. The tiny slice of time carved out by an electronic flash is as effective as an actual fast shutter speed when it comes to freezing action (see figure 6.2).

In contrast, the motion-stopping capabilities of a camera shooting under a continuous light source depend completely on the

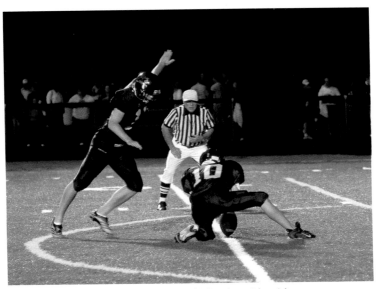

6.2 Electronic flash can freeze this kicker in mid-stride.

shutter speed. And those speeds depend on the amount of light available and your ISO sensitivity setting. For example, if you're shooting sports indoors, there probably isn't enough available light to allow you to use a 1/2000 second shutter speed, but applying that effective speed by using a flash unit is no problem at all.

Of course, any flash exposure is actually two exposures: one from the flash itself, and one from the existing light in a scene admitted to the sensor by the shutter during its leisurely 1/200 second (for the D40x) or 1/500 second (for the D40) trip across the focal plane. If the ambient light levels in a scene are low, only the flash is used to make the image. But if the existing light levels are high, that additional exposure may produce a secondary ghost image in your picture.

That's why electronic flash isn't always a panacea for shooting sports indoors. Yes, the flash's 1/1000 second effective shutter speed will freeze motion, but if the existing

light is bright enough, you also get that ghost image during the 1/200 second "real" exposure. I explain more about this effect later in this chapter.

Syncing capability

The illumination you use must "synchronize" with your camera's shutter. That is, the light must be available throughout the exposure to provide a proper image. Continuous lighting, of course, syncs at any speed; because it is continuous, it is present throughout the exposure, as the shutter exposes the sensor to the incoming light. (I explain this shutter operation later in the chapter.)

However, your D40x or D40's electronic flash is used at shutter speeds no higher than 1/200 second (for the D40x) or 1/500 second (for the D40) for a very good reason. Because of the way the shutter operates — exposing only part of the sensor at a time for exposures briefer than 1/200 or 1/500 second (D40x/D40, respectively) — faster shutter speeds don't synchronize with the flash. The flash must burst when the shutter is fully open (and that's at 1/200 and 1/500 second or slower). At faster speeds, the shutter is only partially open, and flash photography produces only partially exposed frames.

Relative cost

No argument here: incandescent lamps are generally much less expensive than electronic flash units, which can easily cost several hundred dollars. If you want to use more than one light source, the costs mount more quickly with flash. You can pay more than $300 for a Nikon SB-800 electronic flash unit, or $10 for a flexible-necked desk lamp that can double as a macro photography light source. And, of course, sunlight and existing room light is free!

Versatility

Of course, the adaptability and flexibility of a particular light source depends on what type of photography you're doing. If you consider the lighting effect preview question only, incandescent lamps are more versatile than electronic flash units that don't have a modeling light.

But, because incandescent lamps are not as bright as electronic flash, the slower shutter speeds they require mean that you may have to use a tripod more often, especially when shooting portraits or macro photographs, or invest in a Vibration Reduction (VR) lens that counters the camera shake caused by slower shutter speeds. Electronic flash's action-freezing power enables you to work without a tripod, adding flexibility and speed when choosing angles and positions.

This one is almost a tie, depending, as I noted, on what kind of photography you do.

Mastering Continuous Lighting

For most types of photography, continuous lighting is much less complicated to use than flash. The key consideration you need to keep in mind is the illumination's *color temperature* and *white balance*, which are two terms used to describe the same attribute; that is, although light often appears to our eyes as colorless, it actually has a color bias or color balance. The relative color of light is related to its color temperature, and how the digital camera uses white balance controls to adjust for this temperature.

Three types of continuous lighting

As I noted earlier, there are three main types of continuous lighting: daylight, incandescent/tungsten light, and fluorescent light. There are also some oddball light sources, such as sodium vapor illumination, that you won't encounter much outside of parking lots and other urban outdoor nighttime environments.

Daylight

The sun produces daylight even if you can't see the sun directly when it's hidden behind clouds. Direct sunlight can be bright and harsh, causing inky shadows and shiny glare reflecting off some types of subjects. Daylight can also be soft when it's muted by overcast clouds, or diffused when it bounces off matte reflectors, walls, or other nonshiny objects.

Daylight's relative color varies widely, too, from relatively warm and reddish at sunrise and sunset (see figure 6.3), to quite blue at high noon. The temperature part of the equation comes not from the hotness or

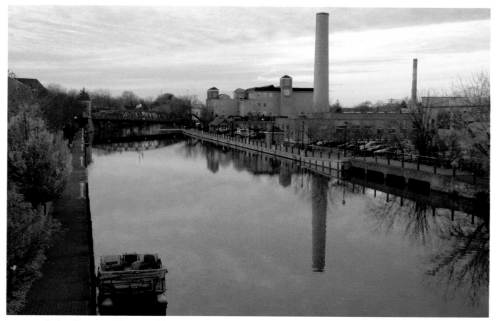

6.3 Early in the morning and late in the afternoon, daylight takes on a warm glow.

coolness of the photons themselves, but from the theoretical source of the illumination, an imaginary object called a *black body radiator*. The "black body" part comes from the object's capability to perfectly absorb all the light that strikes it. The "radiator" portion of the equation is derived from its capability to emit, or radiate, light when heated. At low temperatures, measured in degrees Kelvin, this radiated light is warm and orangeish, like an ember glowing in a fireplace. As the temperature rises, the object eventually reaches a blue-white fury that you might think of as "white hot."

The color temperature of daylight falls along this Kelvin scale. Starting an hour before dusk and an hour after sunrise, the sunlight, filtered by the particles in the air, can range from 4000K to 5000K (the term *degrees* is not used when referring to color temperature). As the day progresses, the color temperature ranges from 5500K to 6000K,

peaking at high noon when the light is most direct and most "bluish."

Because you're likely to take many photos in daylight, you want to learn how to use, or compensate for, the brightness and contrast of sunlight, as well as how to deal with its color temperature. I provide some hints later in this chapter.

Incandescent/tungsten light

Incandescent or tungsten illumination comes from the direct descendents of Thomas Alva Edison's original electric lamp. This illumination consists of a glass bulb that contains a tungsten filament surrounded by vacuum or a halogen gas. The filament is heated by an electrical current, producing photons and heat. Although incandescent illumination isn't a perfect black body radiator, it's close enough that you can precisely calculate the color temperature of such lamps and use them for photography without concerns about color variation for most of the lamp's useful life. (Tungsten bulbs can change color as they age.)

Incandescent lighting generally has a color temperature of 3200K to 3400K. Indeed, before photoflood lamps were largely replaced by electronic flash for studio-type photography, it was possible to purchase bulbs with either 3200K or 3400K output, and films to match those specific color balances (as well as more familiar *daylight-balanced* films for 5500K illumination).

Fluorescent light

Fluorescent light is increasing in popularity for home illumination, generally because fluorescent bulbs and tubes have long lives and low power consumption. When installed in lamps, fluorescent lights may be rated for seven years or more of use, and provide the equivalent illumination of a 60-watt incandescent light in a thrifty 13-watt model. The odd colors and ghastly skin tones that caused homeowners to shy away from fluorescent lights for residential illumination are largely gone, thanks to the latest generation of *warm white* and other types of fluorescent bulbs.

However, digital sensors are less accommodating to variations in the colors present in light than the human eye, so fluorescent lights still can cause the same problems for digital photographers that they did for film photographers in decades past. Fortunately, though, digital cameras are more adept at correcting for the vagaries of this kind of illumination than film is.

Fluorescents generate light through an electrochemical reaction that emits most of its energy as visible light, rather than heat, which is why the bulbs don't get as hot. The precise type and color of light produced varies depending on the phosphor coatings and kind of gas in the tube. Therefore, the illumination fluorescent bulbs produce can vary widely.

That's bad news for photographers. Different varieties of fluorescent lamps have different color temperatures that can't be precisely measured in degrees Kelvin, because the light isn't produced by heating. Worse, fluorescent lamps have a discontinuous spectrum of light that can have some colors missing entirely. A particular type of tube can lack certain shades of red or other colors, which is why fluorescent lamps and other alternative technologies such as sodium-vapor illumination can produce appalling human skin tones. Their spectra can lack the reddish tones we associate with healthy skin and emphasize the blues and greens best-suited for horror movies. Fortunately, you can tame the worst effects of most fluorescent lamps with your camera's white balance features.

Adjusting color temperature

You can use the white balance controls of your Nikon D40 or D40x to adjust the camera for the different types of illumination you'll encounter. I explained in Chapter 3 exactly how to adjust white balance, using the white balance controls found in the Shooting menu. You may recall that you can choose a white balance setting (such as Incandescent, Fluorescent, Daylight, Flash, Cloudy, or Shade), let the camera choose the white balance for you (yet still dial in some color correction), or choose a custom white balance based on the illumination of a particular scene, or the white balance of a photo you've already taken.

All these choices are necessary because digital camera sensors can't always determine the color balance of illumination, although your Nikon can make some pretty good guesses. For example, very bright light is almost always daylight; warmer indoor illumination often produces dim light. The colors the camera detects in the brightest areas of the image (which are supposedly white) can provide additional clues. And, of course, if the camera uses electronic flash to make an exposure, it knows that the electronic equivalent of daylight will provide the illumination.

The ability to change white balance after the shot is taken is one of the best reasons for shooting RAW or RAW+JPEG. When you import the image into Photoshop, Photoshop Elements, or another image editor, you can change the white balance from the "as shot" setting to any other setting you like (see figure 6.4). Although color-balancing filters that fit on the front of the lens still

exist, today they are used primarily with film cameras, because the color balance of film — even color negative film — isn't as extensively adjustable as that of a digital sensor.

If you're not satisfied with the automatic white balance settings you're getting, you can select a manual setting. Use one of the camera's prepared values, or select a custom white balance setting, as I outline in Chapter 3. You should end up with a color setting that's close enough to fall within the range of the fine-tuning you can do in your image editor.

In that case, your biggest white balance problem is likely to occur with mixed light sources. For example, you might take a photo using the flattering soft daylight that filters indoors from a north-facing window and forget that the incandescent room lights are fairly bright, too. You end up with part of your subject illuminated with cool sunlight, and part with warm interior light.

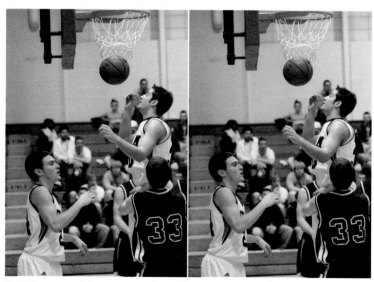

6.4 The greenish tones produced by uncorrected fluorescent lighting aren't flattering to human subjects (left). Fixing the color balance in an image editor produces a much better photo (right).

That's not a good combination, unless you're looking for a special effect. In this case, you might want to turn off the lamps in the room. Consider using a piece of white cardboard or other reflector to bounce some of the daylight into the shadows that result when the lamps are turned off. (Professional photographers might put an orange filter sheet right over the window or perhaps replace the incandescent bulbs in the lamps with special *slave* electronic flash units that are produced as direct replacements.)

Both indoors and outdoors, you can encounter mixed lighting situations when the predominant light source is augmented by another fairly strong light source of a significantly different color. For example, suppose your subject is illuminated primarily by incandescent lamps indoors, but is standing rather near a bright green wall that's spot lit (perhaps to provide extra illumination for some artwork). The green of the wall can change the color of the shadows on the side of the subject closest to it, even if the wall itself does not appear in the photo.

Outdoors, you can find mixed light sources with scenes that include both incandescent lights and daylight (which might happen late in the day or on a cloudy day), as well as colors bounced into a scene from a brightly colored structure outside the frame, or even a blue expanse of sky.

Learn to identify mixed lighting situations and avoid them, or, perhaps, incorporate them into your image as a creative element.

Conquering Electronic Flash

Electronic flash was transformed from a laboratory tool to the ubiquitous photographic device we know today more than 70 years ago by Dr. Harold Edgerton, a professor of electrical engineering at Massachusetts Institute of Technology. His photographs of bullets piercing balloons and the coronets formed by splashing drops of milk helped his patented *stroboscope* gain popularity and evolve into the speedlights and strobes we use today.

Electronic flash illumination is produced by accumulating an electrical charge in a device such as a capacitor, and then directing that charge through a glass flash tube containing an electricity-absorbing gas to emit a bright flash of photons. Such a burst takes 1/1000 second or less and, with the D40/D40x's built-in flash, produces enough illumination to take a photo of a subject 10 feet away at f/5.6 and ISO 200. Indeed, distance, f-stop, and ISO setting are the three important factors that you or your camera must take into account when calculating a flash exposure.

If you're someone who enjoyed learning the multiplication tables even though you're never without a calculator, you should know that you can figure flash exposure manually, too. In the days before automatic electronic flash and TTL (through the lens) exposure metering, flash exposure was calculated using a value called a Guide Number (or GN), which lives on today as a way of rating the power of electronic flash units.

Your D40/D40x's built-in flash, for example, has a guide number of 55 at ISO 200 when the measurement is done using feet. If you're metrically-inclined, the guide number is 17; you'll see why in a moment. To calculate the correct exposure for the D40/D40x's flash at full power and ISO 200, divide the GN by the distance to derive the f-stop. (You may recall from earlier in the chapter that the shutter speed doesn't matter; the flash's "shutter speed" is the duration of the flash.)

So, dividing 55 by 10 feet gives you 5.5, which is close to an actual aperture setting of f/5.6. Doubling the ISO from 200 to 400 enables you to close down one stop to f/8. (Just as a comparison, an external flash like the mighty Nikon SB-800 has a GN in feet of 174 at ISO 200, effectively three to four f-stops more powerful.)

Of course, you generally don't need to calculate flash exposure manually, as the D40/D40x uses its Matrix Meter with a 420-segment RGB sensor to measure a preflash that's triggered just before the main burst. Assuming you're using a flash unit compatible with Nikon's iTTL flash exposure system (as the D40/D40x's built-in flash and recent Nikon external flash are), the proper exposure is calculated and set for you. The camera varies the amount of the flash illumination by dumping some of the electrical energy before it reaches the flash tube. That reduces the power of the flash, and has

the side benefit of making the duration of the flash shorter (as brief as 1/50,000 second with some units).

Because exposure when using a single flash is generally calculated automatically on your behalf, the number of things you have to worry about is sharply reduced. They boil down to three key areas: *light fall-off, flash-sync,* and an aspect related to flash sync, *ghost images.*

Understanding light fall-off

Earlier in this chapter, I mentioned concerns about evenness of illumination with electronic flash, produced as the result of the inverse square law. To recap, light diminishes with the square of the distance from the light source to the subject. An object that is 2 feet from the flash receives four times as much illumination as one that is twice as far, or 4 feet away. That's two full f-stops (see figure 6.5). Conversely, a subject that's twice as far from the flash receives one-quarter as much illumination.

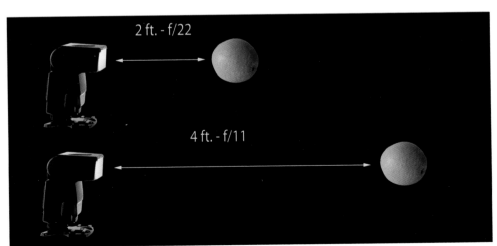

2 ft. - f/22

4 ft. - f/11

6.5 A subject twice as far away receives only one-quarter as much light.

Because the flash pictures you take are likely to have objects that are varying distances from the camera and flash, you need to take this effect into account. A photo of a group of people, as I described at the beginning of this chapter, can be well-exposed or poorly exposed, simply based on the arrangement of the group. Line them up in a row facing you from 10 feet away and they will all be well exposed (assuming you're not using a wide-angle lens that provides a wider view than your flash's coverage can handle).

But if you have one of the group take a few steps backward to the 15-foot position, and another person step forward to a spot 5 feet away, with the same exposure, you'd end up with the closest person two stops overexposed and the farthest one stop underexposed.

You encounter the inverse square law in many other flash situations, such as when you bounce flash off a ceiling and discover that tall subjects receive much more exposure than those of shorter stature standing next to them. When light fall-off bites you, your only recourse may be to rearrange your subjects or use supplemental illumination. But at least you've been warned and now know what to look out for.

Understanding flash sync

The near-instantaneous burst of the flash is supposed to take place only when the D40 or D40x's shutter is fully open. Although digital camera shutters can be both mechanical and electronic, the simplest way to visualize what is happening at flash sync shutter speeds is to visual your camera's shutter as two "curtains" that chase each other across the focal plane at the instant of the exposure. First, the front curtain opens, exposing the leading edge of the sensor as it moves upwards across the focal plane. When the front curtain reaches the other side of the sensor, the sensor is fully uncovered for an instant, and the flash goes off, making the exposure. Then, a rear curtain begins to travel across the focal plane, covering up the sensor again.

To recap, the sequence at shutter speeds of less than 1/200 second (with the D40x) or 1/500 second (with the D40) is this: front curtain opens, pause, rear curtain closes. When shooting photos, the length of the pause determines the shutter speed for exposures from 30 seconds to 1/200 and 1/500 second. The rear curtain may pause for many seconds for longer exposures, and only a fraction of a second for shorter ones. The electronic flash must be tripped during that pause.

For exposures shorter than either 1/200 or 1/500 second, the rear curtain begins its travel before the front curtain has reached the other side of the sensor, so only a slit is exposed at any one instant — a fairly wide slit for a shutter speed like 1/400 second, and a very narrow one for a fast shutter speed, like the D40/D40x's 1/4000 second minimum speed. If the electronic flash is triggered when you're using a shutter speed briefer than 1/200 or 1/500 second, only the portion of the sensor revealed at that instant is exposed (with one exception that I describe shortly).

The camera automatically keeps this from happening most of the time by switching back to the correct fastest shutter speed when you're using flash, even if you've selected a higher shutter speed. The maximum speed that you can use when working with flash is called the camera's *sync speed*.

The sync speed impacts your picture taking in several different ways. For one thing, this limitation means that you can't generally use flash in some situations where it might be desirable. For example, when you're shooting outdoors in sunlight and would like to use the built-in flash to provide fill-in light to brighten shadows, you can only use exposure combinations that require a shutter speed of 1/200/1/500 second or slower. On a bright day, that might mean you're limited to 1/500 second at f/11 at ISO 200 (using a typical daylight exposure). If you'd rather switch to ISO 400 and shoot at 1/1000 second at f/11, you must turn to neutral density filters, or else you're out of luck.

Another situation in which sync speed can be limiting is when you're shooting sports in a brightly lit arena. The flash's brief duration is great for freezing action, but if the ambient light levels are high, you can end up with *ghost* images (which I discuss next). You might prefer to use a higher shutter speed to eliminate the secondary images, but you're stuck with 1/200 second or 1/500 second.

> **Note** The faster 1/500 second sync speed of the D40 is one significant advantage the camera has over its more expensive sibling. The ability to use shutter speeds of up to 1/500 second can reduce the ghost images that can appear when electronic flash is used in environments with higher existing light levels, when compared to the 1/200 sync speed of the D40x model.

Understanding sync modes, flash modes, and ghosts

The flash sync speed determines the maximum shutter speed you can use to provide a complete exposure with your flash. Your camera also has several *sync modes* that

determine how the flash is coordinated with the shutter speed. The three main categories of sync modes are called *front sync*, *rear sync*, and *slow sync*. You can select these sync modes, plus three other flash modes (Off, Red-Eye Reduction, and Auto Flash), by holding down the Flash button on the left side (as you hold the camera) of the viewfinder while scrolling with the command dial.

All six modes can easily confuse you, as some of them are available only when using certain shooting modes among the various Program (P), Aperture Priority (A), Shutter Priority (S), Manual (M), Auto, and DVP/Scene modes possible. Next I describe the sync modes, other flash modes, and their effects, and tell you when you are able to use each.

Front sync

This flash synchronization mode is the default mode for the D40/D40x. You don't really "select" it using the Flash button; when none of the other modes are active, front sync (also called *first curtain* or *front curtain sync*) is what the D40 and D40x uses.

Recall for a moment the flash sync sequence (front curtain, pause, rear curtain) I outlined earlier in the chapter. When front sync is active, the D40/D40x fires the electronic flash as soon as the sensor is fully exposed, before the rear curtain begins its travel to recover the sensor. You can think of the sequence as front curtain, flash, pause, rear curtain. This is actually what happens most of the time.

However, if the light levels are high enough or the exposure is long enough to allow a secondary image (a ghost) to form from the ambient illumination, that second image is exposed after the flash picture. If the subject is moving, you end up with a sharp image (from the flash) and a ghost image in front of the subject in the direction of the movement. Usually that's not what you want. A race car shown chasing its own blurry ghost image is probably not what you think of when you think of motion. In such situations, you can use rear sync instead.

Rear sync

When you've chosen rear sync (also called *second curtain* or *rear curtain sync*), the exposure sequence changes. When you use rear sync, the flash is triggered just before the second curtain begins its travel, producing this sequence: front curtain, pause, flash, rear curtain. There is a pause, during which the ambient light, if it's strong enough, is able to produce an exposure. Then, the flash creates the main exposure. If the subject is moving, you end up with a ghost image that terminates with a sharp

flash exposure in the direction of travel, which is more "realistic."

If you expect to have ghost images and want to incorporate them into your photograph, use rear sync to produce the kind of look that is expected from such dual exposures. Rear sync is available only when you're using Program, Aperture Priority (it's called "Slow Rear" in both), plus Shutter Priority, and Manual exposure modes. S and M modes are the better choices for sports because the slight shadow images that appear are more realistic; the slow shutter speeds that result in Program and Aperture Priority modes exaggerate the ghost images.

Slow sync

Slow sync is not the same kind of sync mode as front sync and rear sync. Slow sync tells the D40/D40x that you want to use slow shutter speeds to increase the chance of

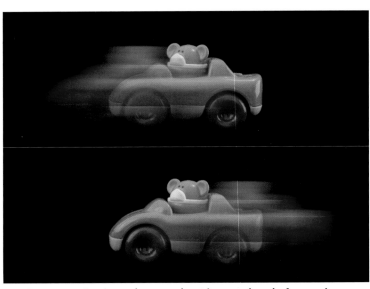

6.6 Front sync (top) produces a ghost image ahead of a moving subject; rear sync (bottom) places the ghost image behind the moving subject.

getting dual exposures: one with the flash, and a second one from the ambient light. You generally use this mode to allow light from the electronic flash to balance with background illumination, avoiding backgrounds that are completely black. (Remember the inverse square law: If the background is far behind the main subject, the background doesn't receive sufficient exposure.)

You should hold the camera very steady (I highly recommend a tripod) when using slow sync mode, to avoid turning the ambient exposure into a ghost image. When slow sync is active, the D40/D40x can program exposures as long as 30 seconds.

Other flash modes

The other three flash modes available with the Flash button/command dial aren't sync modes, but, rather they perform other functions. They are Red-Eye Reduction, Flash Off, and Auto Flash.

+ **Red-Eye Reduction.** This mode uses a preflash of the focus-assist lamp to decrease the chances of red-eye effects (see figure 6.7). Supposedly, the preflash causes a subject's pupils to contract and stifle some of the reflection.

+ **Flash Off.** This mode disables the built-in flash entirely. Use it with modes that automatically pop up the flash when you don't want to accidentally use the flash in situations where it is inappropriate or forbidden, such as museums or some concerts.

+ **Auto Flash.** This mode is available with some DVP/Scene modes, and pops up the flash when you depress the shutter release halfway and the light is dim, or the subject is backlit and could benefit from some fill-in flash.

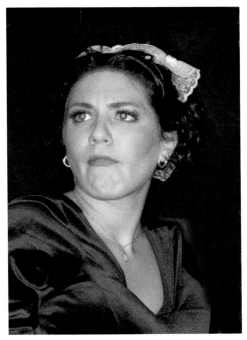

6.7 Your subject doesn't have to be looking directly at the camera for demon red eyes to appear, as long as flash illumination can bounce from the retinas back to the camera, as this photo shows.

Flash mode availability

Not all flash modes are possible with all shooting modes, and the Nikon manual doesn't do a good job of explaining when you can use them. Here's a quick summary:

+ **Front sync.** This mode is used whenever you haven't explicitly selected rear sync (as described next).

+ **Rear sync.** You can select this mode only in S and M modes, or in combination with slow sync (rear curtain+slow sync) in P and A modes.

✦ **Slow sync.** You can choose this mode when using the Night Portrait DVP/Scene mode, as either Auto/slow sync or Auto/slow sync/Red-Eye Reduction. You can also select slow sync in P and A modes in three different combinations: slow sync (alone); slow sync/Red-Eye Reduction; and slow sync/Rear Curtain Sync.

✦ **Red-Eye Reduction.** Red-Eye Reduction is available as an optional mode both for front-sync and slow-sync settings.

✦ **Flash Off.** You can disable the automatic (pop-up) flash feature in Auto, Portrait, Close-Up, and Child DVP/Scene modes. In all other modes, the flash does not pop up automatically and does not need to be disabled; you must push the Flash button to manually elevate the flash in P, A, S, M, Landscape, and Sports.

✦ **Auto Flash.** If you do want the flash to pop up in Auto, Portrait, Close-Up, and Child DVP/Scene modes, choose Auto Flash mode. You can combine auto flash pop-up with slow sync (Auto+slow sync) and slow sync plus red-eye reduction (Auto+slow sync+Red-Eye Reduction) in Night Portrait mode. In Auto, Portrait, and Close-Up modes you can also choose Auto+Red-Eye Reduction.

When you've activated a flash mode, a symbol appears in the LCD representing the active flash mode (see figure 6.8).

Note *To extend the life of your battery, remember to lower the pop-up flash when you no longer need it.*

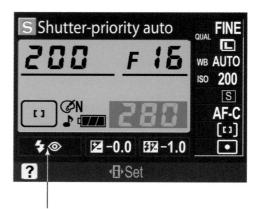

Flash mode

6.8 The current flash mode is shown on the LCD.

Reviewing Key Flash Settings

I outline the various flash settings you can make in the menu system in Chapter 3; in this section, I summarize some of the key options.

Exposure compensation

If you find your flash exposures in a particular shooting situation are consistently over- or underexposed, or you want to dial in a little more fill flash to brighten shadows (or less fill to darken them dramatically), use the D40 or D40x's Flash Exposure Compensation feature. It is available only when you are using Program, Shutter Priority, Aperture Priority, and Manual exposure modes.

There are three ways to add or subtract exposure from the values calculated by the iTTL flash system. You can hold down the Flash button on the left side (as you hold the camera) of the pentaprism while also holding down the Exposure Compensation button located southeast of the shutter release, and then spin the command dial. The Exposure Value (EV) change that you specify, from +1 EV to −3 EV, appears on the panel LCD and an indicator in the viewfinder shows you've changed the flash exposure compensation from the default 0.0 value. To cancel flash EV changes, press the Flash and Exposure Compensation buttons again and turn the command dial until 0 EV appears on the LCD.

You can also set Flash Exposure Compensation by pressing the Info button and navigating to the Flash Exposure Compensation area on the LCD (see figure 6.9.) Press the OK button, and then use the Up/Down keys on the multi selector to choose the amount of Flash EV you want. Finally, you can also set Flash Exposure Compensation using Custom Settings menu option CSM 08 Flash level.

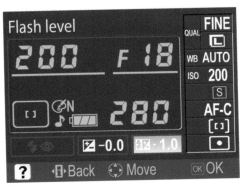

6.9 Adjust the amount of flash exposure using Flash Exposure Compensation.

Flash control

Fill flash is a technique used when shooting photos that combine existing continuous light for the main illumination with a touch of flash to fill in dark shadows. (See Chapter 7 for some examples of fill flash photos.)

Lightening the shadows provides a more pleasing effect and reduces the contrast of the photo under what would otherwise be harsh lighting conditions.

The D40 and D40x use two types of fill flash exposure control when using the built-in flash or the add-on SB-400, SB-600, and SB-800 units. The default is called *i-TTL balanced fill-flash* and allows the camera to adjust the amount of flash to provide an exposure that illuminates both the main subject and its background evenly when possible. This provides the most natural-looking photograph. A second mode, *standard i-TTL fill-flash*, calculates exposure only for the main subject, and does not take the background into account.

The standard fill-flash mode is used by the D40/D40x when you switch to spot metering when using either the built-in flash or one of the external flash units. This mode is also activated when you've connected one of these Speedlights to the camera using an SC-17, SC-28, or SC-29 sync cable (which are connected when the flash is used off-camera), or when you choose standard fill-flash mode using the Speedlight's control panel. The standard fill-flash exposure mode is a good choice when you want to emphasize the main subject and don't care how the background is rendered.

Flash shutter speed

Only certain ranges of shutter speeds are available when using the D40 or D40x's built-in electronic flash. In Auto, Program, Aperture Priority, Portrait, and Child modes, the flash can be used at any shutter speed from 1/60 second up to the sync speed (1/500 second for the D40; 1/200 second for the D40x.) When using the Close-Up DVP/Scene mode, you can choose 1/125 second up to the sync speed; Night Portrait

DVP/Scene mode allows exposures at any shutter speed from 1 second up to the maximum sync speed, and Shutter Priority and Manual mode permit the full range of shutter speeds from 30 seconds to 1/500 and 1/200 second (D40/D40x, respectively).

Built-in flash features

Use Custom Settings menu CSM 14 to choose between iTTL flash mode or Manual flash (with an output level from full power down to 1/32 power). The manual flash setting, with its variable power options, can be useful when you want to use a specific flash exposure for some reason. For example, perhaps you're using multiple non-Nikon flash units as illumination for some studio-type pictures, and would like to use the built-in flash to activate the slave triggering units of the other flashes (more on that in the next section). Set the D40/D40x's built-in flash to manual and 1/32 power, and it emits enough light to set off the other flash units, but doesn't have much effect on the exposure other than to provide a slight amount of fill flash for the shadows.

Using External Flash

The more experience you gain with your D40/D40x, the more you can imagine photos you want to take that just can't be done with the built-in flash. At that point, you want to consider an external flash unit, like the Nikon SB-400, SB-600, or SB-800.

The internal flash is nifty because it's part of your camera (and, thus, is always available), and it uses no additional batteries. The flip side of the coin is that you're stuck with any limitations the D40/D40x's flash has that add-on flash units might not have, and every time you use your flash, you are suck-

ing power out of the camera's batteries that you might well need to take non-flash pictures later on.

Moreover, the internal flash isn't particularly powerful, it can't be swiveled for use as a bounce flash, and its location atop your camera can lead to shadows cast on your subject when you use wide-angle zoom settings, as well as contribute to red-eye problems.

External flash units, on the other hand, usually are more powerful. The Nikon SB-800 Speedlight, for example (see figure 6.10), allows an exposure of about f/18 at 10 feet with an ISO setting of 200, about three stops more light than the D40/D40x's built-in flash. The elevated position of external flash units (or their off-camera capabilities) can virtually eliminate red-eye problems

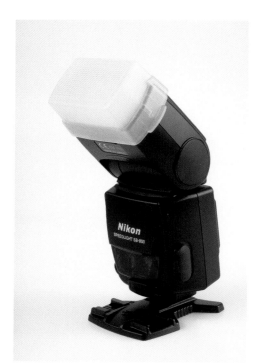

6.10 The Nikon SB-800 Speedlight is a more powerful external flash unit.

and shadows. You can swivel them for bounce flash, and they include features that expand their flash coverage to better suit wide-angle lenses. Although the D40/D40x don't have a built-in wireless Commander mode found in some other Nikon dSLR cameras, the SU-800 or SB-800 can be used to provide this capability and control the other units wirelessly.

Many of the electronic flash's automated functions are available with non-Nikon external flash units as well. A few even support the Nikon iTTL exposure system. However, not all Nikon flashes support all the features of the SB-600/SB-800 and other flash units in the Nikon line.

✦ **SB-400.** This new flash unit, introduced with the Nikon D40, is an inexpensive flash that costs about half as much as the more sophisticated Speedlights in the Nikon line. It operates on two AA batteries, can swivel in four steps up to 90 degrees for bounce flash, and requires an exposure of f/9.0 at ISO 200 for a subject 10 feet from the camera. You cannot use it wirelessly in Commander mode.

✦ **SB-600/SB-800.** These beefier flash units cost $250 to $350, but they have a full line-up of features, including wireless operation and hefty guide numbers. The SB-800 can serve as a commander for other external Nikon flash units, and requires an exposure of about f/18 at ISO 200 for a subject 10 feet from the camera. The SB-600 is only a little less powerful, needing an exposure of about f/13 at the same ISO and distance.

✦ **SB-R200.** This wireless remote Speedlight is triggered solely by an external flash (such as the SU-800 or SB-800) set in Commander mode. It doesn't mount on the D40/D40x's flash accessory shoe and is used entirely as a remote slave flash that you can set on light stands or another support. These are the flash units that are included with the R1C1 wireless close-up flash kit.

Photo Subjects

Whether you're new to digital photography, new to working with a digital single lens reflex (dSLR) like the Nikon D40 or D40x, or an experienced shooter, as you wield your new camera, you'll discover the more pictures you take, the better you become as a photographer. While some of your initial photos may be pleasing, and others might be less successful, every time you press the shutter you're learning how to improve your results and enhance your skills. Practice makes perfection.

You may want to try a different kind of photography, but you might find the new subject matter intimidating. That's where this chapter comes into play. Each section provides a consistent formula for exploring one of the most common shooting situations. You can find tips for choosing a lens, selecting the right ISO setting, and composing the picture. Open this book to any photo subject, and follow the guidelines to get good pictures right off the bat.

This chapter includes a refresher course in the "rules" of good composition, as well as advice on when to break those rules. You can also discover a series of recipes for typical — and atypical — shooting situations, with example photos, tips on getting the best from those photo subjects, and recommendations for lenses, lighting, and more.

Basics of Composition

Legendary American photographer Edward Weston once observed, "Consulting the rules of composition before taking a photograph is like consulting the laws of gravity before going for a walk."

In other words, taking photos that are well-composed should be a natural process, something that you can do without thinking. The very best photos are always carefully planned and executed. Good execution means more than proper exposure and sharp images, especially given some very good pictures are deliberately under- or over-exposed, and include an element of blur in their design. Beyond the technical aspects, good images have good composition; that is, the selection and arrangement of the photo's subject matter within the frame is pleasing.

Such pictures do the best job of telling a story. So, even if you're snapping off a hurried photo with little time to check every last setting, you should try to *compose* the image as well as you can—by instinct or intuition if you have to. Alternatively, you can fine-tune the composition after you've taken the picture, using cropping or other tools in your image editor. But good composition is not something that's optional in a good photograph.

Of course, if you're just starting out in photography, the most time-honored guidelines aren't ingrained yet into your thinking. So, it's a good idea now to absorb these eight simple rules for composing photos effectively. I review each of them in this section.

Achieving simplicity

Just like the sculptor who started with a block of marble and removed everything that didn't look like a discus-thrower, your photograph should be stripped of all elements that don't illustrate your idea. Avoid extraneous subject matter, eliminate confusion, and draw attention to the most important part of your picture. Crop out unimportant objects by moving closer, stepping back, or using your D40 or D40x's zoom lens.

Remember that a wide-angle look emphasizes the foreground, adds sky area in outdoor pictures, and increases the feeling of depth and space. Moving closer adds a feeling of intimacy while emphasizing the texture and details of your subject. A step back might be a good move for a scenic photo; a step forward might be a good move for a picture that includes a person.

Careful cropping when you take the picture means less trimming in your photo editor, and less resolution lost to unnecessary enlargement. You want to waste as few of your D40 or D40x's megapixels as possible. But when you're eliminating "unimportant" aspects of a subject, make sure you truly don't need the portion you're cropping. Removing the trunk and most of the branches of a tree won't work if you leave a stray, unattached branch, floating at the edge of the frame.

Centering interest

Decide on a single center of interest. It doesn't have to be (and probably shouldn't be) the center of your photo, nor necessarily located in the foreground. But no matter where your center of interest is located, a viewer's eye shouldn't have to wander through your picture trying to locate something to focus on. You can actually have several centers of interest to add richness and encourage exploration of your image, but there should be only one main center that immediately attracts the eye.

The center of interest should be the most eye-catching object in the photograph. It can be the largest, the brightest, the most colorful, or the most unusual item within your frame; or it can be one object isolated on a distinct background, as in figure 7.1. A photo of a field with amber waves of grain may have no center of interest at all, but if a bright green combine harvester is busy reaping what has been sown, you're guaranteed an eye-grabbing focal point. Conversely, if you want a certain subject to be the center of attention in your photograph, you should *not* include some competing subject that's larger, brighter, gaudier, or more unusual. If you're photographing your mother-in-law, don't stand her next to a gaudily-dressed circus clown. You should avoid having more than one center of attention; the other subjects in the picture should be subordinate to the main subject.

Choosing an orientation

Although the D40/D40x can be held most comfortably in the horizontal position, that's not always a good idea from a compositional or technical standpoint. If you shoot a vertically-oriented subject in that mode, you waste a lot of image area at either side. Vertical subjects, like trees or buildings (see figure 7.2), often look best when they're shot in a vertical orientation.

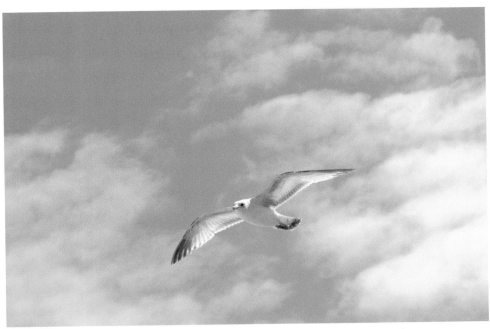

7.1 There's no question about where the center of interest resides in this photo.

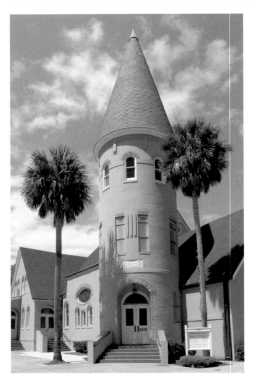

7.2 Tall subjects look best when shot in a vertical orientation.

Many subjects, particularly broad landscape vistas, look best in a horizontal view. A few types of subjects actually lend themselves to a square format (which otherwise tends to look a little static). With the D40 or D40x, you can shoot a horizontal picture and crop the sides.

Applying the Rule of Thirds

Photographers often consciously or unconsciously follow a guideline called the *Rule of Thirds*, which is a way of dividing a picture horizontally and vertically into thirds, as shown in figure 7.3. The best place to position important subject matter is often at one

of the points located one-third of the way from the top, bottom, and sides of the frame.

Other times, you want to break the Rule of Thirds, which, despite its name, is actually just a guideline. For example, you can ignore it when your main subject matter is too large to fit comfortably at one of the imaginary intersection points (like the sea-gull in figure 7.1). Or, you might decide that centering the subject would help illustrate a concept, such as being "surrounded," or placing the subject at one side of the picture implies motion, either into or out of the frame. Perhaps you want to show symmetry in a photograph that uses the subject matter in a geometric pattern. Following the Rule of Thirds usually places emphasis on one intersection over another; breaking the rule can create a more neutral (although static!) composition.

When applying this rule, remember that if your subject includes a person, an animal, a vehicle, or anything else that's mobile and has a definable "front end," it should be arranged in a horizontal composition so that the front of the person or object is facing into the picture. If not, your viewer may wonder what your subject is looking at, or where the animal is going, and may not give your subject the attention you intended. Add some extra space in front of potentially fast-moving objects so it doesn't appear as if the thing is just about to dash from view. It's less important to include this extra space for subjects that don't move, particularly in vertical compositions.

Using lines

Viewers find an image more enjoyable if there is an easy path for their eyes to follow

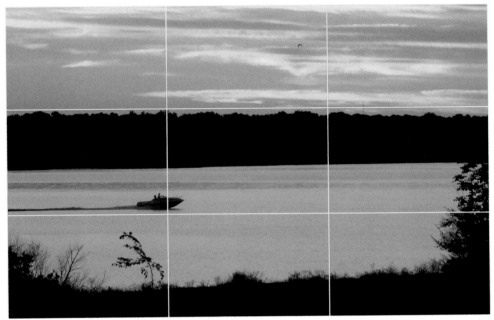

7.3 The "horizon" formed by the trees at the far shore of the lake is located one-third of the way down from the top of the image, while the center of interest — the boat — is placed one third of the way from the bottom and left side of the frame.

to the center of interest. Robust vertical lines lead the eye up and down through an image. Strong horizontal lines draw our eyes from side to side. Repetitive lines form interesting patterns. Diagonal lines conduct our gaze along a more gentle path, and curved lines are the most pleasing of all, as you can see in figure 7.4. Lines in your photograph can be obvious, such as roads or walls, or more subtle, such as the curve of hills on the horizon.

As you compose your images, you want to look for natural lines in your subject matter and take advantage of them. You can move around, change your viewpoint, or even relocate cooperative subjects somewhat to create the lines that enhance your photos. You can arrange lines into simple geometric shapes to create better compositions.

Achieving balance

Balance is the arrangement of shapes, colors, brightness, and darkness so they complement each other, giving the photograph an even, rather than lopsided, look. Balance can be equal, or symmetrical, with equivalent subject matter on each side of the image, or asymmetrical, with a larger, brighter, or more colorful object on one side balanced by a smaller, less bright, or less colorful object on the other.

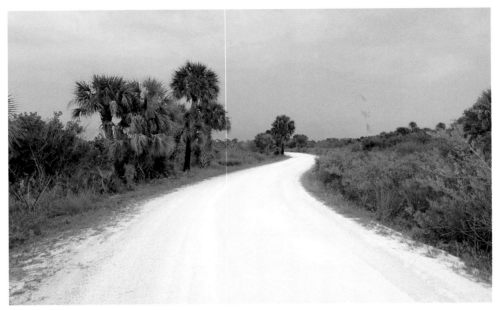

7.4 Curved lines lead the eye through the picture.

Working with framing

Framing is a technique of using objects in the foreground to create an imaginary picture frame around the subject. A frame concentrates our gaze on the center of interest that it contains, plus adds a three-dimensional feeling. You can also use a frame to provide additional information about the subject, such as its surroundings or environment (see figure 7.5).

Use your creativity to look around to find areas that you can use to frame your subject. Windows, doorways, trees, surrounding buildings, and arches are obvious frames. Frames don't have to be perfect or complete geometric shapes.

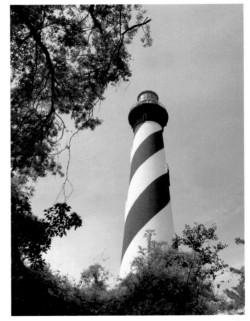

7.5 Surrounding trees form a frame around this lighthouse.

Avoiding fusion and mergers

Two-dimensional photographs tend to flatten the perspective of images we capture. So, although a tree behind the main subject didn't seem obtrusive to the eye, in the final picture, it may appear to be growing out of the roof of a barn. Or, perhaps you framed the image to trim off all of a tree except for one stray branch, and now that branch — detached from the tree that no longer appears in the photo — appears to grow out of the side of the picture. You can see an example of this in figure 7.5, about one-quarter of the way up the right-hand side of the picture, where a branch of a bush appears to spring out of the border of the photo. I could have removed it in an image editor, but there are enough of the remaining branches nearby to indicate the origin of this foliage that I left it in.

Examine your subjects through the viewfinder carefully to make sure you haven't fused two objects that shouldn't be merged, and have provided a comfortable amount of separation between elements. When you encounter this problem, correct it by changing your viewpoint, moving your subject, or using selective focus to blur that objectionable background.

Abstract and Pattern Photography

Photographs that incorporate abstract compositions and patterns are similar in concept. For both, your goal is not to present a realistic representation of a person or object but, rather, to find interest in shapes, colors, and texture. One definition of abstract art says that the artistic content of such images depends on the internal form rather than the pictorial representation. That's another way of saying that the subject of the photo is no longer the subject!

The chief difference between pattern and abstract photography is that in pattern photos, such as the one shown in figure 7.6, the original subject is recognizable, while in abstract photos the actual object pictured may be open to some debate. In fact, some people will tell you that if it's possible to tell what an abstract subject really is, then the image isn't abstract enough.

A droplet of splashing water can become an oddly malleable shape; a cluster of clouds in the sky can represent fantasy creatures as easily as random patterns. When you choose to image an abstract shape, you're giving your vision a tangible form. Image patterns, on the other hand, can consist of recognizable objects, arranged in a repeating or geometric design.

Inspiration

French photographer Arnaud Claass once said, "In painting, the curve is a hill; in photography, the hill is a curve." In other words, while painters attempt to use abstraction and patterns to create an imaginative image of a subject, photographers use these techniques to deconstruct an existing image down to its component parts. Both approaches create art that doesn't look precisely like the original subject, but which evokes feelings related to the subject matter in some way.

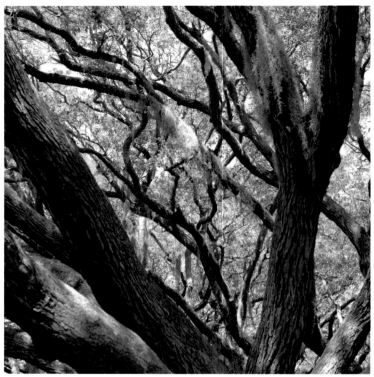

7.6 Familiar objects can form interesting patterns to create an abstract composition.

Look for abstract images in nature and human-made objects by isolating or emphasizing parts of those subjects. You can find suitable patterns in water, plant life, clouds in the sky (always a favorite for imaginary shapes), and objects you may have around the home.

Don't be shy about rearranging found objects in ways that create the patterns you seek. You can photograph familiar objects in unfamiliar ways and unfamiliar subjects in ways that evoke more familiar shapes, winding up with abstract images that are interesting to look at and think about.

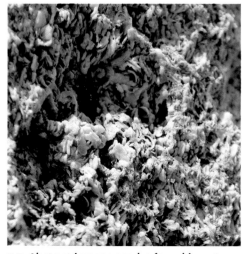

7.7 Abstract images can be found in nature.

Abstract and pattern photography practice

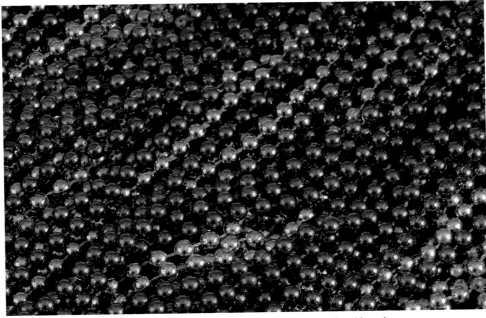

7.8 An extreme close-up creates an abstract image from strands of beads.

Table 7.1
Taking Abstract and Pattern Pictures

Setup	**Practice Picture:** I spied these Mardi Gras beads hanging on a hook after a Fat Tuesday celebration. For figure 7.8, I laid them out on a table, and photographed them in close-up with the D40 mounted on a tripod.
	On Your Own: Wonderful abstract images are hidden in common objects if you look hard enough. A tripod enables you to choose the best angle and distance, then lock the camera into position and focus without risk of losing sharpness from camera shake or unsteady autofocus.
Lighting	**Practice Picture:** I needed high-contrast lighting to emphasize the sheen of the beads, so I took two high-intensity desk lamps, placed them at angles, and illuminated the strands.
	On Your Own: If you're photographing a subject that calls for a softer look, you can use reflectors (a piece of white cardboard will do) to diffuse the light and bounce it into shadows.

Continued

Table 7.1 *(continued)*

Lens	**Practice Picture:** 18-55mm f/3.5-5.6G ED II AF-S DX Zoom-Nikkor at the 55mm zoom setting. You don't need a macro lens to get close enough to capture fine details and abstract patterns in objects. The 60mm f/2.8D AF Micro-Nikkor would also have worked. There's even a popular 105mm f/2.8G ED-IF AF-S VR Micro-Nikkor that includes built-in vibration reduction, which might have partially eliminated the need for a tripod, but I still liked using a camera support to help me frame the image precisely and maintain absolute focus.
	On Your Own: A macro-zoom lens that focuses close enough or even the 50mm f/1.8D AF Nikkor at that lens' minimum 18-inch focus distance might do the job. While the 50mm lens won't autofocus on the D40/D40x, manual focus for close-up work is usually not a handicap.
Camera Settings	**Practice Picture:** RAW capture. Aperture Priority AE with white balance set to Tungsten. Saturation set to Enhanced, and both Sharpness and Contrast set to High. Manual focus fine-tuned for the exact plane of the beads.
	On Your Own: Aperture-priority AE mode lets you choose a small aperture and enables the camera to select a suitable slow shutter speed for the tripod-mounted D40 or D40x. Extra saturation, sharpness, and contrast increase the abstract appearance at the expense of realism. You can also boost these values when converting the RAW image and processing it in your image editor.
Exposure	**Practice Picture:** ISO 200, f/32, 1/30 second.
	On Your Own: A small lens aperture increases the depth of field so that the entire image is sharp. The long exposure means that the D40 or D40x's high-quality ISO 200 sensitivity is sufficient.
Accessories	A tripod lets you lock down the camera once you've found an angle you like, and makes it possible to stop down to a small f-stop without worrying that the long shutter speeds that result are causing image blur. A Nikon ML-L3 wireless remote control is faster for releasing the shutter without jiggling the tripod, but you can also use the self-timer.

Abstract and pattern photography tips

✦ **Turn, turn, turn.** Rotate an image to provide an unfamiliar perspective on a familiar object. Changing the orientation alters the direction of the light as well as your viewpoint of the subject. Just turning the image 90 or 180 degrees might turn an everyday object into an abstract pattern.

✦ **Crop your image.** If you crop tightly or zoom in on your subject, you may find that a smaller portion of the object has abstract qualities that you didn't notice before.

✦ **Exaggerate colors.** Increase the saturation in your camera using the D40 or D40x's Optimize Image options in the Shooting menu, or further enrich the colors in your image editor. Hue controls can shift colors from one shade to another. Exaggerated or modified colors can sometimes be enough to lift an image from the mundane to the abstract.

✦ **Carpe momentum.** Use a high shutter speed to freeze an instant in time to capture an abstract image from things that are ordinarily difficult to see, like the splash of a water drop, or the waves produced when a rock is tossed into a pond.

Action Photography

The Nikon D40 and D40x's fast response and rapid-fire continuous shooting modes (at 2.5 and 3.0 frames per second, respectively) make them a popular tool for capturing sports shots at football or baseball games, soccer and tennis matches, and those sometimes-violent pastimes they call hockey and rugby. But action photography isn't limited to sports, of course. You'll encounter fast-moving action at amusement parks, while swimming at the beach, or while struggling to climb a mountain. Everything from sky-diving to golf to motoring to sledding (see figure 7.9) lends itself to action photography.

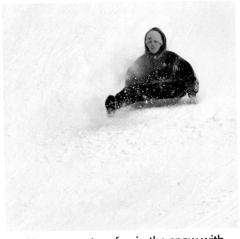

7.9 You can capture fun in the snow with action photographs.

Your Nikon D40/D40x simplifies action photography. You can have it powered up and ready to shoot at all times, bringing the exposure meter and autofocus instantly to life by pressing the shutter release down halfway. Once the camera is at eye level, the autofocus and auto exposure systems work so quickly that you can depress the release button the rest of the way and take a picture in an instant, without the frustrating shutter lag that plagues so many point-and-shoot digital cameras. And the D40 and D40x's continuous shooting mode can squeeze off bursts of shots, so even if your timing is slightly off, you can still improve your chances of grabbing the exact shot you want.

Inspiration

The two main components of a good action photo (in addition to good composition!) are capturing the right subject and capturing the right instant. A shot of a sub off the bench taking a foul shot after a basketball team has piled up a 40-point lead is much less exciting than a picture of the winning basket being dunked at the last second.

Similarly, a shot of a basketball player going up for a shot, with a defender attempting to block, needs to be captured at just the right instant, as you can see in figure 7.10. A fraction of a second later, and the shooter's right arm would probably obscure his face as he releases the ball.

When you're shooting action, it's always useful to have some understanding of what's going on so that you can anticipate just where the most exciting moments will take place; this way you're ready to snap the shutter at the perfect instant. With that much preparation, your D40 or D40x's

action-ready features handle the rest of the job for you.

Action photography freezes a moment in time, capturing a critical instant that sums up the excitement of the sport or activity. But that's not to say that every action photo has to be razor sharp, with all subject motion at an absolutely standstill. Indeed, a little blur can add a feeling of urgency and realism. Auto racing, for example, is traditionally shot using a slightly slower shutter speed to produce tire blur; otherwise the image may look like the vehicle is parked.

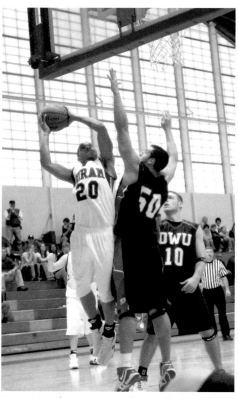

7.10 A peak moment is the perfect instant to capture an exciting action photo.

Action photography practice

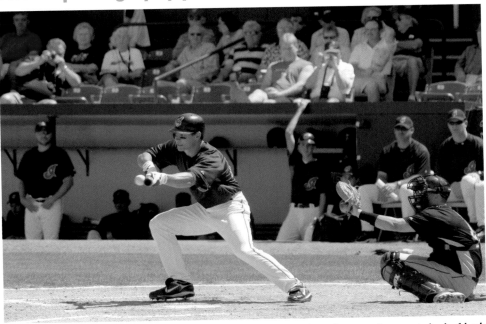

7.11 A combination of a seat next to the home dugout, a long lens, and a great deal of luck produced this perfect shot of a bunter making contact with the ball.

	Table 7.2
	Taking Action Pictures
Setup	**Practice Picture:** I mounted my camera on a monopod, sat in the first row next to the home dugout, and was able to cover home plate, first base, the pitcher's mound, and third base for the whole game. Thanks to the D40's continuous shooting mode, I was able to take hundreds of photos of batters' swings during the game. It was pure luck that I captured the shot, seen in figure 7.11, of the batter making contact with the ball. No photographer's reflexes are that good, and even the D40's burst mode isn't fast enough to grab more than a frame or two of a blazing fastball's flight.

Continued

Table 7.2 *(continued)*

	On Your Own: Knowing where to stand or sit is half the battle. Near the dugouts is good for baseball. If you can't wangle a spot behind the baseline, you can cover basketball games from a floor or second-row seat, especially one near the bench. Most of the action at a soccer game takes place near the net. At football games, don't stand at the line of scrimmage: Position yourself 10 yards in front of or behind the line to catch a receiver snaring a pass, a runner breaking through, or a quarterback dropping back to throw.
Lighting	**Practice Picture:** Daylight, mixed with some occasional overcast that softened shadows, was perfect for this afternoon baseball game.
	On Your Own: Whether shooting outdoors or indoors, you usually have to work with the light you have. You may have to increase the ISO slightly to allow high enough shutter speeds, and indoors use settings as high as ISO 1600 in very poor illumination.
Lens	**Practice Picture:** 55-200mm f/4.5-5.6G ED AF-S VR DX Zoom-Nikkor at 200mm.
	On Your Own: Outdoor sports often call for lenses with at least 200mm of reach if you're in a fixed position far from the action, and even longer is better. But if you have some mobility, a 55-200mm or 70-200mm zoom lens may be better. Indoor action may require wider lenses to take everything in or faster lenses to allow higher shutter speeds. An 85mm f/1.8 lens can be perfect for some kinds of indoor activities.
Camera Settings	**Practice Picture:** JPEG Fine. Shutter Priority AE and continuous shooting mode.
	On Your Own: The D40 and D40x store JPEG Fine images more quickly than RAW format images, so when you're taking photos quickly and continuously, you gain some shooting speed with very little quality loss by choosing Fine. Using Shutter Priority mode allows you to choose the highest appropriate shutter speed when you want to stop action. Under reduced light levels, you want to drop down to a slower shutter speed or boost the ISO setting.
Exposure	**Practice Picture:** ISO 400, f/11, 1/1000 second.
	On Your Own: At 400mm, the f/11 aperture allowed the people in the stands to blur, and 1/1000 second was fast enough to freeze the ball as it struck the bat. Noise isn't a problem with the D40/D40x at ISO 400.
Accessories	A tripod isn't usually a good choice for action photography, because it reduces your mobility and may even make you a hazard to the participants if you're standing along the sidelines. A compact monopod can steady a long lens and produce sharper results. If you do a lot of action photography, look at lightweight monopods made of carbon fiber or magnesium.

Action and sports photography tips

✦ **Anticipate action.** Become sensitive to the rhythm of a sport and learn exactly when to be ready to press the shutter release to capture the peak moment.

✦ **Be ready to use manual focus or focus lock.** Autofocus works great, particularly the D40/D40x's Predictive Autofocus feature that tries to anticipate where your subject will be at the time the picture is taken. However, don't be afraid to turn off the autofocus feature, manually focus or lock focus on a position where you think action will be taking place, and then snap the picture when your subjects are in position.

✦ **Take advantage of peak action.** Many sports involve action peaks that coincide with the most decisive moment. A pole vaulter pauses at the top of a leap for a fraction of a second before tumbling over to the other side. A quarterback may fake a pass, then hesitate before unleashing the ball. A tennis player poised at the net for a smash is another moment of peak action. These moments all make great pictures.

✦ **Freeze oncoming action.** Any movement that's coming directly toward the camera can be frozen at a slower shutter speed than action that's across the width of the frame. Instead of using the D40/D40x's highest shutter speeds (from 1/1000 to 1/4000 second) at large apertures, stop down to an f-stop with more depth of field, use a shutter speed like 1/500 second, and freeze oncoming action instead.

Animal Photography

We're surrounded by animals, both domestic and wild. If you live in Florida, you'd probably estimate that there are at least 40 million alligators, like the one shown in figure 7.12. If you like your fauna smaller and less menacing, there are 360,000 different species of beetles.

If you don't want to occupy your time shooting landscapes, photographing flowers, or capturing portraits of your friends, colleagues, and family, opportunities abound for photo creativity when taking pictures of animals. You can visit a zoo (virtually any nearby metropolitan area has one), or photograph animals in a nearby park, water creatures in a lake or stream, rabbits in your back yard, or even your own pets.

Inspiration

The key to attractive photos of animals is to picture them in natural-looking surroundings, whether they are wild animals, pets at home, or animals being showcased in a zoo exhibit. Nobody particularly cares for pictures of animals in cages or with other unnatural surroundings. A photograph of a deer that's wandered into your backyard may be mildly interesting because of the incongruity, but if you're able to use the patch of woods that borders your property as a backdrop instead, the image will seem more natural and compelling.

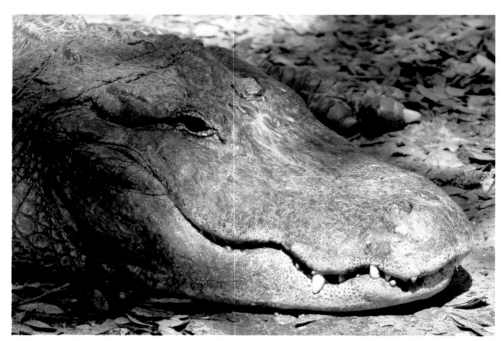

7.12 A telephoto lens lets you get good shots of animals you'd probably rather not approach too closely.

Similarly, you should photograph a zoo animal as if it were in its natural habitat, with nary a bar or moat in sight. Those who view your photographs probably won't think you traveled to some exotic place to take the picture, but the natural surroundings encourage them to suspend their disbelief and enjoy the photo on its own merits.

The quest for natural appearance extends to the animals' behavior, too. Once you've selected and tracked down your quarry, wait until the creature is engaged in behavior that's both typical and revealing. It may take awhile (our cats seem to sleep all day long) but eventually an animal will spring into action. You can count on dogs as willing participants for any activity you choose to offer them. More timid animals may act nervous, but you can still capture them if you're patient and don't act in a threatening manner (see figure 7.13). Be patient and you'll be rewarded with a great animal picture.

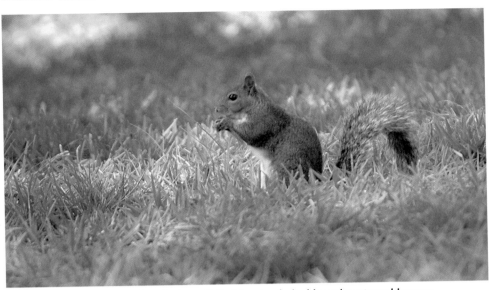

7.13 You may have to wait quietly until timid animals feel less threatened by you.

Animal photography practice

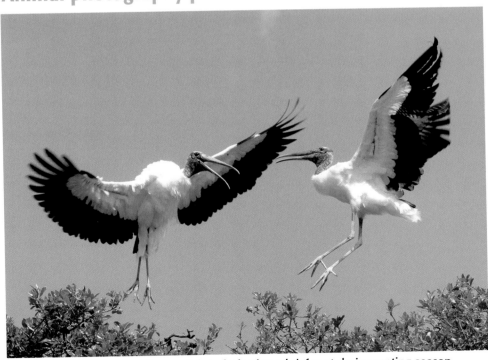

7.14 A long lens captured these wild storks having a brief spat during mating season.

Table 7.3
Taking Animal Pictures

Setup	**Practice Picture:** Perched near a rookery frequented by large birds, I set up my D40 with a long lens on a tripod and waited for the chance to capture the two storks shown in figure 7.14. One was building a nest in the top of a tall tree, and fended off an invasion by a rival bird as I snapped away. **On Your Own:** Patience is its own reward when photographing animals. In the wild, you might want to set up a blind to hide in wait near a watering place. Food or salt blocks can attract wild creatures. At zoos, spend the morning when the animals are most active observing and taking pictures, and return at late evening or feeding times, if necessary, when the creatures are active again.
Lighting	**Practice Picture:** The bright sunlight was perfect for showing off the birds' plumage. **On Your Own:** You work with the available light most of the time, although some photographers have been known to set up flash units with remote wireless triggers for photographing animals in the late evening or nighttime.
Lens	**Practice Picture:** 70-300mm f/4.5-5.6G ED-IF AF-S VR Zoom-Nikkor at 300mm. **On Your Own:** You can use a long lens to shoot close-up photos of animals that won't come closer to you than 20 or 30 yards. Wide-angle lenses aren't much use for wildlife photos, but longer lenses—either zooms or prime lenses with focal lengths of 300mm or more—will do the job. If you'll be shooting under dimmer light (say, in the woods), a fixed focal-length lens with a large maximum aperture, such as f/4 or f/2.8, will be better than a slower zoom lens.
Camera Settings	**Practice Picture:** RAW capture. Shutter Priority AE. Saturation set to Enhanced. **On Your Own:** Shooting in RAW format enables you to adjust the exposure when importing the picture in your image editor. Shutter Priority mode enables you to specify a fast shutter speed to freeze a fast-moving or skittish animal.
Exposure	**Practice Picture:** ISO 200, f/8, 1/1000 second. **On Your Own:** Using a fast shutter speed serves a triple purpose: the high speed minimizes camera shake (in case you're not using a tripod), reduces the amount of vibration that a typical long lens produces, and lets you work with a fairly large aperture so a distracting background is out of focus.
Accessories	Carry a tripod or monopod when using a long lens. A rain poncho and umbrella can come in handy if the weather turns bad and you're far from your transportation.

Animal photography tips

✦ **Early to rise.** Whether you're going to the zoo or venturing out into the boonies, get up early and arrive when the animals are active. By noon, they're ready for a nap.

✦ **Go outdoors.** Even domestic animals look their best outdoors, so take your pets outside to your yard or to a nearby park for their portraits. In zoos, if the animals have gone inside to feed, wait until they emerge again to shoot them against a more natural outdoor backdrop.

✦ **Shoot low.** Humans are taller than most wild animals, and so the tendency is to photograph them from an unnatural standing position. Get down low and take pictures of wildlife from their own vantage point for a more natural photograph.

✦ **Accentuate the habitat.** If you're photographing in a zoo, use a long lens and wide aperture to throw the bars or fence (if present) out of focus. Scant depth of field can disguise those walls and fake rocks in the background, too. If you're forced to shoot through glass, take your pictures at an angle to avoid reflections.

Architectural Photography

Professional architectural photography is specialized and involves complex guidelines and sophisticated equipment. There are no such strictures on the kind of informal amateur architectural photography you can do just for fun with your D40 or D40x and a few lenses. Whether you're taking some snapshots of existing homes you'd like to offer as suggestions to your architect, or looking to document historic structures, taking photos of interior and exterior architecture is fun and easy.

Architectural photos can also be used for documentation, to provide a record of construction progress, or show how a building has changed through the years. It's also fun to capture details of interesting structures, such as a tower like the one shown in figure 7.15. Some of the most dramatic architectural photos are taken at night, using long time exposures or techniques like painting with light.

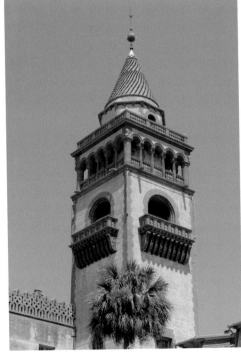

7.15 A detail of an interesting building can show the character of a structure more vividly than an overall shot.

The best architectural photographs involve a bit of planning, even if that's nothing more than walking around the site to choose the best location for the shot. Or, you might want to take some test shots and come back at a specific time, say, to photograph an urban building on a Sunday morning when automobile and foot traffic is light. A particular structure might look best at sunset.

However, the biggest challenge to plan for is illumination. The existing lighting can be dim, uneven, or harsh. You may encounter mixed illumination with daylight streaming in windows that blends with incandescent room illumination, or lighting that is tinted. You can counter some of these problems by mounting your camera on a tripod and using a long exposure.

Inspiration

You can also use architectural photography to capture the designer's art or to create abstract patterns from a section of a complex structure. You can take architectural photos at virtually any time and in any weather. Indeed, some of the most interesting photos are taken in the rain or after a snowfall, or at night when interior and exterior illumination combine to show off the building. I have some favorite structures that I return to over and over, months and years apart, and I always come away with a new image and new perspective.

One example is the old mansion, now a museum, shown in figure 7.16, which I visit several times a year to photograph along with

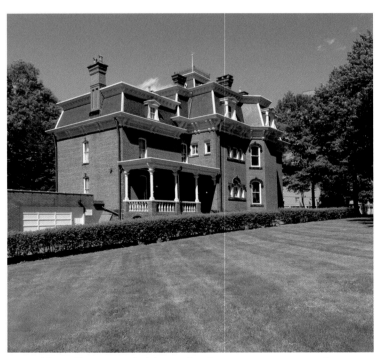

7.16 This well-preserved old mansion is now a museum and serves as bridge to the past for photographers interested in architecture of the 19th century.

its well-kept grounds. It looks good from several different angles, both in overall shots and pictures of architectural details. You should be able to find multiple ways of photographing any building if you think creatively.

Photography of building interiors is particularly challenging for owners of dSLRs like the Nikon D40 or D40x because the lighting aspects can be complex, you may need extremely wide (and extremely expensive) lenses, and indoor shots frequently require the kind of perspective adjustments that are easiest with specialized cameras and equipment. That doesn't mean you can't attempt indoor architectural photography — only that you may find photographing exteriors less frustrating and more rewarding.

Architectural photography practice

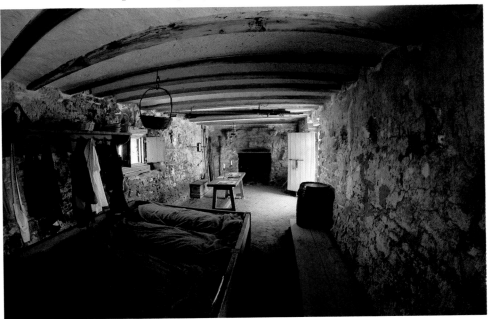

7.17 The bunkhouse of this old fort lent itself to an interior photo using only the available light.

Table 7.4
Taking Architectural Pictures

Setup	**Practice Picture:** This 1740 Spanish fort fended off British attacks in the New World, and now is maintained as a U.S. National Monument. While on a guided tour of the bunkhouse, I waited until the last stragglers in my group had gone back outside, then snapped the quick photograph shown in figure 7.17.

Continued

Table 7.4 *(continued)*

	On Your Own: Shooting interiors almost always backs you up against a wall, so bring your widest lens. Outdoors, if you're not shooting a detail of a structure, you need to find a location that enables you to photograph the entire building without obstructions and with a clean background.
Lighting	**Practice Picture:** It was midday and the brilliant sunlight coming in the open doorway and window lit the far end of the bunkhouse, with enough light diffusing toward the near end to provide softer illumination.
	On Your Own: Indoors, you may have to provide auxiliary lighting of your own. Outdoors, in most cases you want to avoid harsh shadows, so slight cloud cover might be desirable to provide slightly more diffuse illumination.
Lens	**Practice Picture:** Tokina 10-17/3.5-4.5 DX fish-eye zoom set to 10mm to include almost the whole interior of the bunkhouse. Unfortunately, this fun lens doesn't have an internal focusing motor, and so you must manually focus it with the D40 or D40x. However, it has so much depth of field at its ultra-short focal lengths that careful focus isn't critical.
	On Your Own: The best lens depends on whether there is enough interior room or, if you are outside, you are able to back away from the building enough to take in the entire structure without tilting the camera back and introducing perspective distortion. Very wide-angle lenses like the 14mm f/2.8D ED AF Nikkor are quite expensive, however, and don't provide autofocus with the D40 or D40x. A more reasonably priced alternative is the 10.5mm f/2.8G ED AF DX Fisheye-Nikkor, which produces a curved view that can be straightened out with some success in Nikon Capture NX. Further, it's not an autofocus lens on the D40/D40x, either, but may not require much focusing because of its prodigious depth of field.
Camera Settings	**Practice Picture:** RAW capture. Shutter Priority AE. Saturation set to Enhanced and Sharpening set to Medium High.
	On Your Own: Outdoors in bright sun, you can usually use Shutter Priority to specify a speed that nullifies camera shake, and lets the camera choose the appropriate aperture.
Exposure	**Practice Picture:** ISO 200, f/16, 1/200 second.
	On Your Own: Center-weighted or spot metering can help ensure that the exposure is made for the building itself and not any bright surroundings such as sky or snow.
Accessories	A tripod can be helpful to enable you to carefully compose your photo. I like to remove the camera after the shot and take a picture of where the tripod was set up, so I can repeat the picture from that position on a visit on a different day and different time of year.

Architectural photography tips

✦ **Do your architectural planning.** Walk around a location to choose the best position for a shot. If the weather isn't ideal, plan to come back at a better time — but take a few test shots you can use to map out what you're going to do.

✦ **Choose the best time.** For buildings in urban settings, Sunday mornings are often the best time to shoot structures (other than churches) without the intrusion of automobile or foot traffic. Other buildings might look their best at sunrise or sunset.

✦ **Avoid perspective distortion.** You don't want to end up with that tipping-over look that results when the camera is tilted back, unless you plan to use the effect as part of your image. Instead, step back as far as you can, using the widest lens you have available. Sometimes shooting from a slight elevation enables you to take in the entire structure without needing to tip the camera back.

✦ **Ask permission.** In these security-conscious days, it's often a good idea to ask permission to shoot a particular building, especially government edifices and commercial structures. The laws of most states don't require getting permission to shoot and use photographs of buildings that are clearly visible from public areas, but doing so can avoid potential problems.

Black-and-White and Monochrome Photography

Stripping away all the color in your images — or perhaps providing new hues — can make for some interesting photographs. Your D40 or D40x has a mode (available under Optimize Image in the Shooting menu) that allows you to originate photos in black-and-white. You can also convert your pictures in the camera after they are taken to black-and-white or a toned monochrome scheme such as sepia (brownish) or cyanotype (bluish) using the Retouch menu's Monochrome options.

You can also convert a RAW color image into a black-and-white picture using Nikon Capture NX or another RAW converter such as Adobe Camera Raw; and every image editor includes tools for removing the color from images (in any file format, including JPEG) and choosing or mixing color channels down into a grayscale version.

For photographers who grew up in the age of color, black-and-white and monochrome photography is a new way of seeing; a way to reduce an image down to its essentials, as in the African mask shown in figure 7.18; and a method for concentrating on the tones, play of light and shadows, and texture rather than the hues in an image.

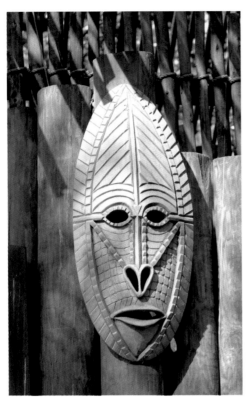

7.18 Black-and-white photography strips away distracting color to provide a simpler image.

If you're willing to explore photography at a new level, black-and-white photography can add excitement and new creative options to your work.

Inspiration

Until the 1950s, monochrome images dominated movies, television, advertisements, and even publications like *Life Magazine* that featured photojournalism. Until *USA Today* launched in 1982, black-and-white photos were the rule in our daily newspapers, too. Affordable desktop scanners introduced late in that decade were monochrome only, and the first image editing programs I worked with in the late 1980s could handle only black-and-white.

Today, many digital photographers have never taken a black-and-white picture, and, thanks to full color imaging, often fret more about getting just the right colors than about capturing a rich tonal scale. And yet, the range of tones is one of the most important aspects of a good picture: The amount of detail in the shadows, midtones, and highlights is just as important with a color photograph as it is for a black-and-white picture. Monochrome photography makes it possible to explore tonal relationships without the distraction of color.

I also like monochrome photography because of its ability to add a period flavor to photographs. Sepia-toned images, for example, more closely resemble 19th century photographs, particularly if the picture shows old-timey subject matter, such as people in Civil War garb. Or, you can evoke a flavor of the mid 20th century simply by switching to black-and-white. Monochrome toning can even be used for a visual pun, as for the "moon is blue" photograph shown in figure 7.19, which was taken with a 500mm lens and the camera mounted on a tripod for the exposure of 1/250 second at f/11. (Oddly enough, the moon can be photographed using roughly the same exposure as you'd use in bright daylight; the reflected light from the sun is that bright.)

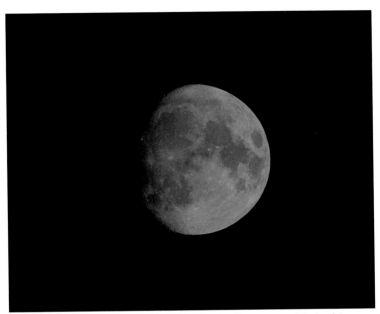

7.19 The concept of "once in a blue moon" comes to life in this cyanotype-toned visual pun, created using the D40's Retouch menu features.

Black-and-white and monochrome photography practice

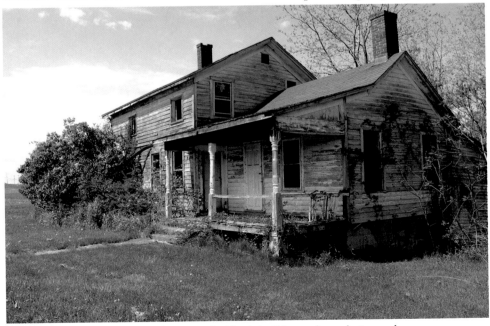

7.20 Using black-and-white gives a period look to this modern photograph.

Table 7.5
Taking Black-and-White and Monochrome Pictures

Setup	**Practice Picture:** The old farmhouse shown in figure 7.20 provided a stark reminder of life in the Great Depression, so I decided to picture it in stark black-and-white.
	On Your Own: Train your eye to look for subjects that would look especially good in black-and-white. In addition to historical objects and scenes, any subject with strong interplay of light and shadows has great possibilities, as well as high contrast scenes with pure whites and blacks.
Lighting	**Practice Picture:** Bright daylight with a dappling of shade from trees provided enough contrast to show the texture of the old farmhouse without excessive harshness.
	On Your Own: Black-and-white photography is your chance to experiment with light. Use the existing lighting, or add your own (including bounce light from reflectors or fill flash), to manipulate the highlights and shadows for the tonal rendition you want.
Lens	**Practice Picture:** 18-55mm f/3.5-5.6G ED II AF-S DX Zoom-Nikkor at 25mm.
	On Your Own: The particular lens you choose for black-and-white photography has no effect on the monochrome rendition itself; select your lens to best suit the subject matter, whether you're shooting a portrait, landscape photo, or close-up.
Camera Settings	**Practice Picture:** RAW+JPEG Basic. Black-and-white mode. Aperture Priority AE with white balance set for Daylight.
	On Your Own: Using RAW+JPEG Basic gives you the best of both worlds. When you play back the image, the black-and-white version appears on the D40/D40x's LCD so you can judge exposure and tonal rendition. You can further manipulate the image — or even convert it back to color — when you import the RAW version into your image editor.
Exposure	**Practice Picture:** ISO 200, f/11, 1/500 second.
	On Your Own: Because color isn't available to provide tonal separation, if you want to isolate a black-and-white subject from its background you need to use a large lens opening; if you want the foreground, subject, and background all in focus, use a smaller f-stop.
Accessories	Black-and-white photography can be contemplative (think Ansel Adams) or fast-moving photojournalism (think Eddie Adams). So, your accessories might range from a sturdy tripod to a photojournalist's vest with pockets for lenses, flash, and other gear.

Black-and-white and monochrome photography tips

✦ **Watch for unintended fusion and mergers.** While your D40 or D40x captures images in black-and-white, you can still see the scene through the viewfinder in full color. Unless you're careful, you may miss mergers of tones that are similar in brightness and texture, but differ in color. Until you learn to "see" in black-and-white, check your shots on the LCD to make sure that what you end up with is what you intended.

✦ **Look for a moment.** Black-and-white photography is a great tool for capturing the essence of a moment. You may discover that if your snapshot captures an interesting moment, viewers don't care if the exposure or focus isn't absolutely perfect, and a few imperfections might even make the photo appear to be more natural.

✦ **Tell a story.** Traditionally, some of the best black-and-white photos have been photojournalist-style images that tell a story about the people and their activities in the urban area you picture.

✦ **Travel light.** The purity of black-and-white photography often lends itself to working simply, sometimes with a single camera or lens. That's especially true of street photography in cities, when you're on foot much of the time, scooting between locations by bus or taxi. You don't want to be lugging every lens and accessory around with you. Decide in advance what sort of pictures you're looking for, and take only your camera and a few suitable lenses and accessories.

Event Photography

Events are a welcome respite from the daily humdrum, especially happenings like Mardi Gras or county fairs, which happen only once a year. But more frequent events like concerts, parades, and festivals are fun, too. For the photographer, these events offer a cornucopia of photo opportunities, concentrated in a few hours, spread over a day or two, or even lasting a week for larger festivities.

Live music and stage productions have a lot of visual excitement that you don't get from recorded performances on CD or DVD, and they make perfect venues for photography as well. It doesn't matter whether you're attending a concert by an internationally known artist or enjoying the earnest efforts of a high school musical. You can get interesting results, as shown in figure 7.21, at any performance.

Inspiration

You don't need to attend a mammoth extravaganza to get good event photos. A company picnic, class reunion, or local art festival offer great opportunities for memorable photos. You may get the chance to photograph exotic automobiles or aircraft, too, up close and from unusual angles.

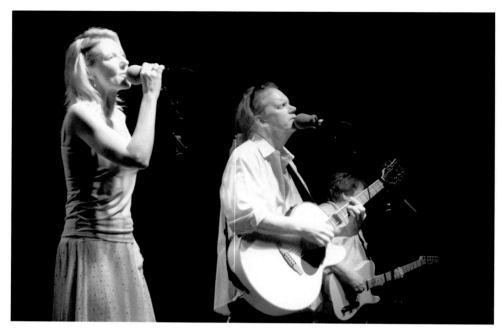

7.21 Low angles next to the stage can provide an interesting perspective.

Try to take photos that capture the theme of the special event. Show the overall event and its environment; photograph the people, capture an awards ceremony, and get close-ups of the automobiles, airplanes, or crafts on display. Your photos should tell a story and help the viewer understand the event itself. Most day-long (or longer) events have a schedule, often available from the promoter's Web site, that you can use to plan which things you want to see, and map out the logistics for seeing them.

Historical reenactments are another kind of event with endless photographic possibilities. Living-history buffs spend a great deal of their own money purchasing costumes, equipment, camping gear, and weapons, or making their own authentic reproductions. Typically, reenactments are all-day or several-day events, during which you have the chance to see every aspect of the historical drama as it unfolds. Many participants take on the identity of a particular historical character to represent, which is the case with the Revolutionary War soldier pictured in figure 7.22.

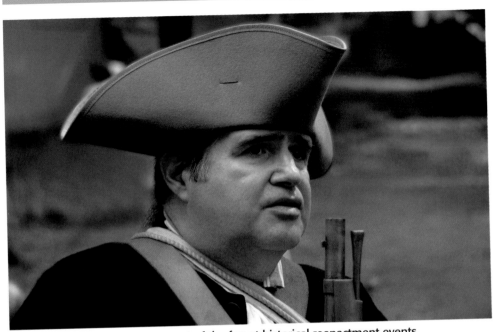

7.22 Interesting costumes are part of the fun at historical reenactment events.

Event photography practice

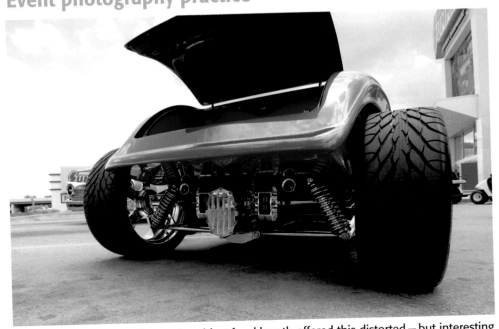

7.23 A 12-24mm zoom lens at its widest focal length offered this distorted—but interesting—view of a customized automobile.

Table 7.6
Taking Event Pictures

Setup	**Practice Picture:** A large number of customized vehicles are always on display at car shows. This one's hot engine, tuned suspension, and aggressive tires provided all the detail needed for the photo shown in figure 7.23.
	On Your Own: Even if the midday schedule is filled with the most action, if a particular outdoor event has activities extending from full daylight to after dark, you'll be rewarded if you stick around for the late-evening happenings. Interesting displays, rides, or things like a county fair's midway are transformed when the sun goes down and the lights come on.
Lighting	**Practice Picture:** Daylight provided the light required for this photo, and there was enough bouncing off the pavement to provide illumination to highlight the auto's undercarriage.
	On Your Own: The natural lighting at most events provides a look that's consistent with the event itself, especially after dark, when the illumination is sometimes garish and filled with color. You wouldn't like that kind of lighting when shooting a portrait, but it's perfect for gala outdoor events.
Lens	**Practice Picture:** 12-24mm f/4G ED-IF AF-S DX Zoom-Nikkor set to 12mm.
	On Your Own: I needed a special-purpose super-wide-angle lens for this intentionally distorted shot, but you want to travel light at most events. A single lens that has a variety of focal lengths from wide to medium-long can eliminate a lot of lens swapping. The 18-135mm f/3.5-5.6G ED-IF AF-S DX Zoom-Nikkor or 18-200mm f/3.5-5.6 G ED-IF AF-S VR DX Zoom-Nikkor with vibration reduction are also good choices.
Camera Settings	**Practice Picture:** Aperture Priority AE mode. The white balance was set to daylight. This exposure mode let me select an f-stop that would provide the extra depth of field needed to render all parts of the vehicle sharp.
	On Your Own: If you want to control the depth of field tightly, switch to Aperture Priority AE mode and set the white balance to the type of light in the scene. If the light is low, switch to Shutter Priority AE mode, and choose the slowest shutter speed that will do the job of preventing blur from camera shake.

Exposure	**Practice Picture:** ISO 200, f/16 1/200 second.
	On Your Own: Nighttime events usually call for higher ISO ratings, and the D40/D40x does provide acceptable images at settings as high as ISO 1600. Don't rule out that ISO 1600 in very low light or when you need faster shutter speeds. A monopod can steady the camera to make it possible to use slower shutter speeds.
Accessories	A tripod isn't practical at most events, because the events are crowded, you move around a lot, and there may be scant space to set up a three-legged camera support. On the other hand, a monopod is compact and has a very small "footprint" while shooting and is extremely portable. You might have some limited use for flash, either as the main illumination or for fill flash during the day, so either use the D40 or D40x's built-in strobe or bring along a detachable external flash unit.

Event photography tips

✦ **Ask for permission before photographing adults or children at most events.** A smile and a nod is usually all you need to gain the confidence of your photo subject. But it's always best to explicitly ask for permission from a parent or guardian before photographing a child.

✦ **Get there early.** As with concerts and plays, do yourself a favor by showing up early enough to scout around, get the lay of the land, and locate the best spots for photography. Just don't get in the way of event workers who are setting up equipment or displays, or making last-minute touch-ups on their automobiles or aircraft.

✦ **Most events look best photographed from a variety of angles.** Don't waste your time in the front row of a performance; you can take the most interesting photos at the sides of any stage. Nor should you remain stuck at street-level for a parade, or around the barbeque grill at a tailgate party. Roam around. Shoot from higher vantage points and from down low. Use both wide-angle and telephoto lenses.

✦ **For outdoor events, plan for changing light conditions.** Bright sunlight at high noon calls for positioning yourself to avoid glare and squinting visitors. Late afternoon through sunset is a great time for more dramatic photos. Night pictures can be interesting, too, if you've brought along a tripod or monopod, or can use flash.

Fireworks and Light Trails Photography

Fireworks and other types of light trails are especially fun to capture, because you never quite know what you are going to get. You can point your camera at just about any subject with its own illumination, take a photograph at an exposure of anywhere from 1/30 second to a minute or more, and then examine your results. If the picture looks good, you can save it, tell everyone "I meant to do that!" and congratulate yourself on your artistic sensibilities.

I like to shoot photographs of moving lights from various vantage points. For figure 7.24, I grabbed a series of pictures of headlights and tail-lights of cars, allowing the motion of the vehicle I was riding in to provide an interesting wavy effect to the light trails. You can get even better effects by pointing your camera at lights and moving it intentionally.

The cool thing about light trail photography is that the light itself becomes your subject. Every point of illumination writes its own "path" on the sensor. You can lock down the camera on a tripod and shoot a fixed scene such as an overlook view of a city in a valley below, with only the lights of moving cars as they move down the streets forming trails.

Inspiration

Let your imagination run free in transforming any type of illumination into your own

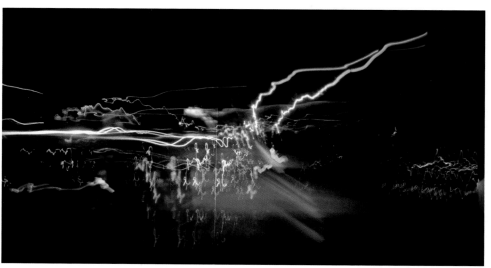

7.24 I shot through the front window of my car, and captured these light streaks with a four-second exposure with the D40x on a monopod to provide a modicum of steadiness.

personal drawing-with-light tool. All you need is a dark background and either a moving camera, moving lights, or both, to produce interesting light trails.

For example, you can mount the camera on a tripod, focus sharply on some interesting lights (a neon sign, holiday lights, or the lights of a building), choose an exposure of several seconds, and then press the shutter release down fully. Allow the image to record for about 25 to 50 percent of the full exposure (I count off one-Mississippi, two-Mississippi...), then carefully rotate the zoom ring, as I did for the photo shown in figure 7.25. You get different results when you start the zoom at the maximum focal length, and then zoom in, than when you shoot the picture using the reverse strategy. Try both.

Another favorite technique of mine is to point the camera at a busy street, use a low ISO setting (such as ISO 100), a small f-stop, and set the exposure for 30 seconds. All sorts of interesting and unpredictable photos result. If traffic lights are in the frame, you can end up with a picture showing red, yellow, and green lights illuminated. Automobiles that stop for a red light appear in the photo more clearly than those that were just passing through. Pedestrians might be entirely invisible, unless they stopped moving during the exposure long enough to register.

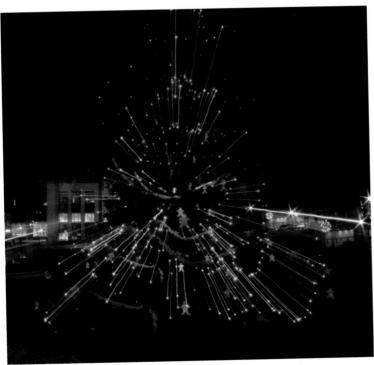

7.25 I mounted the camera on a tripod and zoomed during the long exposure to create this moving image of a fir tree bedecked with holiday lights.

Fireworks and light trails photography practice

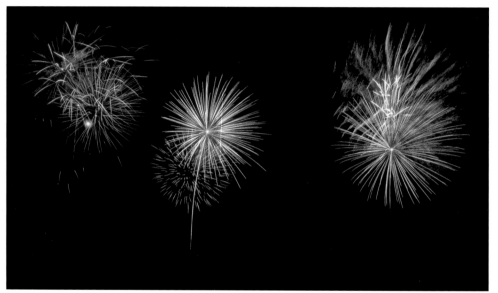

7.26 A tripod and a 30-second exposure captured multiple fireworks bursts.

Table 7.7
Taking Fireworks Pictures

Setup	**Practice Picture:** I got to the fireworks show early so I could pick out a prime location on a hill slightly elevated above the crowd; this way I could set up a tripod without obstructing the view of the crowds seated in the vicinity. Figure 7.26 resulted from a 30-second exposure.
	On Your Own: A position close to where the fireworks are set off will let you point the camera up at the sky's canopy and capture all the streaks and flares with ease. On the other hand, a more distant location will let you photograph fireworks against a city's skyline. Both positions are excellent, but you won't have time to use both for one fireworks show. Choose one for a particular display, then try out the other strategy at the next show.
Lighting	**Practice Picture:** The fireworks provide all the light you need.
	On Your Own: This is one type of photography that doesn't require making many lighting decisions.

Lens	**Practice Picture:** 18-55mm f/3.5-5.6G ED II AF-S DX Zoom-Nikkor set to 28mm. **On Your Own:** A wide-angle lens is usually required to catch the area of the sky that's exploding with light and color. Even a fish-eye lens can be used to interesting effect. If you're farther away from the display, you may need a telephoto lens to capture only the fireworks.
Camera Settings	**Practice Picture:** RAW capture. Manual exposure, with both shutter speed and aperture set by hand. Saturation set to Enhanced. **On Your Own:** Depth of field and action stopping are not considerations. Don't be tempted to use Noise Reduction to decrease noise in the long exposures; the extra time the reduction step takes will cause you to miss some shots.
Exposure	**Practice Picture:** ISO 200, f/11, 30 seconds. **On Your Own:** Don't try to rely on any auto exposure mode. Your best bet is to try a few manual exposure settings and adjust as necessary.
Accessories	A steady tripod is a must. You also should have a penlight so you can locate the control buttons in the dark! Carry an umbrella so your camera won't be drenched if it rains unexpectedly. The infrared remote control can be used to trip the shutter.

Fireworks and light trails photography tips

✦ **You must use a tripod.** Fireworks exposures usually require a second or two to make, and nobody can handhold a camera for that long. Set up the tripod and point the camera at the part of the sky where you expect the fireworks to unfold, and be ready to trip the shutter.

✦ **Review the first one or two shots you take on your LCD to see if the fireworks are being imaged as you like.** Decrease the f-stop if the colored streaks appear to be too washed out, or increase the exposure if the display appears too dark. Experiment with different exposure times to capture more or fewer streaks in one picture.

✦ **Track the skyrockets in flight so you can time the start of your exposure for the moment just before they reach the top of their arc and explode.** Then, trip the shutter. An exposure of one to four seconds will capture single displays. You can use longer exposures if you want to image a series of bursts in one shot.

✦ **Don't worry about noise.** It's almost unavoidable at longer exposures, and won't be evident once you start playing with the brightness and contrast of your shots in your image editor.

Flower and Plant Photography

For many, flowers and plant life are the only living things that are as much fun to photograph as people. Like people, each blossom has its own personality. Flowers come in endless varieties, and their infinite variety of textures and shapes can be photographed from any number of angles. If you like colors, flowers and fruits provide hues that are so unique that many of our colors — from rose to lilac to peach to orange — are named for them.

Best of all, flowers and plants are the most patient subjects imaginable. They'll sit for hours without flinching or moving, other than to follow the track of the sun across the sky. You adjust them into "poses," change their backgrounds, and even trim off a few stray fronds without hearing a single complaint. You can photograph them in any season, including indoors in the dead of winter. Floral photographs are universal, too, as flowers are loved in every country of the world.

Because of their popularity, you won't have to look far for subject matter. Your own garden might provide fodder (see figure 7.27), but if you're looking for more exotic plants, there are bound to be public gardens and herbariums you can visit for your photo shoots. Photography is so likely to be part of the experience at such venues that you'll find maps leading you to the most popular

exhibits, along with tips on the best vantage points for taking pictures. Take a few overall photos to show the garden's environment, then get closer for floral "portraits" of your favorites.

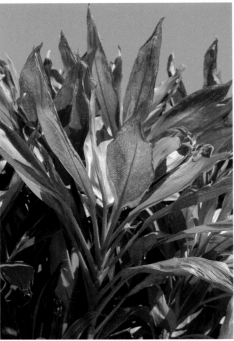

7.27 You can find "wild" flowers and plants everywhere, including your home garden.

Inspiration

Flower photography is an excellent opportunity to apply your creative and compositional skills. Use color, shape, lines, and texture to create both abstract and concrete images. Experiment with selective focus and lighting (just move to another angle — and the lighting changes!). It's always fun to find plants and flowers that look like people or other objects when you want to add a little mystery or humor to your photographs.

When shooting flowers, you can capture individual blossoms, as in figure 7.28, or photograph groups of them together. As every professional or amateur flower arranger knows, floral groups of different types of plant life can be put together creatively in bouquets to form one-of-a-kind compositions.

If you have a macro lens, you can isolate an individual part of a flower to explore the mysteries of how these small-scale miracles are constructed. It's possible to spend an entire career doing nothing but photographing flowers, and many photographers do. Surely, you'll find many hours of enjoyment tackling this most interesting subject on your own.

Although some photographers specialize in flower photography, many of us turn to shooting blossoms when we have nothing else to inspire us or need a creative spark. Certainly, the fresh flowers of springtime, the mature blooming plants of summer, and the last bursts of color in the fall can be invigorating, but there's no need to eschew flower photography in the dead of winter. You can drop by your local florist and purchase a bouquet, a blooming plant, or

selected individual flowers to brighten your home as well as your photographic efforts.

Public gardens, greenhouses, and herbariums are also open year round. If you read your newspaper, you can find dates for exhibits and flower shows that are an opportunity to shoot digital portraits of some of the most beautiful living things.

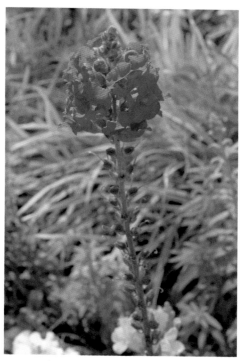

7.28 Isolate an individual flower to focus attention on its colors and shape.

Flower and plant photography practice

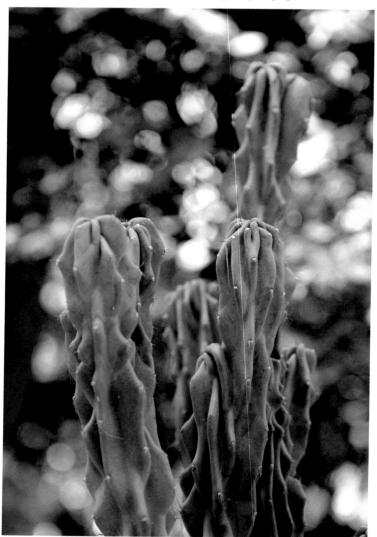

7.29 While flowers and plants themselves can make a great background for your photos, sometimes the play of light behind them can serve as an interesting counterpoint.

Table 7.8
Taking Flower and Plant Pictures

Setup	**Practice Picture:** I wanted to capture this healthy succulent, and when I squatted down to focus, I noticed how the multicolored out-of-focus points of light behind it made the interesting background you can see in figure 7.29.
	On Your Own: It's tempting to shoot down on plants flowers, to better capture those opulent blooms. But you can also get interesting views by getting down and looking at the plant from its own level, or by shooting upwards to include a contrasting blue sky in the image. Don't be locked into one position, and thus limit your creative possibilities.
Lighting	**Practice Picture:** I waited for a slightly overcast day with no breeze so I could capture this cactus in a softer light.
	On Your Own: Full sunlight brings out the brightest colors and adds contrast that highlights detail, but also produces dark shadows. You may need reflectors to soften the light, or fill flash to illuminate the shadows. Use the diffuse light of overcast days for a softer look, but keep in mind that the colors will be muted. You might need to adjust the saturation by using your D40 or D40x's Optimize Image feature or your image editor.
Lens	**Practice Picture:** 17-35mm f/2.8D ED-IF AF-S Zoom-Nikkor set at 35mm.
	On Your Own: If you're serious about flower photography, you might want to invest in some serious lenses, although the D40/D40x's 18-55mm kit lens will do a good job. I used a pricier wide-angle zoom "borrowed" from the arsenal of one of my other Nikon dSLRs, because it focuses as close as 12 inches. You might prefer the 105mm f/2.8G ED-IF AF-S VR Micro-Nikkor, which has some significant advantages, including its Vibration Reduction feature that reduces the need for a tripod. Unlike shorter focal length lenses (like the 60mm f/2.8D AF Micro-Nikkor), which exaggerate the proportions of parts of the flower closest to the lens, a telephoto macro lens lets you step back, and throws the background out of focus. A close-focusing telephoto in the 100mm range also works well.
Camera Settings	**Practice Picture:** Aperture Priority AE. The white balance was set to Auto. Color saturation was set to Enhanced.
	On Your Own: For all types of close-up photography, you usually want to select the aperture yourself, either to control depth of field for selective focus effects, or to increase it to bring more of the frame into sharp focus.

Continued

Table 7.8 *(continued)*

Exposure	**Practice Picture:** ISO 400, f/5.6, 1/400 second.
	On Your Own: A sensitivity setting of ISO 200 is a good starting point for most outdoor lighting conditions. You can increase the setting if you find you need a faster shutter speed or more depth of field. To blur the background, start with an f/5.6 aperture. For more generous depth of field, use an f/8 or f/11 aperture.
Accessories	In addition to a tripod, you want to have the Nikon ML-L3 wireless remote control to release the shutter without shaking the camera. You can also use the D40/D40x's self-timer.

Flower and plant photography tips

✦ **Rely on manual focus.** Autofocus is great, but your D40 or D40x isn't necessarily smart enough to know exactly what portion of a flower you want to focus on. There are situations where you want to focus on the center of a blossom, and the camera might tend to focus on the closest petal instead. You can manually select one of the three available autofocus areas, of course, but with a nonmoving subject, it's usually quicker to switch into manual focus mode and set your plane of focus by hand.

✦ **Increase saturation.** Boost the richness of the colors by visiting the Shooting menu and setting the saturation to Enhanced under Optimize Image. If the sky appears in your photos, use a polarizing filter to add saturation to the flowers and sky.

✦ **Experiment with lighting.** Simply changing your position can alter the lighting dramatically. You can use reflectors and (indoors) lights of your own. Backlighting can be especially interesting to show off translucent petals and leaves.

Infrared Photography

Infrared (IR) photography shows familiar scenes and subjects in a new way, using only the illumination in the infrared spectrum. IR photography with the Nikon D40 or D40x requires a special filter to emphasize the *near infrared* portion of the spectrum (although some visible light sneaks through) when making exposures.

Subjects are reproduced with tones that depend on how much IR illumination they reflect; this creates images with very light foliage, dark skies with fluffy white clouds, and other effects. The strange images result from the tendency of plant life to reflect IR light extremely well, while the sky doesn't reflect much IR at all.

Because of the stunning effects it creates in landscape images, IR photography is most often used for scenic pictures. Filtering out most of the visible light also means that you need to shoot IR pictures with your camera mounted on a tripod, and, for the most part, shoot blind. That's a hefty price to pay, but one that is well worth it once you see the unusual images you end up with.

IR photography requires a bit of technical skill, and tweaking of the D40/D40x's white balance controls. For example, initially your shots will have a reddish cast to them, but you can eliminate that by converting the picture to grayscale or by isolating the red channel in your image editor, or by changing to a preset white balance (described later in this section). If you use a special white balance, your infrared photos will have the color scheme shown in figure 7.30.

Inspiration

Landscape photos are traditional fodder for IR photography, because such images are static and accommodate procedures that involve setting up the tripod, composing the image through the viewfinder, and then attaching the IR filter (which makes D40 or D40x's viewfinder appear totally black). However, there are plenty of other subjects for IR photography, including architecture (see figure 7.31), portraits (IR photography tends to smooth out complexions), and pictures taken by candlelight.

You don't need a lot of special equipment. An IR filter, such as a Hoya R72 or Wratten #89B, is required, and you must use a tripod for the long exposures (frequently four seconds or more) that IR photos call for.

Setting the white balance for IR is a good idea. For figure 7.31, I adjusted white balance by pointing the D40/D40x at the leaves on a stand of trees and using the preset white-balance facility (described in Chapter 3) to eliminate the reddish cast and create a more offbeat color-but-not-color IR picture. You can also reduce IR pictures to straight grayscale images if you like, or capture false-color IR pictures with *channel swapping* in your image editor (as detailed later in this section).

IR photography can be especially interesting as a photojournalism tool because its grainy look, black-and-white tones, and motion blur add an artful look. With the odd tonal shifts, common subjects take on unusual looks that you can use creatively. Some things appear to be darker in an IR photo than you might expect, while others are lighter.

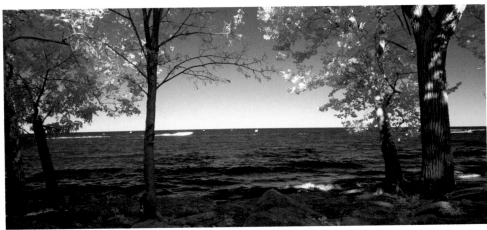

7.30 With the white balance set especially for IR photos, the colors will have a strong sepia tone.

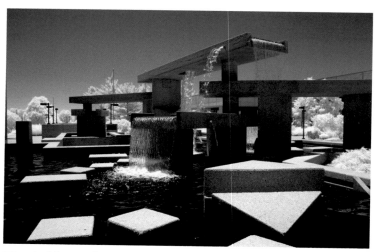

7.31 Architectural subjects often lend themselves to the stark look IR photography provides.

Infrared photography practice

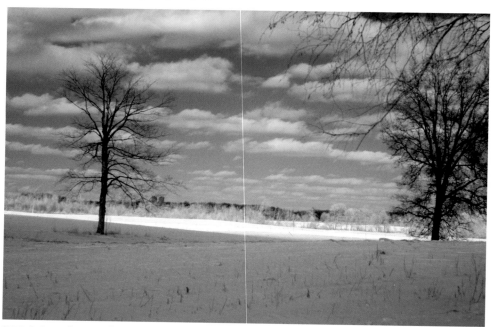

7.32 Interesting IR pictures can be as close as your backyard, as you can see in this false-color IR photo.

Table 7.9
Taking Infrared Pictures

Setup	**Practice Picture:** To take the photo shown in figure 7.32, I wandered out into my own backyard towards a field located behind my property one winter day. I set the camera up on a tripod, composed my image, and then mounted my Hoya #72 IR filter.
	On Your Own: In non-winter situations, look for subjects outdoors with a lot of foliage and grass to make the most of the dramatic pale look that IR photography provides.
Lighting	**Practice Picture:** Daylight illumination.
	On Your Own: Brightly lit days are best for outdoor IR photography, but you can also get good results on slightly foggy days, too, because IR illumination cuts right through the haze.
Lens	**Practice Picture:** 12-24mm f/4G ED-IF AF-S DX Zoom-Nikkor set to 12mm to exaggerate the foreground, making the field look even larger.
	On Your Own: Unfortunately, you may find your choices of lenses limited by the need to have an IR filter for each lens. The Nikon 12-24mm zoom uses an expensive 77mm filter, but many other Nikkors accept 52mm, 62mm, or 67mm filters. You can buy a single 67mm filter for, say the 18-135mm f/3.5–5.6G ED-IF AF-S DX Zoom-Nikkor, and use it with a step-down ring or two (available at camera stores for about $10) so it can be mounted on lenses that use the smaller 62mm or 52mm filter size. If you can live with using just one lens, the 18-55mm f/3.5-5.6G ED II AF-S DX Zoom-Nikkor uses relatively inexpensive 52mm filters.
Camera Settings	**Practice Picture:** I used RAW capture and manual exposure. The previous summer I had set white balance manually for infrared, saved a couple photos, and then used them in wintery weather (when nary a patch of grass could be found) using the D40's Preset capability.
	On Your Own: Manual exposure and manual bracketing (use several different exposures, such as one second, two seconds, and four seconds) make it easier to get the correct settings. Review your images on the camera's LCD, and then adjust for subsequent exposures.
Exposure	**Practice Picture:** ISO 200, f/11, 8 seconds.
	On Your Own: Increase the ISO setting to allow shutter speeds within a range of a few seconds. Otherwise, moving objects such as tree branches or clouds can blur.
Accessories	A tripod is essential for IR photos.

Infrared photography tips

✦ **Use channel swapping for false color infrared.** It's easy if you own Adobe Photoshop. Just use the Channel Mixer to set the Red Channel's Red value to 0 percent and its Blue value slider to 100 percent. Then switch to the Blue channel and set the Red slider to 100 percent and the Blue slider to 0 percent. That's all you need to do.

✦ **Bracket exposures.** Even small exposure increments can change an IR photo dramatically. Set your basic exposure, say f/11 at 4 seconds, then shoot additional pictures at 1, 2, 8, and 12 seconds.

✦ **Use motion blur creatively.** The long exposures needed for IR photos can be used creatively. Waterfalls take on a satiny texture with exposures of one second or longer. People walking and vehicles driving past blur in an interesting way. Use a small f-stop and a very long exposure (perhaps 30 seconds), and those moving subjects may vanish entirely, turning your urban IR scene into a ghost town!

Landscape Photography

Landscape photography provides you with a universe of photo subjects, there for the taking, courtesy of Mother Nature. This kind of photography provides a dual joy: the thrill of the hunt as you track down suitable scenic locations to shoot — whether remote or close to home — and then the challenge of using your creativity to capture the scene in a new and interesting way.

Landscapes are an ever-changing subject, too. The same scene can be photographed in summer, winter, fall, or spring, and look different each time. Indeed, a series of these photos of a favorite vista in different seasons makes an interesting and rewarding project.

This kind of photography can take many forms. You can photograph a landscape as it really is, capturing a view exactly as you saw it in a moment in time. Or, you can look for an unusual view or perspective, like the one shown in figure 7.33, that adds a fantasy world quality.

Look for wildlife to populate your landscape, or shoot a scene with only the trees and plants, rocks, sky, and bodies of water to fill the view. Choose the time of day or season of the year. You may be working with the raw materials nature provides you, but your options are almost endless.

Inspiration

The three basic styles of landscape photography actually have names: *representational* (realistic scenery with no manipulation); *impressionistic* (using photographic techniques such as filters or special exposures that provide a less realistic impression of the landscape); and *abstract* (the landscape is reduced to its essential components so that the photo may not resemble the original scene at all).

You can apply any of these to the landscape locations you find. You can get a good start

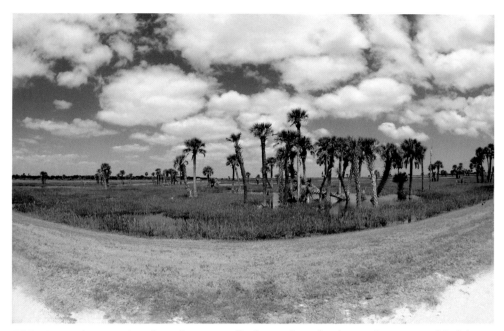

7.33 Human intervention doesn't necessarily detract from landscape images, as this fisheye shot of what is actually a series of human-made water treatment ponds demonstrates.

by photographing the landscapes around your home area. If you don't live close to majestic mountains or the thunderous surf of an ocean, you still can find good locations among forests, lakes, deserts, or even swamps (they're called *wetlands* these days) near your home.

When you travel outside your home base, you can get good tips on scenic locations from the staff of a camping or sporting goods store, or from the friendly folks who operate a fishing tackle shop. Buy a map or make another small purchase, and then get the real scoop on hiking trails or scenic fishing spots from the local experts.

At locations near the sea coast, newspapers always have listings of high and low tides, and a schedule of sunrises and sunsets, so you know when the beaches might be at their best, and what times the sun is lower in the sky and better able to emphasize the texture of the scenery. I very rarely photograph landscapes at high noon; more often I'm out there shooting in the two or three hours before sunset, and a couple hours after sunrise.

It's easy to get lost in unfamiliar territory, so carry a compass. Better yet, use the compass with sunrise/sunset tables to determine exactly where the sun disappears in the evening and reappears in the morning, so you can be positioned to catch it illuminating a mountain, lake, or other scenic feature.

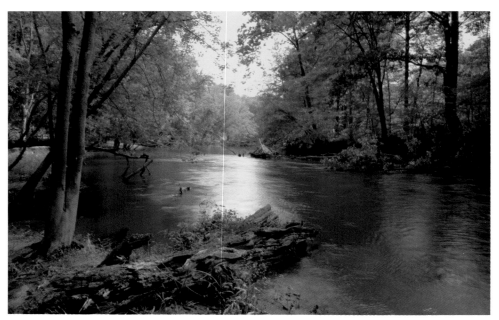

7.34 This quiet river scene makes a peaceful landscape vista.

One special kind of landscape photography that you might want to explore is the *panorama*. All that's required is to take a series of overlapping photos, and then stitch them together. Most image editors have that capability, and Photoshop and Photoshop Elements' PhotoMerge facility is particularly good. But you'll also find stand-alone programs that do nothing but stitch together panoramas.

Landscape photography practice

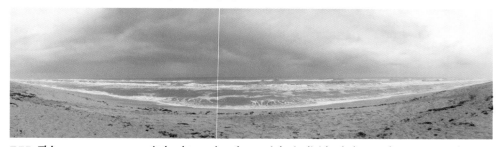

7.35 This panorama was stitched together from eight individual shots taken at a seashore. It had to be cropped to fit the page.

Note　*If you want to see the entire panorama in figure 7.35, go to www.nikonguides.com/ images/seascape.jpg.*

Table 7.10
Taking Landscape Pictures

Setup	**Practice Picture:** The beach was deserted, and I couldn't resist capturing a 180-degree panorama (shown in figure 7.35) covering the shore from north (left) to south (right). I didn't use a tripod or any special equipment. I just visually overlapped each photo slightly as I took eight different shots, using the D40's focus bracket marks as a guide to position the horizon at roughly the same place in each shot. Photoshop Elements 5.0's PhotoMerge facility automatically grouped them together, and I cropped out a little of the top and bottom to create this finished shot.
	On Your Own: You don't need to find a remote location to find unspoiled wilderness. Even sites close to home can make attractive scenic photos if the signs of civilization are rustic and/or historic.
Lighting	**Practice Picture:** Fortunately, it was an overcast day, so I didn't have to contend with sharp shadows that would be converging at different angles in a panorama shot.
	On Your Own: You don't have a lot of control over the available illumination when shooting landscapes. Your best bet is to choose your time and place, and take your shots when the light is best for the kind of photography you want to capture.
Lens	**Practice Picture:** 18-55mm f/3.5-5.6G ED II AF-S DX Zoom-Nikkor set to 18mm.
	On Your Own: While you can use a wide-angle lens to take in a broad view, you should remember that the foreground will be emphasized. If you're far enough from your chosen scene, a telephoto lens can capture more of the landscape, and less of the foreground.
Camera Settings	**Practice Picture:** RAW capture. Shutter Priority AE. Saturation set to Enhanced.
	On Your Own: Shutter Priority mode lets you set a high enough shutter speed to freeze your landscape and counteract any camera or photographer shake if you're not using a tripod.
Exposure	**Practice Picture:** ISO 200, f11, 1/500 second. Slight underexposure helped make the colors appear even richer.
	On Your Own: On this overcast day, an ISO setting of 200 was enough to allow an appropriately higher shutter speed.
Accessories	Use a tripod for scenic photographs whenever possible, and they are especially good for helping you frame overlapping photos when shooting panoramas. If you want to do a lot of panorama work, there are special heads for tripods that help you swivel the camera in appropriate increments. Use a quick-release plate so you can experiment with various angles and views and then lock down the camera on the tripod only when you've decided on a basic composition.

Landscape photography tips

✦ **Bracket your exposures.** It may be a long time before you're back at the same location for a reshoot, so expend the effort to shoot several different exposures to increase your odds that one is exactly right. A given scene can look different when you photograph it with a half-stop to a full-stop (or more) extra exposure, or with a similar amount of underexposure. An ordinary dusk scene can turn into a dramatic silhouette.

✦ **Learn to use your filters.** Landscape photographers have two favorite filters. One is a graduated neutral density filter that you can orient so the top half of the image receives a stop or two less exposure than the bottom half. That lets you reduce the exposure of the sky, so clouds appear more readily, without causing the foreground to darken too much. The other favored filter is a polarizer, which can remove reflections from the water, reduce haze when you're photographing distant scenes, and boost color saturation.

✦ **Be prepared for the weather.** Scenic photos often involve a bit of hiking, and it's easy to find yourself a mile or two from your car when an unexpected shower becomes a downpour. Carry an umbrella, a rain poncho, gloves, or other protective gear even if you think you don't need them.

Macro Photography

Close-up, or *macro*, photography is another chance for you to cut loose and let your imagination run free. This type of picture taking is closely related to floral photography and still-life photography, which also can involve shooting up-close and personal. However, the emphasis here is on getting really, *really* close.

Although you can have lots of fun shooting close-ups out in the field, as I did at a zoo with a macro-zoom lens for figure 7.36, macro photography is one of those rainy-day activities that you can do at home. You don't need to travel by plane to find something out of the ordinary to shoot. That weird crystal salt shaker you unearthed at a garage sale might be perfect for an imaginative close-up that captures its brilliance and texture. Or you can photograph something that is important to you, such as your coin or stamp collection.

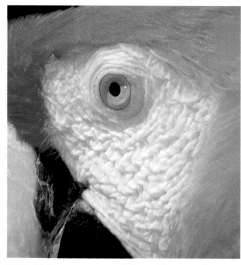

7.36 This parrot wasn't fazed by my close approach, so I used a macro-zoom lens to capture this close-up of his alert, intelligent eye regarding me.

You need some special equipment for the most flexibility in shooting macros, but you should not have to spend a great deal of money. Your current lens might focus close enough for macro photos. If not, the 50mm f/1.8D AF Nikkor costs about $100, and you can outfit it with extension tubes or a lens reversing ring that let you focus manually to within a few inches of your subject with great results. (It's a very sharp lens, too.) You can fit inexpensive filter-like close-up lenses (despite their name, these are not stand-alone optics themselves) to the front of your existing lens. If you really enjoy macro photography and have a few hundred dollars to spend, you can purchase a macro lens, such as the 60mm f/2.8D AF Micro-Nikkor. While neither of these lenses will autofocus on the D40 or D40x, that's not usually much of a drawback for macro work. Unless you already own one of them, you might want to wait. I expect Nikon to introduce AF-S versions of both in the future.

Inspiration

It's important to keep in mind that magnification, not focusing distance, is paramount in macro photography. That's because the size of the subject in the finished photo, not how far you were away when the picture was taken, is key. For example, you might be able to fill the frame with a stack of coins using a 60mm macro lens at a distance of two inches, or take virtually the same picture using a 105mm macro lens from five inches away (see figure 7.37).

Indeed, macro lenses are often described using the magnification they produce at their closest focusing distance. For example, a lens capable of creating a 1:1 (also known as 1X magnification) image would produce an image that's *life-size*; that is, a subject measuring one-half-inch across would be one-half-inch wide on the sensor. A 1:2 magnification (1/2X) would create an image that's half life-size, and so on.

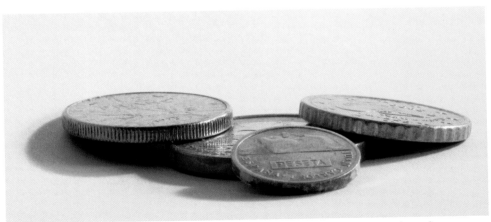

7.37 Toss some old coins on a table, set up a few high-intensity lamps, and you have a macro subject to experiment with.

For flat objects, you probably can't tell which lens or focal length was used. That's not the case with three-dimensional subjects, because the closer you get, the more those parts of the subject that are closer to the lens appear disproportionately large compared to more distant parts of the subject.

You might find a longer focal length (say, 105mm instead of 60mm) preferable to avoid this distortion. Plus a longer focal length gives you a greater working distance and more elbow room to light the subject, both of which can be important if you're photographing living creatures.

Macro photography practice

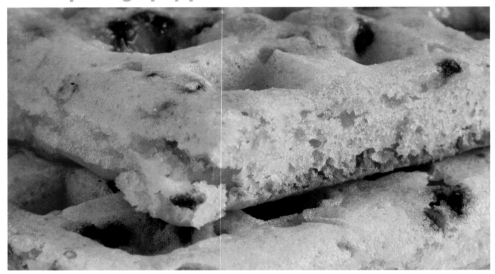

7.38 Food often can be used for interesting macro photos.

Table 7.11
Taking Macro Pictures

Setup	**Practice Picture:** Food can be used for excellent close-up photos. I set the breakfast treat in figure 7.38 on a plate placed on a piece of seamless white cardboard. The texture and color made for an interest, almost abstract, macro photo.
	On Your Own: You can use poster board, fabric, or other backgrounds to isolate your macro subjects, and pose them on a tabletop or other flat surface.

Lighting	**Practice Picture:** I used a pair of external electronic flash units connected to slave triggers, bounced off umbrellas, and activated by the D40's built-in flash, which was set to 1/32 power.
	On Your Own: You can also use desk lamps to light small setups, with reflectors to fill in the shadows.
Lens	**Practice Picture:** 50mm f/1.8D AF Nikkor.
	On Your Own: Any macro lens, close-focusing prime or zoom lens, or an ordinary lens on extension tubes or outfitted with close-up attachments can do the job.
Camera Settings	**Practice Picture:** RAW capture. Manual exposure. Although Nikon's Creative Lighting System and iTTL flash exposure could have adjusted the flash output automatically, it was just as much fun to set the flash units' output manually and experiment.
	On Your Own: If you're using incandescent illumination, use Aperture Priority AE mode and allow the D40 or D40x to choose the right shutter speed appropriate for the f-stop you select.
Exposure	**Practice Picture:** ISO 100, f/32, 1/200 second.
	On Your Own: For maximum depth of field, chose a small aperture such as f/16 to f/22. If you want to blur the background, choose a wider aperture such as f/8 to f/11. Use ISO 100 for maximum sharpness and the least amount of noise. You don't need higher ISOs when your camera is mounted on a tripod.
Accessories	Use a tripod for macro photography. The Nikon ML-L3 infrared remote helps prevent camera shake, but you can also use the self-timer.

Macro photography tips

✦ **Close-up attachments are cheap.** Filter-like close-up attachments that screw onto the front of a lens provide additional magnification and can cost about $50. They do come with a sharpness penalty and, unlike extension tubes, only work with a lens that has a matching filter thread size. If you want to use close-up attachments with lenses having different filter sizes, you need step-up or step-down rings, available from your camera supplier.

✦ **Buy some automatic extension tubes.** I use the Kenko brand that preserves the camera's autofocus and auto exposure features. You can purchase them individually for as little as $50, in sizes ranging from about 12mm to 36mm in length, or in sets of three for about $150. Combine tubes to achieve longer extensions.

✦ **Always review your first shots.** That's especially important when you're taking photos using electronic flash that don't have modeling lights that let you preview your close-ups. It takes a long time to set up a close-up photo, so you want to get it right the first time rather than have to set up everything again later.

Night Scene Photography

There's not much to see after dark — but there's a lot to photograph. The same inky blackness that's illuminated by artificial lights or moonlight offers lots of possibilities if you look carefully enough. At night and during the early evening, the reduced illumination serves to cloak some of your surroundings in darkness, while further accentuating the scene that remains.

Add-on light sources, particularly flash, may not always be the answer, because artificial light makes night scenes seem ... artificial. It's often best to work with the illumination that's naturally there, as was done for the image shown in figure 7.39, which shows off the garish lights of a county fair amusement ride.

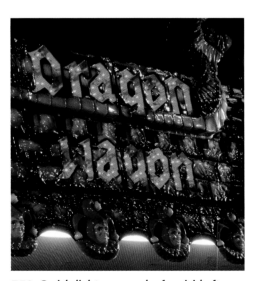

7.39 Garish lights can make for vivid after-dark photos.

Night and evening photography is challenging technically, because a combination of slow shutter speeds, higher-than-normal ISO sensitivity settings, the potential for using camera supports like tripods, and, as a last resort, auxiliary lighting, can pose a complex puzzle to solve. Those hurdles make night photography that much more satisfying when you do a good job.

Inspiration

Getting good exposures at night is the most significant technical challenge you need to tackle. There's simply not enough light to use the best f-stop at a low ISO setting with a shutter speed that's fast enough to prevent blurry pictures from camera shake. You often need to make compromises in one or all three of these settings. Here are some possible solutions:

✦ **Use fast lenses.** The typical zoom lens has a maximum aperture of f/3.5 to f/4.5. More expensive zoom lenses might have f/2.8 as their largest f-stop. Nikon makes several fixed focal length (prime) lenses with maximum apertures of f/1.8 or faster, including a very affordable 50mm f/1.8 optic, a medium-priced 85mm f/1.8 lens, and more costly 50mm and 85mm f/1.4 lenses. Any of these can let you shoot at night without using oppressively slow shutter speeds (1/30 second or longer) or especially noisy ISO settings (ISO 800 and higher).

✦ **Use vibration reduction.**
Although some people claim to be able to handhold exposures with wide-angle lenses at 1/30 second or even longer, few can actually pull it off. But lenses with built-in vibration reduction, such as the 24-120mm f/3.5-/5.6 VR Zoom-Nikkor or 18–200mm f/3.5-5.6 G ED-IF AF-S VR DX Zoom-Nikkor can be reliably handheld for exposures of 1/15 second or longer.

✦ **Use a tripod, monopod, or other support.** Brace your camera well enough, and you can take sharp photos with exposures of several seconds to 30 seconds or longer.

✦ **Use ISO settings wisely.** You can boost your camera's sensor's response to light by increasing the ISO value, but at the cost of additional visual noise in your photos. If image quality is important, use ISO increases as a last resort, and use the D40/D40x's noise-reduction features when appropriate. Use the ISO Auto function, described in Chapter 3, to intelligently rein in the automatic application of ISO increases.

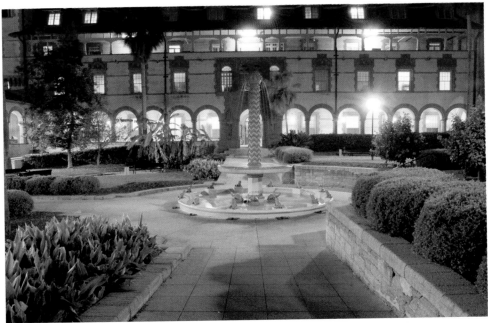

7.40 A lengthy exposure was required to capture this courtyard scene at night.

Night scene photography practice

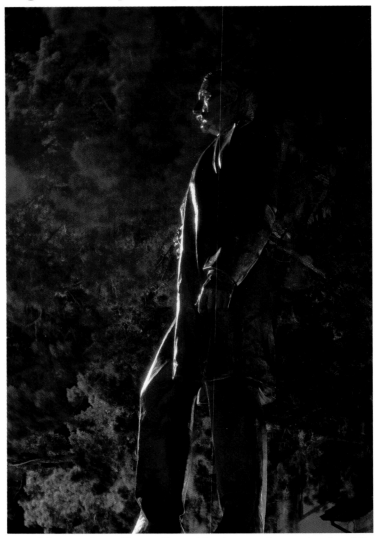

7.41 This statue's profile was limned by the streetlamps that faced it.

Table 7.12
Taking Night Scene Pictures

Setup	**Practice Picture:** As I passed this statue of Henry Flagler, one of the founders of Standard Oil, I was struck by how the streetlamps that faced the statue outlined the industrialist's profile. A long exposure with my camera on a tripod yielded the eerie "portrait" shown in figure 7.41. **On Your Own:** Although I used one, you don't necessarily need a tripod for night scenes. Rest your camera on an available object to steady it. If your scene is relatively unmoving, use the self-timer to trigger the shot and avoid shaking the camera with your trigger finger.
Lighting	**Practice Picture:** The streetlamps provided the main sidelighting, while other lamps in the vicinity added enough "fill" to make the main figure of the statue visible. **On Your Own:** Try to work with the available light at night. If you must use supplementary illumination, bounce it off reflectors and try not to overpower the existing light. Use your extra light as fill for dark shadows, which can be helpful when the available light is overhead and high in contrast.
Lens	**Practice Picture:** 18-55mm f/3.5-5.6G ED II AF-S DX Zoom-Nikkor set to 18mm. **On Your Own:** Wide-angle lenses and zooms at their wide-angle settings generally afford the fastest f-stop available. Even short telephoto lenses saddle you with a double penalty: a smaller maximum aperture and the need for a faster shutter speed to minimize camera shake.
Camera Settings	**Practice Picture:** RAW+JPEG Basic capture. Manual exposure with Optimize Image set to Vivid and white balance set to tungsten. **On Your Own:** As your exposures approach one second or longer, manual mode and some minor tweaking of shutter speed between shots yield the most accurate exposures.
Exposure	**Practice Picture:** ISO 200, f/16, 20 seconds. **On Your Own:** For exposures longer than about 1/30 second, you might want to bracket exposures to get different looks.
Accessories	A tripod, a monopod, a clamp with a camera tripod mount attached, or even a beanbag, can serve as a support for your camera during long nighttime exposures.

Night scene photography tips

✦ **Slow Sync helps dark backgrounds.** If you use flash, the D40 or D40x's Slow Sync mode is available when using the Night Scene or Program or Aperture Priority modes. It allows the use of longer shutter speeds with flash so that existing light in a scene can supplement the flash illumination in the background areas.

✦ **Twilight: The other nighttime.** If you shoot at twilight, you get a nighttime look, but will have the remaining illumination from the setting sun to fill in your scene, reducing the inky blackness. A full moon can also provide a little fill light when you're shooting exposures of one second or longer.

✦ **Readjust, or bracket.** Whether you're estimating exposure, using histograms to zero in, or letting your camera choose the night exposure for you, it's a smart idea to review your shots and make adjustments, or to use the camera's bracketing feature to automatically create overexposures and underexposures that might later turn out to be spot on when you get the photo into your image editor.

People Photography

Photographs of people are one of the most popular subjects for both casual and avid photographers. Such photos are a way of documenting our activities and showing how our lives change as we grow and develop. People can be portrayed as friendly, glamorous, adventuresome, hopeful, or even sinister, at the whim of the photographer or, maybe, the mood of the subject.

Photographing people is always challenging because everybody's a critic. You as the photographer have to please yourself with your results; you have to please the person you've photographed; and please everyone who knows that person. Photographs never really show people as they are, but rather as we see them, and as they see themselves. People pictures can be posed or candid, capturing an individual in a deliberate stance, or caught in an unguarded moment.

Outdoors, you can work with the environment and the light that is available. You might find it a challenge to choose the best background and angle so the lighting is

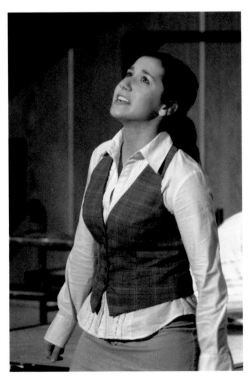

7.42 People pictures can capture a person in moments of great expression, as in a play.

flattering. However, you're not stuck with what you have. A piece of cardboard can be used outdoors to bounce light into inky shadows. You can use your D40 or D40x's pop-up flash to fill in dark areas, too.

In contrast, shooting indoors is a perfect opportunity to experiment with lighting, because you have complete command of the illumination and can, if you like, set up lights or electronic flash units under conditions that are more easily controlled than outdoors. A mini studio set up at home lets you adjust poses, backgrounds, and lighting in dozens of ways, all in the space of a few minutes.

Inspiration

You may find that photographing people is your inspiration to experiment, because the feedback from your subjects will be gratifying if you achieve a particularly good result. Don't be afraid to try capturing people in deliberate poses, work with props, shoot from different angles, or try out different kinds of backgrounds.

You can also see what happens when you exclude or include parts of your subjects' environment, and experiment with various types of illumination. For example, you might want to see how people appear during late afternoon or dusk, discovering that humans look their best at that time of day, compared to the stark, bluish tones found at midday.

As sunset approaches, you may find the color of the light too reddish for your tastes, but if you go with the flow you can get romantic images of people with an almost candle-lit quality. Early-evening sunlight is much different from what you'd get by simply applying a warming tone using your camera's or image editor's controls.

People photography practice

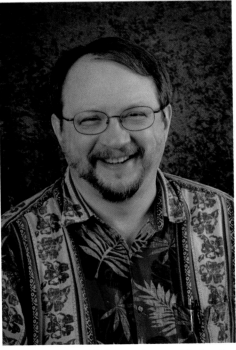

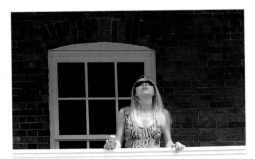

7.43 Posed snapshots are the perfect opportunity for your subject to ham it up, as in this photo of a young lady striking a model-esque pose.

7.44 A couple of lights and a stool helped produce this portrait.

Table 7.13
Taking a Head Shot

Setup	**Practice Picture:** My friend Brian needed a new head shot for his Wikipedia user page, so I draped a length of fabric over a curtain as a background, set up a couple off-camera electronic flash units, and posed him on a stool to bring him up to camera-eye level for the photo in figure 7.44.
	On Your Own: You'll find that fabric, at a few dollars a yard, makes a great background for indoor portraits. Purchase two or three yards of solid or textured fabrics in blues, neutral browns, or grays. A transparent piece of plastic placed over your background line can turn a gray background into any color of the rainbow.
Lighting	**Practice Picture:** I set the D40's built-in flash to Manual and 1/32 power and used a remote to trigger a pair of off-camera flash units each equipped with a light-sensing slave unit. One of the flash units was positioned three feet to the right of the camera and bounced off a 40-inch white umbrella. The second flash was bounced off a white reflector positioned to the left of the camera to provide fill light.
	On Your Own: If you don't own a brace of strobes, you can use incandescent lights and white cardboard to achieve the same effect if you mount the D40 or D40x on a tripod to hold the camera steady.
Lens	**Practice Picture:** 18–55mm f/3.5–5.6G ED II AF-S DX Zoom-Nikkor set to 55mm.
	On Your Own: The kit lens actually makes a nice portrait lens at its longest zoom setting. However, you can choose any lens or zoom setting in the 50–70mm range for most individual portraits.
Camera Settings	**Practice Picture:** RAW capture. Aperture-priority AE.
	On Your Own: If you're using flash, the shutter speed isn't crucial, so you'll want to use aperture-priority AE mode to let you specify the f-stop and control the amount of depth of field.
Exposure	**Practice Picture:** ISO 200, f/11, 1/500 second.
	On Your Own: For most portraits, you want enough depth of field to ensure your model's entire face is in sharp focus (especially the eyes!), but is shallow enough to throw the background partially out of focus. So, f/11 is a good place to start, but you can use f/8 or f/5.6 if you want more selective focus.
Accessories	White or silver reflectors or umbrellas are essential for providing indirect lighting that is softer and more flattering. Use soft white for women and teenagers who want their skin to look creamy-soft. Silver might be a better choice for men or older folks who are proud of their character lines. Gold reflectors add a warmer look that is beneficial for glamour shots.

People photography tips

✦ Although a bald head has become a fashion statement these days, if your subject is sensitive about a bare pate, elevate your victim's chin and lower your camera slightly to minimize the top of the head.

✦ If your subject has a long, large, or angular nose, have him or her face directly into the camera.

✦ To minimize prominent ears, shoot your subject in profile, or try to arrange the lighting so the ear nearest the camera is in shadow.

✦ To minimize wrinkles or facial defects such as scars or a bad complexion, use softer, more diffuse lighting. A reflector, such as a piece of white cardboard, is a good idea.

✦ People wearing glasses are a perennial problem for photographers. Watch for reflections and ask your subject to raise or lower her chin slightly so the light bounces off the lenses at an angle, rather than right back at the camera.

Seasonal Photography

Most photographers would agree with Pete Seeger, the Byrds, and the Book of Ecclesiastes that every season has its purpose. Pictorially, the change of seasons brings renewed opportunities for different kinds of photos four times every year. So, just when you tire of photographing basketball games and snow scenes (or slush scenes where I live), spring comes along and there are new indoor and outdoor photographic prospects.

Indeed, I feel bad for those who don't live in areas that have the full range of seasonal transitions, from winter to spring to summer to fall. That was one of the reasons I moved some time ago back to the Midwest from Rochester, New York. It's a joy to record the varied weather, the changes in wildlife and moods, and the other changes as the seasons progress.

Each new season has new activities, as people celebrate the rebirth of spring, the freedom of summer, the changes of fall, and the beauty of new-fallen snow. These seasons all present a wonderful array of photo ideas, and even if you've seen dozens of seasonal changes in your lifetime, each new transition is bound to get your creative ideas flowing.

Something as simple as a decorated Christmas tree can inspire you to try new things. We didn't have much of a snowfall in my area during the early part of last winter (this deficit was heartily resolved in January), so when we had an unexpected snowfall, I rushed outside to capture the image of a hedge burdened with a blanket of white stuff shown in figure 7.45.

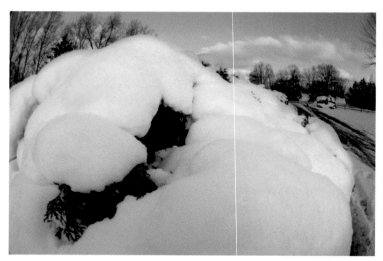

7.45 In northern climes, winter usually means pictures of snow.

Inspiration

Each new season presents its own roster of opportunities. Here are some idea starters to think about:

Winter

Each year kicks off in the dead of winter, and it might seem like a good idea to stay indoors and take macro photographs of your hobby collection or flowers purchased from the florist shop. That's especially true on dreary days filled with more slush and rain than snow. So, when the snow does arrive, it's time to get out and take photos of snowy landscapes, tree branches caked with ice, and fields buried under a blanket of white. You can take some of the best shots at sunset, with its dramatic colors contrasting with the monochrome landscape. It may be chilly in winter, but you can go out, take a few sunset photos, and still be home in time for dinner.

Winter is also a good time to shoot wildlife photos, because the tracks in the snow make it easier to discover where deer, rabbits, and other hardy species congregate. Dress warmly, and you can have more fun than you expect. Just remember to protect your D40 or D40x from the elements; cold weather depletes battery power quickly.

If you happen to be a winter sports enthusiast, you can combine your interest in outdoor activities with your affection for photography.

Winter is a good time for traveling light, because it's never fun to change lenses or lug around a lot of equipment when the weather is cold. Decide on one "walking around lens" and perhaps an alternate, and stick to that, if possible.

Spring

I always get excited when spring approaches, because by March or April I've taken about as many winter pictures as I care to, and am eager to photograph something that's not white. Emerging greenery can be invigorating.

It's easy to jump the gun. I'm usually out there photographing crocuses and other spring flowers the instant they poke their petals above the snow. Eventually, though, the flowers emerge, leaves reappear on the trees, and you can find lots of vibrant colors for your photography. New plants and wildlife are emerging from hibernation or restricted activity, ready for you to capture with your camera.

Just remember that, as in the fall, weather can be fickle throughout the springtime, especially in March and April. Carry protective rain and wind gear for yourself and your camera and dress in layers so you can add or remove clothing to keep warm or cool as required.

During your spring shooting, it may be more convenient to carry along a bit of additional gear, giving yourself a full complement of lenses, flash units, tripods, and other essentials to choose from.

Summer

Summers are great, as long as they're not too hot; I don't even mind the heat because I like to concentrate my outdoor shooting in early morning or late evening hours because the light is better. Summer days are longer, so you do have more time to shoot.

There's always a lot going on in summer, including swimming, baseball, motor sports, outdoor plays and musicals, as well as active animal life both in the wild and in zoos (if you're smart like the animals and avoid the heat of midday). There are always tempting shots of sunsets, water activities, and rich landscapes full of mature plant life.

Fall

Many photographers find fall to be their favorite time of year. The weather is cooler, but still summer-like at the tail end of September. Indeed, last September I found myself shooting photos at a professional baseball game and a high school football game in the same week, then two weeks later photographing fall colors in a nearby national park.

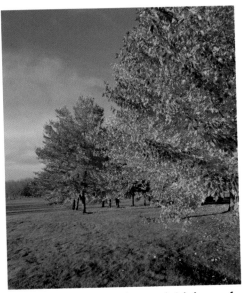

7.46 Fall brings the colors and rich hues of changing foliage as the leaves turn.

Of course, the fall foliage, as it changes from green to vivid reds, oranges, and yellows, is always the main attraction during autumn. It's a great time for a road trip, given the colors change as you travel from north to south, or even just from one state to another. Check with tourist boards in most areas to pinpoint when each area's fall colors are at their peak. Set your camera's saturation level to Enhanced or Vivid in the Optimize Image options of the Shooting menu during this time of year to get the most of the rich colors.

Every other year, I like to spend a couple weeks in the fall on photo safaris to Europe, as October is absolutely the best time to visit many countries on the Continent. Most of the tourists have gone home, but the weather is still warm and comfortable, and most of the attractions and monuments maintain their summer schedules for a few weeks more.

When planning your fall shooting activities, don't forget the key autumn holidays, including Halloween and Thanksgiving, and the activities that accompany them.

Seasonal photography practice

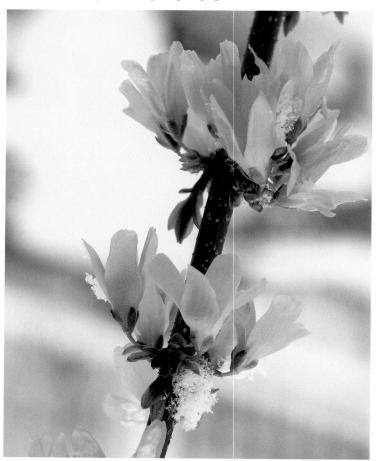

7.47 These early spring blossoms are caked in snow, which provides a poignant contrast.

Table 7.14
Taking Seasonal Pictures

Setup	**Practice Picture:** An unexpected mid-April snowfall covered the ground and these sturdy blossoms with a coat of snow. I ventured out in the cold to take the photograph shown in figure 7.47, remaining high enough to show the out-of-focus snow in the background.
	On Your Own: Your own seasonal photography can include fireworks in the summer, snow scenes in the winter, and the rich colors of changing leaves in the fall. It's a challenge to find seasonal themes that haven't been done to death, but you can rise to the challenge by emphasizing good composition, color, or distinctive patterns.
Lighting	**Practice Picture:** Midday sunlight.
	On Your Own: Learn to work with outdoor lighting, or to supplement it with fill flash or a bit of brightening up with reflectors.
Lens	**Practice Picture:** 105mm f/2.8G ED-IF AF-S VR Micro-Nikkor.
	On Your Own: Wide-angle lenses are very popular for seasonal landscape photos. You need a telephoto to pull in distant views or for sports photos.
Camera Settings	**Practice Picture:** Aperture Priority AE mode with white balance set to Daylight.
	On Your Own: In bright daylight, your shutter speed is likely to be short enough to freeze movement, so you can use Aperture Priority AE mode to select a suitable f-stop. If the light is low, switch to Shutter Priority AE mode. Be sure to set the white balance to match the type of light in the scene.
Exposure	**Practice Picture:** ISO 200, f/16, 1/200 second.
	On Your Own: Outdoors during the day, ISO settings of 100 or 200 should be sufficient for most seasonal photographs. Choose f/8 or f/11 to give you enough depth of field, or stop down to f/16 when you need extra DOF for a close-up photo. As the light wanes, switch to Shutter Priority and select a speed no slower than 1/60th second.
Accessories	Use a tripod or monopod for longer exposures. Carry reflectors with you to fill in dark shadows.

Seasonal photography tips

✦ **Winter.** During snowfalls, use slower shutter speeds so the flakes appear as white streaks.

✦ **Spring.** On dewy mornings, search for new plant life that's still covered with moisture, and possibly surrounded by mist and fog.

✦ **Summer.** In bright daylight you can find contrasty scenes that must be compensated for with careful exposure. Reflectors can fill in shadows, but for scenic photos you might be better off with a graduated neutral density filter to darken the sky and balance it with the foreground.

✦ **Fall.** Capture colors at their most brilliant by shooting late in the day.

Still Life and Product Photography

Still life photos don't have to include baskets of fruit anymore! These medium-close photographs, typically taken of tabletop arrangements of inanimate objects, are enjoying a Renaissance of popularity thanks to online auctions. The groupings and objects you photograph are as likely to include that ceramic piece or old photographic gear you have up for sale as a vase of flowers or cornucopia filled with the fall's harvest. The techniques for shooting these images are identical in all cases.

Of course, still life subjects and product photos make a great training ground for photographers, too. Anyone looking for infinitely patient models that can become the basis for images that explore form and light to its fullest will love this type of photography. The best thing about still life photography is that, sometimes, after you're finished, you don't need to buy your model lunch … it can *be* lunch!

You'll find shooting still lifes and product shots a perfect rainy day activity. A quick visit to your collection of porcelain figurines, pewter soldiers, or artificial flowers can yield enough subject matter to keep you busy for hours. Or, you might find the subject matter you need in the refrigerator.

The most labor-intensive part of this kind of photography is coming up with pleasing arrangements that lend themselves to creative compositions. Count on spending time positioning your objects, perhaps adding something here, or removing an item that doesn't quite work. Setting up a still life arrangement is the closest a photographer can come to sculpting or painting.

You may be attempting to create photographic art, illustrate a cookbook, or lure a buyer for your junk at an online auction, but still life photography is challenging under any circumstances.

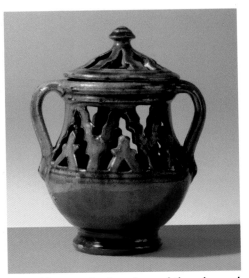

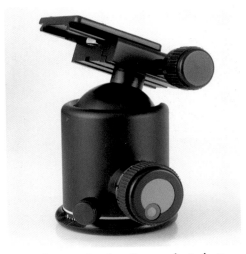

7.48 This ceramic piece has subtle color and an interesting shape that can be used in a variety of still life setups, either alone or with other objects.

7.49 When you're shooting product photos, such as this photo I used to sell an unneeded tripod head on eBay, it's important to show all the details, texture, and color of the item up for sale.

Inspiration

Still life photography is like macro photography but a step or two farther from your subject. Your subject matter is likely to be a bit larger, sometimes covering an entire table top, especially if it's an item you're offering for sale in an auction. You probably don't need a macro lens to focus close enough. Yet, the same principles of lighting and composition apply. Use auxiliary lighting such as flash or incandescent lights, maintain control with umbrellas or reflectors, and, once you've selected the best composition, lock your camera down on a tripod.

Unless you're mimicking an impressionistic painting, your artistic still lifes should be sharp and full of detail. That's even more important when your goal is a product shot for an online auction. Buyers should be able to see exactly what they are getting.

One way to think about a still life or product shot is to imagine it as a portrait of the object or grouping you're photographing. Indeed, you can light many of these setups as you would a portrait sitting; for example:

✦ Use a main light off to one side (a desk lamp will often do) to create shadows that provide your subject with shape and form.

✦ Illuminate the shadows with reflectors or fill lights.

✦ Consider lighting the background on its own to provide separation between your subject and its surroundings.

Still life and product photography practice

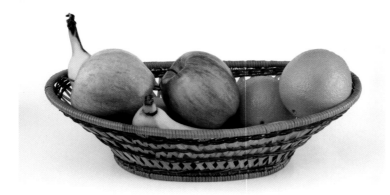

7.50 Simple setups such as this are easy and quick to create.

Table 7.15
Taking Still Life and Product Pictures

Setup	**Practice Picture:** A basket of fruit that greets guests ended up as a temporary guest star for a still life photography exercise. I placed the basket on a piece of poster board that had been curved to form a seamless background, as you can see in figure 7.50.
	On Your Own: Some of the best still life photos are the simplest. Use the natural beauty of food or a hand-crafted object, and don't clutter up the picture with other props.
Lighting	**Practice Picture:** I used a pair of white umbrellas placed to the left and right of the camera, and turned them around to shoot *through* the fabric to create extra-soft lighting.
	On Your Own: Many umbrellas are backed with black fabric (often removable) to reduce light loss. If your electronic flash is powerful enough, you can use the extra diffusion from shooting through the umbrellas to produce an even softer lighting arrangement. You'll find add-ons called *soft boxes* that produce even smoother, broad lighting.
Lens	**Practice Picture:** 60mm f/2.8D AF Micro-Nikkor.
	On Your Own: A close-up macro lens has the advantage of extra sharpness and the ability to focus close, but you don't necessarily need such a lens for your still life photography. Any zoom lens that focuses down to a foot or two is suitable for all but the tightest compositions.

Camera Settings	**Practice Picture:** RAW capture. Aperture-priority AE with a custom white balance. Saturation set to Enhanced.
	On Your Own: You'll want to control the depth of field, so choose Aperture-priority AE mode and set the white balance to the type of light in the scene, either tungsten or flash.
Exposure	**Practice Picture:** ISO 200, f/16, 1/200 second.
	On Your Own: Close-up photos call for smaller f-stops and extra depth of field, and most still life pictures are in that distance range.
Accessories	Umbrellas with external flash units are your best choice, but desk lamps and reflectors can also be used. A tripod is handy for locking down a composition and holding the camera steady if the exposure time is longer than 1/125 second.

Still life and product photography tips

✦ **Use your imagination.** Seek out still life subjects and backgrounds that you might not think of immediately. For example, an end table carefully arranged with a lamp, television remote control, newspaper folded open to the crossword puzzle, and pencil could become an interesting still life, rather than a picture of some cluttered furniture.

✦ **Inject the element of surprise**. A little bit of the unexpected or a humorous touch can spice up a mundane still life. An arrangement of green peppers with one yellow pepper in the middle will attract attention. A cluster of stainless-steel nuts making a nest for a single walnut is a visual pun that can tickle the funny bone — especially if you can work a confused stuffed toy squirrel into the picture.

✦ **Small touches mean a lot.** Spritzing a little water on food can make it seem more appetizing. The difference between a suitable background and the *perfect* background can be significant. For example, a layout of a picnic basket and its contents on a checkered tablecloth might be interesting, but a background of an old slab of wood from a weathered picnic table resting on a few tufts of grass might be better.

✦ **Try different angles.** Even if you've meticulously set up your still life or product shot, you might find that another angle you hadn't considered looks even better. Don't ignore the possibility of happy accidents.

Sunset and Sunrise Photography

It's no accident that this chapter is packed with photo subjects that relate to landscape and scenic photography in some way. Sunsets and sunrises are classic subgenres of the larger landscape photography arena, and especially beloved by photographers for some very good reasons.

One is that it's very difficult to shoot a bad sunset or sunrise. The most mundane sunset is gorgeous, and any sunrise is likely to be stunning just on the basis of its rich colors and the broad strokes from nature's palette on the skies. Sunsets can survive a wide range of overexposures and underexposures, and each and every day provides a sunset and a sunrise in infinite varieties. You can shoot a sunset from a single location five evenings in a row and come up with a different picture every time. On every trip I take, I always try to shoot sunrises and sunsets as often as possible, usually from a different vantage point every morning or

evening. None of my shots resembles any of the others.

Sunsets and sunrises can be dressed up, too. You can shoot them with nothing but the sky and horizon, or include foreground objects, such as mountains, lakes, or even shoreline fences, as in figure 7.51.

Inspiration

Sunsets and sunrises are a treasure that you shouldn't waste, and which should be photographed at every possible opportunity. That's especially true because these natural wonders are so beautiful; they make even an average photographer seem brilliant.

Sunsets and sunrises tend to resemble each other a great deal, but there are some small differences. Dawn in the early morning occurs after the cool of the night, so there may be haze or mist in the distance as the sun comes up. Sunsets take place after the heat of the day, so mist may be replaced by smog if you're near an urban area. The differences are likely to be important only to

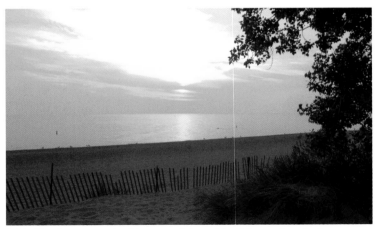

7.51 The foreground adds some interest to this sunrise shot.

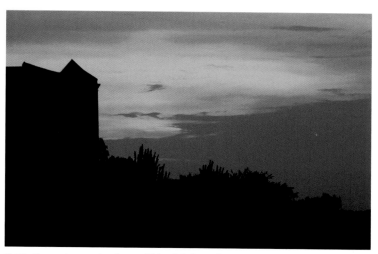

7.52 Sunsets can be incredibly rich in colors, and also incorporate other subject matter, such as the castle shown in this photo.

those who live on the East and West Coasts, where, if you want to picture the sun at the horizon over water, you generally must take your photos in the morning (in the East) or at dusk (in the West). Those of us who live along the Great Lakes can often position ourselves to capture both sunrises and sunsets above our respective bodies of water.

Sunset and sunrise photography practice

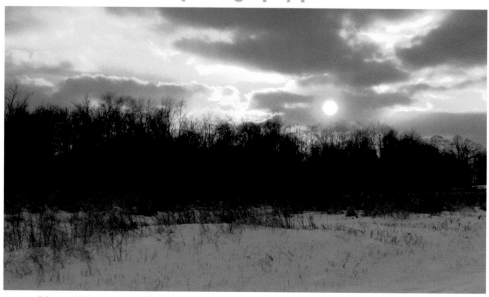

7.53 Although the sun was low in the sky on this crisp winter day, it was still an hour from sunset. I created a dusk photo by underexposing the picture by three f-stops.

Table 7.16
Taking Sunset and Sunrise Pictures

Setup	**Practice Picture:** I pass by this field often, and have photographed it at sunset frequently, but this day the sun was still an hour away from sunset. I decided the composition would work better as a sunset silhouette, as shown in figure 7.53.
	On Your Own: If you can't come back to a locale when the lighting is perfect, you can frequently use underexposure to simulate a sunset when the real thing won't happen in time to suit your schedule. But, if you can, wait until the time is perfect, or, alternatively, come back another day to capture the sunrise or sunset properly.
Lighting	**Practice Picture:** I found a spot where the sun would silhouette the trees.
	On Your Own: Taking a few steps to the left or right can dramatically change the composition of the photo and allow foreground objects to frame a sunset or sunrise in an interesting way.
Lens	**Practice Picture:** 18-70mm f/3.5-4.5G ED-IF AF-S DX Zoom Nikkor at 50mm.
	On Your Own: Wide-angle lenses are excellent if you want to take in a large area of sky. A telephoto setting is a better choice to emphasize the sun and exclude more of the foreground.
Camera Settings	**Practice Picture:** RAW capture. Shutter Priority AE.
	On Your Own: Use a high shutter speed to minimize camera shake, and a small f-stop at least two or three stops under the correct exposure to underexpose the foreground in a silhouette.
Exposure	**Practice Picture:** ISO 200, f/16, 1/800 second.
	On Your Own: Underexpose by two f-stops or more to create your silhouette effect.
Accessories	Carry along your tripod, and a selection of filters, such as a polarizer, star filter, and split density filter.

Sunset and sunrise photography tips

✦ **Use underexposure creatively.** Silhouettes consist of black outlines against a bright background, so you usually have to underexpose from what the camera considers the ideal exposure. Use the Exposure Value compensation to reduce exposure by two stops or more.

✦ **Shoot sharp.** Silhouettes usually look best when the outlined subject is sharp, so watch your focus, locking it in, or use manual focus.

✦ **Vary your composition.** Sunsets and sunrises don't have to be shot in a horizontal format. Actively look for vertical compositions to create an unusual-looking dusk or dawn image.

✦ **Experiment with filters.** You can apply diffraction grating filters (which split the light into rainbows), split-density filters, polarizers, and colored filters to sunset and sunrise images creatively.

Water Scene Photography

The final landscape subject in this chapter is water scenes, which can include seascapes, waterfalls, and pictures taken along rivers or alongside lakes. Water makes a great photographic subject because of its purity and the interesting reflections that result when nearby objects are mirrored in the water itself.

Photographers either live near an ocean or are willing to travel to one expressly for the photographic opportunities. A seashore, with its marine life, the beach, and the relentless lapping of the waves, provides picture opportunities nearly as varied as those offered by sunsets.

Lakes can be interesting subjects, too, because they are, in some ways, gentler on the environment surrounding them, so you can find a greater variety of trees, forests, swampland, and other habitats next to their shores.

Rivers and waterfalls have their own charms, because the water is livelier and ever-changing, appearing different at different times of day and in changing seasons. These dynamic

bodies of water can be pictured in a variety of ways, as you can see in figure 7.54. I mounted my favorite fish-eye lens and walked right down to the water's edge to capture this distorted, but interesting view.

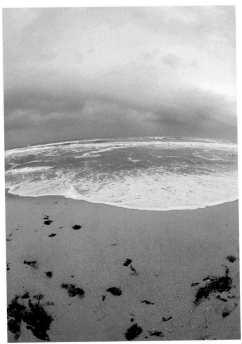

7.54 A fish-eye lens let me get to within a few feet of the incoming tide, and still show the sand, surf, sea, and sky.

Inspiration

As with other types of scenic photography, sea, lake, and river photos are often at their best when the human touch is not obviously present. If you can find a spot without people, structures (other than, perhaps, the rustic cabin or seaside grass hut or two) and other artifacts, your photograph can be viewed through rose-colored glasses that might suggest an uncharted desert isle or a remote mountain stream. You may have to take a short trek to provide such a vista, or confine your visit to the early morning or late evening hours, but it should be worth it. I like to visit such areas after the tourist season has ended.

On the other hand, some artifacts or signs of human habitation, such as beach huts or the boat shown in figure 7.55, can add a little interest to your photograph.

In one sense, most waterside photos have already been done to death, so you have to use your ingenuity to come up with new angles and perspectives. For example, you can shoot from offshore looking towards the beach, rather than from the beach looking seaward. Fishing piers or boats can provide good vantage points.

Or, shoot from overhead. Photographer Felix Hug, who contributed several exceptional photos to my book *Digital Travel Photography Digital Field Guide*, provided a couple of excellent ocean pictures taken from high vantage points, looking down into crystal-clear water. Alternatively, you can get

down low, almost at water level to emphasize the watery foreground and/or beach. (Keep your camera dry, or consider renting a waterproof housing for your camera.)

Use long shutter speeds (a neutral density filter might be necessary) to allow waves to merge, or a waterfall to blur, as I did for figure 7.56. Mix in some wildlife of the non-human variety: Seagulls, crabs, or other natural creatures in their own environment don't detract from your waterside nirvana.

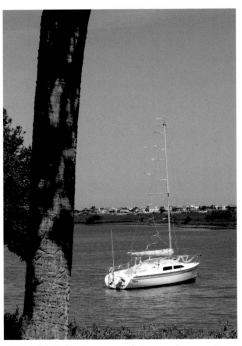

7.55 This inlet is a popular mooring spot, and always has at least one boat to make for a more interesting shot.

Water scene photography practice

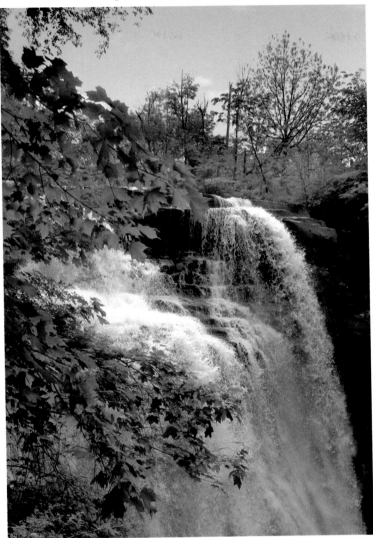

7.56 This waterfall is the tallest in this particular national park, and well worth the hike needed to reach it.

Table 7.17
Taking Water Scene Pictures

Setup	**Practice Picture:** It was a long trek to this waterfall, but worth it. An overlook provided a sturdy platform for my tripod as I took the photo shown in figure 7.56 using a slow shutter speed to allow the water in the waterfall to blur slightly.
	On Your Own: You may have to do some exploring to find suitable waterside scenes to shoot. Rough-looking roads and trails leading off the main highway often dead end at scenic overlooks and interesting hiking routes right on an ocean, lake, or river.
Lighting	**Practice Picture:** It was midafternoon, skies were clear, and the sunlight was perfect for this photo.
	On Your Own: As with other types of landscape photography, you usually can't choose your lighting, but you can choose to wait until the illumination looks good. Sometimes you have to come back on a different day, but when the lighting is just right, it's worth being patient.
Lens	**Practice Picture:** 18-55mm f/3.5-5.6G ED II AF-S DX Zoom-Nikkor set to 28mm, with an ND8 neutral density filter over the lens to reduce the light by three f-stops and allow a longer shutter speed.
	On Your Own: Wide-angle lenses work well with seascapes, and a zoom is handy to have if your photographic perch makes it difficult to move closer to or farther away from your favored vista. You need a telephoto zoom only to pull in distant views.
Camera Settings	**Practice Picture:** RAW+JPEG Basic capture. Shutter Priority AE.
	On Your Own: Choose a shutter speed that counters camera/photographer shake and let the exposure system choose the f-stop. For my photo, I selected a long shutter speed to allow the water in the waterfall to blur.
Exposure	**Practice Picture:** ISO 200, f/22, 1/15 second.
	On Your Own: Your D40 or D40x usually does a good job of calculating the exposure for you, but be prepared to use the EV compensation feature to add or subtract a little exposure if the metering system is misled by bright water or extra dark surroundings. Switch to center-weighted or spot metering if necessary.
Accessories	You should have some sort of waterproof bag to carry your equipment, as splashing water is one of the dangers inherent in photographing water scenes. In hot weather, have a cooler in your vehicle to protect your camera from high temperatures. Digital cameras don't have film that can be spoiled by heat, but a hot sensor is a noisy sensor.

Water scene photography tips

✦ **Watch the horizon.** It's easy to tilt the camera slightly, and you must fix a sloping horizon in an image editor, probably wasting pixels, and perhaps forcing you to crop out some portion of your image that you didn't want to part with.

✦ **Watch your environment.** Water scenes are fraught with sand, which can play havoc with the delicate mirror and shutter mechanism of your camera should a few grains sneak in during lens swaps. Water, especially salt water, is not good for your D40 or D40x, either, which isn't weather sealed to the extent of its high-end D200 and D2Xs siblings. If you keep splashes and sprays of sand from your camera, and are careful when changing lenses, you should be okay.

✦ **Follow the tides.** For ocean pictures, you want to track the tides and remember that a high tide cleans the beach, and a low tide exposes a treasure-trove of picturesque seashells, seaweed, scrambling sea creatures, and a few old shoes, tires, and soda cans. You'll soon learn which times of day provide the best and most photogenic seashore for your photographic endeavors.

Downloading and Editing Images

Why mention software in a *field guide*? That's a good question. I expect most readers of this book to relax with it in an armchair, their Nikon D40 or D40x in hand, and work their way through most of the chapters before heading out into the field, inflamed with creative inspiration. Okay, maybe taking photos as soon as the camera is ripped from its packaging will have a higher priority. I also hope this book goes along with you into the field, to provide tips on taking specific types of pictures you encounter.

What I don't expect most of you to do is sit down at your computer and use this book as a software instruction manual. And, unless you have a laptop that you drag along on your shooting expeditions, I don't think you'll be doing much downloading and picture editing in the field.

Finally, I want this book to help you get great pictures *in your camera*, without much need for an image editor to fix those goofs that needn't have existed at all if you knew what you were doing.

Despite all that, working with various software applications and utilities is often a necessary part of the process. You need to download your images to your computer, organize them for display, prep them for printing, and perhaps do a little cropping and resizing. Beyond that, many pictures can benefit from a little judicious editing to tweak unanticipated defects.

So, field guide or not, I devote this chapter to introducing you to the most common applications, including Nikon PictureProject, which is furnished with the D40 and D40x, and more sophisticated tools such as Nikon Capture NX and Nikon Camera Control Pro, that you can put to work after you have already taken your picture. Don't expect extensive instructions on how to use any of these programs: This is still a field guide, after all.

Starting with Nikon PictureProject

If you aren't currently heavily involved in photo editing and organizing, Nikon PictureProject is a good place to start. Packaged on a CD right in the box with your D40 or D40x camera, it offers an easy-to-use set of basic functions for importing your photos to your computer, organizing them into albums, (as shown in figure 8.1) and doing simple image editing. Even if you intend to graduate to another application, PictureProject enables you to perform the most common functions without the need

to spend hours learning to use a new program. If you're new to digital cameras or image editing, PictureProject gives you a quick way to perform many of the basic functions involved in importing, touching up, and organizing your photos.

The basic functions of PictureProject are image transfer, organization of photos into albums, basic image editing, and the capability to share images as prints, slide shows, e-mail, or other forms. PictureProject also includes a button that links the program to the Nikon Camera Control Pro, which for an additional cost enables the camera to operate remotely, downloading photos immediately as they are shot, and uploading camera settings files to the D40 and D40x.

PictureProject is furnished with the Nikon D40 and D40x on two CDs: one disc for the

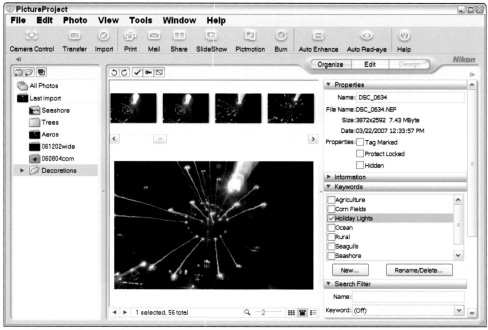

8.1 PictureProject enables easy organization of photos without having to learn a complex program.

application and another for the user manual. The two discs also contain Nikon Fotoshare, a photo sharing program, and a trial version of Nikon Capture NX.

Transferring pictures

PictureProject can transfer images directly from your D40 or D40x to your computer using the USB cable. The program also recognizes when a memory card has been inserted in your card reader, and pops up to offer to transfer those photos, too. You can specify PictureProject as your default photo importing utility, or choose to work with another program, such as Adobe Photoshop Elements' Photo Downloader, or the facilities built into Microsoft Windows XP, Microsoft Windows Vista, or Mac OS X's iPhoto.

If you decide to rely on one of the other image transfer options, you can prevent PictureProject from popping up when a camera or memory card is detected by choosing Tools ➪ Options in the Picture Project main screen. In the Auto Launch area of the dialog box, uncheck the Auto launch PictureProject when a camera or memory card is connected box. You can still use PictureProject Transfer at any time by launching the application manually and then clicking the Transfer button in the toolbar. Whether the transfer utility is started automatically or manually, the Picture Project Transfer wizard shown in figure 8.2 appears.

Click the Show Thumbnails button in the transfer wizard's toolbar to inspect miniature views of each picture in the dialog box's main pane. Choose which images you want to transfer by clicking to select individual photos, Ctrl/cmd+click to add additional photos or to remove them from the selection, or click the Select All button to choose all the thumbnails the wizard detects.

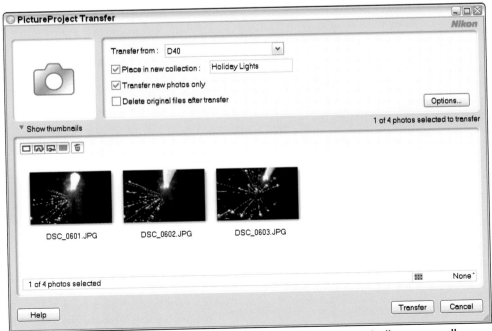

8.2 The PictureProject Transfer dialog box can launch either automatically or manually.

A check box is available to enable you to place the imported photos in a new collection (album) with a name of your choice, or to append the new images to an existing album you specify. You can also choose to import only new images from the camera or memory card, ignoring those that were imported earlier. If you want, the PictureProject Transfer wizard can erase the photos from the camera or memory card after they've been copied. Click the Options button to select additional choices (described next). When you've returned from the Options dialogs, click the Transfer button in the lower-right corner of the dialog box to initiate importation of your photos.

Knowing your transfer options

The PictureProject Transfer wizard has options of its own. Click the Options button at the upper right of the screen to view the Transfer Options dialog box with tabs for General, Transfer Destination, Rename Photos, and Pictmotion choices. (Pictmotion is available only with Windows and is not used with the D40 or D40x. Why does it appear? It's used with Nikon's point-and-shoot digital cameras, which also are furnished with PictureProject.) The options for the four tabs are as follows:

✦ **General.** This tab includes options for copying hidden files, embedding the color profile information in the file, adding a preview to RAW Nikon Electronic File (NEF) images, rotating images shot in vertical orientation (if you've selected that option in the camera), and synchronizing your camera to the computer's clock (only when the camera is connected via the USB cable). You can also elect to copy the photos into a single

new collection (*album*) on your hard disk, separate them based on the folders you've created for images on your memory card, or segregate them by the date the images were shot.

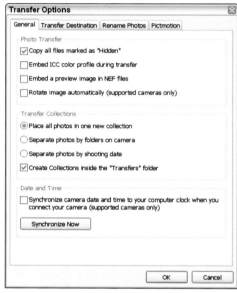

8.3 The General parameters tab helps you transfer and collect images.

✦ **Transfer Destination.** Here you specify the names of the folders used to store the transferred pictures on your computer. You can tell PictureProject Transfer to create a new folder each time photos are transferred, which can make it simpler to organize the fruits of your various shooting sessions. The utility can also use the folder names created in your camera (in case you've stored images in more than one user-named folder). You can specify the prefix used to create the folder names, too. For example, with travel photography, you might want to use prefixes like Paris, New York, or Geauga Lake. You can also append a sequential number to folders and apply a suffix to the end of folder names.

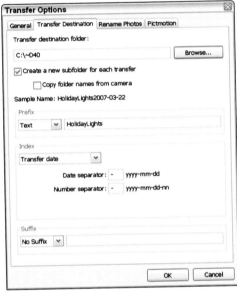

8.4 Specify the file destination with the Transfer Destination tab.

✦ **Rename Photos.** This tab gives you a lot of flexibility when you create new descriptive names for your image files as they are copied — or you can retain the name applied by the camera. Here you tell PictureProject Transfer whether to use the file name the camera created, or to rename each photo using a name you specify. File names can begin with a text label you specify, use a numbering scheme with one to nine digits, and begin the numbering at a value you enter. You can also add a suffix to renamed files.

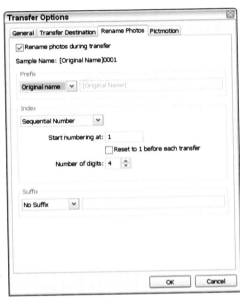

8.5 Specify the file name in the Rename Photos tab.

✦ **Pictmotion.** Windows users who own Nikon point-and-shoot digital cameras that support Pictmotion can have PictureProject Transfer assemble copied photos into a minimovie of stills, using either Windows Media Video (WMV) or MPEG1 (MPG) formats. Several quality levels are available, as well as resolutions from 160 x 120 pixels up to 640 x 480 pixels (which is near TV quality). The D40 and D40x don't support this function, but I'm describing it for completeness.

Organizing and viewing pictures

PictureProject's album functions enable you to create album-like collections, and then organize images by file name, date, or keywords that you enter to classify your shots. You can drag and drop images to organize your album collections, and preview your images as thumbnails, thumbnails with an enlarged image of the current frame, or thumbnails with photo information. You can click one of the icons at the bottom of the preview pane to switch views.

PictureProject lets you examine individual images, organize them into collections, or view a series of photos in a slideshow. The window is set up as follows:

✦ **Picture collections.** The left side of the PictureProject window shows a list of available picture collections. Just click on a collection name to view all the images in that collection in a scrolling thumbnail panel in the center of the PictureProject window. Click the All Photos or Last Import buttons to see all the images in all your collections, or only the most recently imported images.

✦ **Thumbnail area.** A zoom slider at the bottom of the preview area enables you to change the size of the thumbnails, and you can choose whether to view thumbnails only, view a larger preview of a selected image below the thumbnails in addition, or see thumbnails accompanied by shooting information for those images.

✦ **Information area.** At the right side of the screen are expandable/collapsible panels that show more information about a selected photo, and search boxes for finding specific images using the file name, a keyword you've previously entered, or the date when the image was taken. Click the Information and Properties bars (shown collapsed in figure 8.6) to see additional data about a selected image.

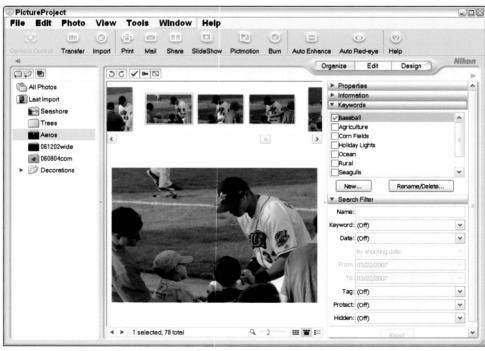

8.6 PictureProject makes it easy to place your images into albums.

✦ **SlideShow button.** Select a collection or folder of images and click the SlideShow button in the PictureProject toolbar to view a series of selected images one after another.

✦ **Import button.** Although PictureProject automatically loads the pictures it transfers into collections, you can also add photos already residing on your hard drive by clicking the Import button in the top tool bar.

Retouching pictures

PictureProject has some limited picture-retouching features that you can use when you don't want to work on your images in a more advanced image editor. Editing changes are always applied to a duplicate image instead of the original, so if you change your mind you can always return to the original photo. Click the Edit button at the right side just below the tool bar or the Auto Enhance button in the tool bar itself.

To edit in PictureProject, double-click any photo in a collection, or select a photo and click the Edit button. You can choose from the following functions:

✦ **Auto Enhance button.** PictureProject makes its best effort to automatically fix the brightness, color saturation (under the option Color Booster), and sharpening for the image.

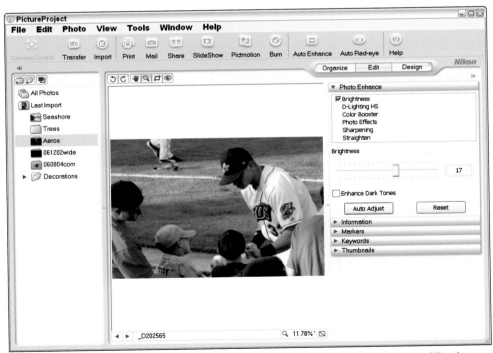

8.7. PictureProject offers basic editing features you can use to make simple modifications to your JPEG images.

✦ **Auto Red-eye button.** PictureProject automatically removes glowing red eyes from pictures of humans. This tool doesn't work on the eyes of animals, which usually glow yellow or green.

✦ **Photo Enhance section.** Click the Brightness, D-Lighting HS (a shadow brightener), Color Booster (for saturation), Photo Effects, Sharpening, or Straighten boxes, and then use the slider and/or options offered for each to make the adjustments manually.

✦ **Tool buttons.** Six buttons appear immediately above the editing preview window. They enable you to rotate the image counterclockwise or clockwise, move it around, zoom in or out, crop, or remove red eye.

Sharing pictures

PictureProject also includes functions you can use to share your photos through PictureProject InTouch. You need to create an account with the PictureProject InTouch Web site, but it's free, and you can set it up the first time you use PictureProject InTouch. To use the feature, click the Share button in the toolbar and wait for the program to launch. PictureProject InTouch enables you to do the following:

✦ **Print.** Output one photo, or a selection of them, from a collection.

✦ **E-mail.** Send one or more photos by e-mail using Outlook, Outlook Express, or Eudora (Windows); or Entourage X, Mail, or Eudora (Macintosh).

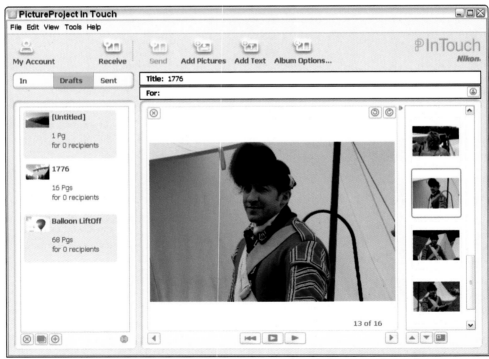

8.8 You can use PictureProject InTouch to print, e-mail, and share your best photos.

✦ **Organize.** Arrange photos into a layout to print or e-mail.

✦ **Share.** Share album collections with friends, using up to 50MB of free Web space provided to you by Nikon each week. After two weeks, your photos are deleted from the Nikon Web site, freeing up space for additional images.

Looking at Nikon Capture NX

Nikon Capture NX replaces the earlier version, Nikon Capture, and is not so much an upgrade as a completely new application built from the ground up with much more sophisticated editing features and lots of new capabilities. The original Nikon Capture was a useful tool for manipulating Nikon NEF (RAW) image files, converting files in batches, uploading/downloading and transferring images, as well as controlling the camera remotely through a USB cable (for time-lapse photography and other kinds of remote shooting). Capture NX gives you much more powerful editing tools that you can use for *non-destructive* modifications (meaning that you can always return to the original picture) of selected regions of the picture you can isolate using *U control points*.

If this all sounds complex, it is. Capture NX is definitely a highly optional tool for Nikon D40 and D40x owners. That is so true that Nikon has unbundled one of the most-used portions of the old Nikon Capture program, the camera communication facility, and now provides it as yet another optional utility under the name Camera Control Pro. This utility works with both PictureProject and Capture NX, so you can purchase it (about $70) and use it without needing to make

the hefty $149 investment in Capture NX itself. (You can try it out for 30 days for free before you have to buy it.)

If you do need the advanced features of Capture NX, they are impressive. Developed using technologies from Nikon partner Nik Software, Capture NX features new Brush, Lasso, and Marquee selection tools, advanced layering features, and the aforementioned U Point control points so that you can modify color, dynamic range, and other parameters only in selected areas. This new program has improved tools for correcting aberrations such as barrel distortion, vignetting, and fish-eye distortions found in Nikkor lenses. The new Edit List provides better control over image processing workflow by listing each manipulation as it is applied, and allowing individual steps to be undone in any order. Also included is a new Capture NX Browser for labeling and sorting images, and applying settings to batches of photos.

Advanced photographers will like the color management controls that aid printing images that more closely match what you saw through the camera and on the display screen, and new, sophisticated noise reduction algorithms.

Nikon Capture NX users can import RAW/NEF images and save them in a standard format such as TIFF, either using the original settings from the camera file or fine-tuned settings for things such as sharpening, tonal compensation, color mode, color saturation, white balance, or noise reduction. Capture NX has a useful *image dust off* feature for subtracting dust spots caused by particles that settle on the sensor. Just take a blank dust reference photo and the application "subtracts" dust artifacts in the same location in additional images you import.

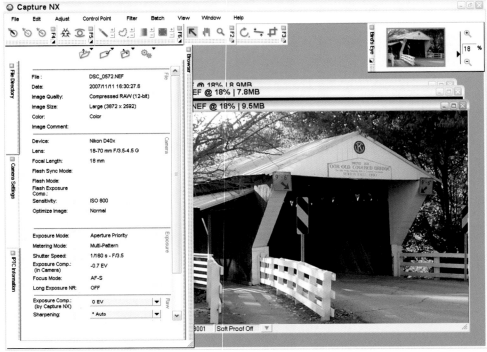

8.9 Nikon Capture NX has a full set of features for importing and converting NEF files, and making a host of fine-tuning adjustments.

Using Nikon Camera Control Pro

Nikon Camera Control Pro, an extra-cost utility priced at about $69, gives you a way to communicate directly with your D40 or D40x when the camera is linked to your computer with a USB cable, just as if you had your eye glued to the viewfinder and were manipulating the controls on the camera itself. (Unfortunately, you can't preview the image you're about to take using your computer.)

For example, if you have a squirrel that visits your outdoor deck frequently, you can set up your camera on a tripod close to a feeder, link it to your computer with a USB

cable, and trip the shutter when the creature approaches. Camera Control Pro lets you see the viewfinder's LED readout from your computer, and even change the shooting mode and other settings without touching your camera. There are five tabs in the Camera Control Pro window, shown in figure 8.10:

✦ **Exposure 1.** Here you can choose the exposure mode (Aperture Priority, Shutter Priority, or Manual), and then adjust the aperture itself if you're using a lens that sets the f-stop electronically; or can adjust the shutter speed (in Shutter Priority or Manual mode). You can add exposure compensation (EV) or flash exposure compensation (FEV) if you want to override the camera's exposure settings. If you want to keep the metered exposure, but use a different combination of shutter speed and f-stop, use the Flexible Program slider. The two buttons at the bottom of this tab activate the autofocus system and take a picture (AF and Start) or simply take the picture at the current focus setting (Start). These two buttons, as well as the viewfinder LED readout, are repeated on the other tabs.

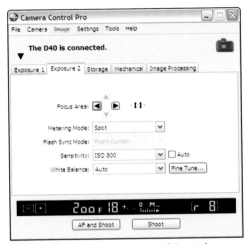

8.11 Select the Focus Area, White Balance, or ISO settings in the Exposure 2 tab.

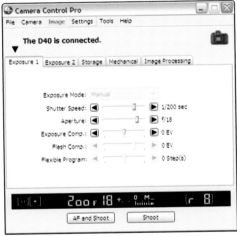

8.10 Camera Control Pro enables you to control your D40/D40x over a USB cable.

✦ **Exposure 2.** Here you can move the Focus Area using directional buttons that mimic the D40/D40x's multi controller. There is even a thumbnail of the focus zones as they appear in your viewfinder that shifts brackets as you change the focus area. You can also choose a Metering Mode or Flash Synch Mode, and change ISO settings (Sensitivity) or White Balance (including making fine adjustments to White Balance).

✦ **Storage.** Use this tab to specify the file format used to take your photo (JPEG, RAW, or RAW+JPEG), and resolution settings of the camera (L, M, and S).

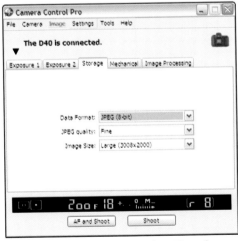

8.12 Choose file format and JPEG options in the Storage tab.

✦ **Mechanical.** This is an important tab that enables you to specify many frequently changed settings. You can choose from single shot or continuous shooting modes, as well as perform automatic bracketing (and select whether to bracket exposure, flash, or both) while choosing other bracketing parameters such as number of shots, bracket increment, and bracket order. It enables you to access single and continuous shooting modes, set up bracketing options, choose the autofocus mode (dynamic area, single area, and auto area selection; plus AF-C, AF-S, or AF-A). There's even a battery level indicator, which is an excellent idea, because running your camera through a USB connection consumes a lot of power.

✦ **Image Processing.** You can use this tab to fine-tune your image even before you take it — just like the Optimize Image controls in the D40/D40x's Shooting menu. Choose Softer, Normal, Vivid, Black-and-White, or one of the other custom looks the D40/D40x offers, and change sharpening, tonal compensation, color mode, saturation, and hue. Select User-Defined Custom Curve in the Tone Comp area and click the edit button to create your own custom tonal curve, as shown in figure 8.15.

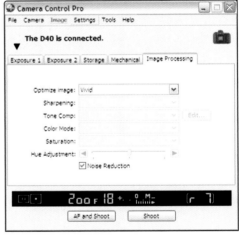

8.14 Manipulate the fine-tuning process your camera performs in the Image Processing tab.

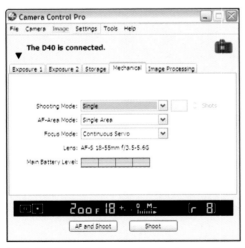

8.13 Fiddle with the mechanical controls of your camera, including focus options, in the Mechanical tab.

Camera Control Pro also lets you change settings, including those that are clumsy to enter using the camera controls alone, such as the image comment appended to every photo. Perhaps the most interesting capability is the

Time Lapse facility (choose Camera ⇨ Time Lapse Photography), which enables you to take a series of pictures at intervals that range from seconds to days. The time lapse utility can shoot from two to 9,999 shots, stored directly to your computer's hard drive, using a delay from one second to 99 hours, 59 minutes, and 59 seconds between shots. You can even bracket exposure or white balance between pictures. If you're shooting a very long time-lapse sequence, it's a good idea to use the D40 and D40x's optional EH-5 AC power supply to avoid having your battery run out before you finish your sequence. And keep your camera protected from the weather if you're shooting time-lapse photos outdoors!

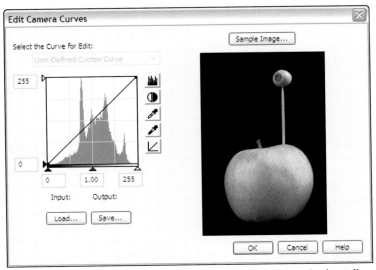

8.15 Create custom curves for uploading to your camera in the Edit Camera Curves dialog box.

Troubleshooting

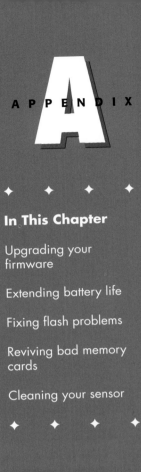

Your new Nikon D40/D40x should give you years of trouble-free use. The compact, robust body that these two tiny cameras share has few mechanical parts that can fail. There is no film transport, wind lever, or motor drive; and the D40 line, which eschews the internal autofocus motor found in other Nikon dSLRs, has simplified linkages from the camera to the lenses.

The only major moving parts in the camera are the shutter and the viewfinder's flip-up mirror, and both are designed to provide tens of thousands of picture-taking cycles with no problems. The various switches, dials, and buttons, as well as the memory card door and flip-up electronic flash, are quite sturdy and should last the life of your camera. Unlike cameras that accept CompactFlash cards (with their array of tiny connectors in the camera socket), the SD cards that the D40/D40x use have broader, more rugged card edge contacts that can't be bent or easily damaged in normal use.

Even so, certain components, ranging from the battery, to memory cards, to the D40/D40x's programming (which is a kind of operating system), do require some attention from time to time. Eventually, the D40 or/D40x's sensor will pick up some dust and need a quick and easy cleaning.

In this appendix, I cover useful alerts that warn you about potential problems, and offer advice for troubleshooting and maintaining your camera.

Upgrading Your Firmware

Firmware is the D40/D40x's operating system, which oversees all the operations of the camera, from the menu display — including fonts, colors, and the actual entries themselves — to all the camera's features that call for processing in the camera, to the support for devices that link with the camera, such as the memory card and your computer (when you've connected using the USB cable).

In This Chapter

Upgrading your firmware

Extending battery life

Fixing flash problems

Reviving bad memory cards

Cleaning your sensor

From time to time Nikon issues firmware upgrades that you can install yourself, and, in fact, has done so already for the D40 (only) to provide updates that were incorporated in the D40x's operating system. In the past, upgrades for other Nikon models have fixed bugs in the firmware itself, improved the performance of features such as autofocus, and added options for printing images directly from the camera. Other upgrades have even given cameras entirely new features, as when the D40/D40x's big brother, the D200, was gifted with a new black-and-white imaging mode that later models already have.

Upgrading your firmware is easy. If you're computer savvy, you might wonder how your D40/D40x is able to overwrite its own operating system. Nikon's secret method is to perform the upgrade in two steps, so the entire camera operating system is not replaced in one fell swoop. Each of the two pieces of the firmware is fully capable of managing the camera's basic firmware update functions without the other, so you can replace one half of the firmware, and then the other in turn. It's a little like an airplane with a pilot and copilot. You can replace either of them with another crew member with no dire results, as long as the other remains in control at all times. It's actually possible to operate the camera with only one or the other parts of the firmware updated (rather than both), but I don't recommend that. (A partial firmware upgrade sometimes happens when a camera owner forgets to load the second part, or is temporarily unable to do so because of an interruption.)

Performing updates

When the time comes to update your firmware, the process is easy. Follow these steps:

1. **First, check the version number of your current firmware to confirm that a later version is available.** In the Setup menu, scroll to Firmware version and press OK or the right directional key. The current version displays on a screen (see figure AA.1).

2. **Turn the D40/D40x off.**

3. **Make sure you have a freshly charged EN-EL9 battery inserted in the camera, or are using the optional AC adapter.** You don't want the D40/D40x to run out of juice during the upgrade process.

4. **Download the new firmware from the Nikon Web site and place it into a new folder on your computer's hard disk drive.** The firmware is in two files: Camera A firmware and Camera B firmware. The names of the files will be something like the names used for the Firmware 1.1 fix introduced for the D40 early in 2007:

   AD400110.bin

   BD400110.bin

5. **Turn the D40/D40x on and format a memory card so that it is empty of image files or (most important) any other firmware files left over from the last time you upgraded.**

6. **Copy either of the two firmware files to the top (root) directory or folder of the memory card.** You can copy the files using a direct USB connection from your computer to the D40/D40x, or can turn off the D40/D40x and remove the memory card so you can copy from your computer using a memory card reader. It makes no difference which of the two BIN files

you copy first, although I always like to start with Camera A firmware to avoid any chance of confusion.

7. **When the firmware is copied, either turn off the camera (if you're using a direct link), or remove the memory card from your card reader.** Insert the card into the D40/D40x.

8. **Turn the D40/D40x on.**

9. **Press the Menu button and find Firmware version in the Setup menu.** Press OK or the right directional control.

10. **From the screen, choose Update and press OK or the right directional control.** Select Yes from the screen that appears next to start the upgrade. The firmware is updated. Do not turn the camera off, open the memory card door, or use any of the controls while the upgrade is processing. It may take a minute or two.

11. **When the Update Complete message appears, you can turn the D40/D40x off.**

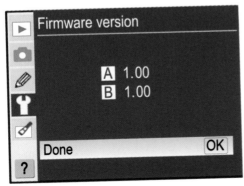

AA.1 You can determine the current firmware version from the Setup menu.

12. **You can then turn the D40/D40x back on, and access the Firmware version screen from the Setup menu to confirm that the update has been completed.**

13. **Format the memory card once again, and repeat steps 6 through 12 with the second firmware file.**

Extending Battery Life

The D40/D40x's EN-EL9 lithium ion battery should provide you with at least 500 shots per charge (or even more), depending on how you are using the camera. However, certain features, such as the LCD or built-in flash, are more of a drain on the battery. When the battery is depleted, you need to pop it into the Nikon MH-23 charger for about two and a half hours to revitalize it and bring it back to full power. You can recharge the D40/D40x's battery at any time, even after just a few shots, with no danger of the battery building a memory of reduced capacity (which was the case with old-style nickel-cadmium batteries). It's fine to recharge daily, or to charge just before heading out for a new shooting session. I've gotten more than 1,000 pictures from a single charge, and always carry a spare battery or two with me, so power is rarely a concern.

To maximize the number of shots you can get from a single charge, minimize the use of features that use the most power. You can review the status of the battery at any time on the back panel LCD, which has an icon that shows the approximate percentage of battery life left (see figure AA.2). In approximate order of impact on battery life, these features are as follows:

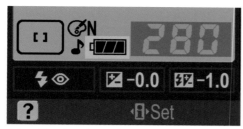

AA.2 The D40/D40x's LCD provides current power-status information.

✦ **Built-in flash.** The D40/D40x's built-in flash is ample for most picture-taking situations, but it provides quite a drain on the battery. If you'd like to stretch the useful life of the D40/D40x's internal battery, either reduce your use of the internal flash, or switch to an external flash such as the Nikon SB-400, SB-600, or SB-800, which uses its own battery supply.

✦ **LCD.** That big, beautiful 2.5-inch color LCD on the back of your D40 or D40x pulls a lot of power. You absolutely must use it to make settings changes and to review photos that might need some exposure tweaks. But do you really need to stare at each and every picture you shoot for 10 or 20 seconds? You can save a lot of battery power by turning off the automatic display of each shot after exposure. Turn off Image review in the Custom Setting menu (CSM 07) and crank down the LCD brightness setting in the Setup menu.

✦ **Autofocus and vibration reduction.** Refocusing the lens in and out of focus requires power. You can save a little juice by using AF-S (Single-servo Autofocus) to avoid focusing and refocusing constantly when you don't need to. Vibration Reduction (VR) also eats up power.

If you're using a VR lens, turn off the Vibration Reduction feature when you don't need it, especially when the camera is mounted on a tripod or you're already using high shutter speeds at shorter focal lengths that don't benefit much from VR.

✦ **RAW drainage.** Nikon cameras seem to use more power when saving files in RAW mode. If you don't need a RAW version of your image, but do need to take a lot of pictures on a single charge, consider using JPEG Fine instead of RAW or RAW+JPEG.

✦ **New battery.** It just might take a new battery several charge/discharge cycles to achieve its maximum capacity. Some D40/D40x owners report getting 10 to 20 percent more shots per charge after they've seasoned their new batteries.

Fixing Flash Problems

The D40/D40x's built-in flash is reliable, so much so that any problems you're likely to have will probably be caused by incorrect settings or other human errors. If one of the following situations occurs, my diagnosis and suggested cures should help you put things right quickly.

✦ **Consistent under- or overexposure.** There are several possible causes for flash exposures that are always wrong. You have used Flash Exposure Compensation and forgotten. Press the Flash button on the left side of the D40/D40x's prism while holding down the

Exposure Compensation button located on top of the camera southeast of the shutter release, and use the command dial to return Flash EV to 0.0. It's also possible you've switched the flash to Manual mode using CSM 14.

✦ **Consistent underexposure.** Accidental Manual mode can also be the problem if you have consistently dark flash photos, without occasional overexposures. Check CSM 14 to make sure you haven't manually set the flash to reduced power. You can adjust the D40/D40x from full power down to 1/32 its normal output. The latter setting is almost guaranteed to give you underexposures in your flash pictures.

✦ **Unsightly shadows.** The flip-up flash may not have enough elevation to prevent casting a shadow of the lens hood or even the lens itself in your subject area when you use the 18-200mm, 18-70mm, 18-55mm, 17-55mm, or similar zooms at their widest settings, especially for pictures of close subjects. You can try removing the lens hood or zooming in slightly.

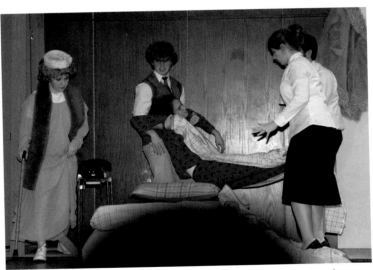

AA.3 Oops! The dark shadow at the bottom of this close-up photo was caused by a lens's hood blocking the flash.

Reviving Bad Memory Cards

Memory cards, including the SD cards used in your D40/D40x (they aren't called *Secure Digital* cards for nothing!) rarely fail on their own. You're far more likely to lose one, step on it, or run it through the wash or rinse cycle of your washing machine than have it fail during use. There's not really anything that can wear out within these solid-state devices.

Preventing trouble with memory cards starts with what you do or don't do. SD cards are small and easy to misplace if you're not careful. For that reason, it's a good idea to keep them in their original cases or a *card safe* offered by Gepe (www.gepecard-safe.com), Pelican (www.pelican.com), and others.

It's also wise to use them carefully. Don't remove the card while the camera is writing images to the card. If you do, you lose any photos in the buffer and may damage the file structure of the card, making it difficult or impossible to retrieve the other pictures you've taken. The same thing can happen if you remove the card from your computer's card reader while the computer is writing to it.

If you are having problems with a memory card and the images on it are important to you, stop using that card immediately. Don't take another picture. Safely power down your D40/D40x and remove the card and, as soon as possible, insert it into a card reader on your computer and attempt to copy the files to a safe folder on the computer. Avoid the temptation to link your D40/D40x and computer with the USB cable and copy the files that way: It's possible that a camera/card incompatibility is at work that might not be present if you transfer the images with your card reader instead.

If your computer's card reader doesn't let you transfer the images, and those images are very valuable (say, a wedding that might be difficult to restage), you can always consult a professional data recovery firm, which will charge you hundreds of dollars and still might be unable to recover your photos. You can also find software online specifically for salvaging photos from memory cards or from other media, such as floppy disks or hard disks. Although I've never used any of them and so can't recommend a specific solution, some of the best-regarded include Photo Rescue 2, Digital Image Recovery, MediaRecover, Image Recall, and Recover My Photos. For more ideas and links, check out www.ultimateslr.com/memory-card-recovery.php.

Cleaning Your Sensor

No matter how careful you are, dust will eventually find its way inside your camera and onto the sensor. Although sensor dust is annoying, it's not a serious problem—unless you use a very small f-stop (on the order of f/16 or f/22), you may not even spot it—and it can easily be cleaned off. Unfortunately, many D40/D40x owners panic at the first sign of sensor dust, and pale at the thought of reaching inside their cameras to work on an exposed sensor. Panic isn't necessary. First, the sensor itself is protected behind a hard glass filter. Second, if you're new to owning a dSLR, what you think is sensor dust might in fact be something else.

If you see tiny specks in your viewfinder or dust on your camera's mirror, that isn't sensor dust. Neither has any effect on your photographs, and you can often quickly remove the dust with an air blower. (Avoid touching the mirror with any sort of cleaning tissue or cloth as it's easy to scratch its front-surfaced mirror coating.)

A bright spot in the same location in all your photos is not sensor dust either (see figure AA.4). That's most likely a *hot pixel* (one that turns on when the sensor becomes warm from a long exposure, regardless of whether there is picture information in that spot), or a *stuck pixel* (one that is permanently on or off).

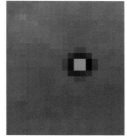

AA.4 A hot or stuck pixel is usually surrounded by other erroneous pixels that aren't defective, but which are incorrectly activated by the sensor's processing algorithms and misinterpret the truly errant photosite.

A few bad pixels may not be noticeable, but if you have more than a couple, they can be removed by a process called *pixel mapping*, which any Nikon Service Center can do for you. Pixel mapping involves identifying these errant pixels and telling the camera to ignore them in the future. This kind of pixel defect can also show up on your D40/D40x's color LCD panel, but unless they are abundant, the wisest course is to just ignore them. They harm nothing, and the pixels on the LCD have absolutely nothing to do with your sensor's image.

Actual sensor dust is likely to show up as an irregular out-of-focus blob that appears in the same place in every photo. Such artifacts may be visible only at smaller f-stops and

vanish at larger apertures. They're easiest to see in areas without much detail, such as sky. To test for sensor dust, take some test shots of a plain, blank surface (such as a piece of paper or a cloudless sky) at small f-stops, such as f/22 and a few wide open. Open your image editor, copy several shots into a single document in separate layers, and then flip back and forth between layers to see if any spots you see are present in all layers. You may have to boost contrast and sharpness to make the dust easier to spot.

Your best bet for dealing with sensor dust is to avoid it entirely: work only in clean areas when possible and don't change your lenses when you're in areas prone to dust. Keep your lenses clean — it's easy for dust specks on the rear bayonet to infiltrate farther, past the shutter, and onto your sensor. Minimize the time your camera has no lens mounted, and when you do change lenses, point the D40/ D40x downwards so that any dust tends to fall away from the inside of the camera. Keep the mirror box area clean with a rubber bulb blower to reduce the amount of dust that might get past the shutter.

You can clone out any tiny or infrequent dust spots on your images using an image editor or eliminate them using a tool such as Photoshop's Dust & Scratches filter. When the spots really become bothersome, it's time to consider an actual cleaning. You might find that your local camera shop will do it for you and show you how to do it in the future; though you might be apprehensive at first, cleaning is really not that big a deal.

To clean your sensor, first make sure that your D40/D40x is operating on a full-charged battery or is attached to an AC adapter. Then, move on to the Setup menu and choose the Mirror Lock-Up option.

Select On and press the OK button. You see a message:

When shutter button is pressed, the mirror lifts and the shutter opens. To lower mirror, turn camera off.

Go ahead press the shutter release, remove the lens from the D40/D40x, and clean the sensor using one of the following methods:

✦ **Air cleaning.** Use a strong blast of air from a tool designed especially for cleaning sensors, such as the Giottos Rocket (see figure AA.5). You can also use a clean nasal aspirator or ear syringe. Do not use canned air, which can baste your sensor with propellant, or compressed air, which may be too strong and end up forcing dust underneath the sensor's protective filter. This works well for dust that's not clinging stubbornly to your sensor and should probably always be your first approach.

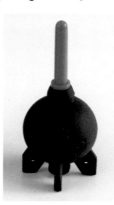

AA.5 An air blower can safely blast off sensor dust.

✦ **Brushing.** Pass a soft, very fine brush across the surface of the sensor's filter, dislodging mildly persistent dust particles and sweeping them off the imager. You can find special brushes designed especially for cleaning sensors that are free of contaminants that might adhere to the sensor.

✦ **Liquid cleaning.** Use a soft swab dipped in a cleaning solution such as ethanol to wipe the sensor filter, removing more obstinate particles. Photographic Solutions' Eclipse is an especially pure solution for this process. You can find inexpensive swabs and other supplies at Web sites such as www.visibledust.com and www.copperhillimages.com.

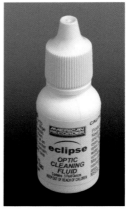

AA.6 Use only a pure solution designed for digital camera cleaning when using swabs to wet-clean your sensor.

Glossary

additive primary colors The red, green, and blue hues that are used alone or in combination to create all other colors that you capture with a digital camera, view on a computer monitor, or work with in an image-editing program, such as Photoshop. See also *CMYK color model*.

AE/AF lock A control on the D40 and D40x that lets you lock the current auto exposure (AE) and/or autofocus (AF) settings prior to taking a picture, freeing you from having to hold the shutter release partially depressed, although you must depress and hold the shutter release partially to apply the feature.

ambient lighting Diffused, nondirectional lighting that doesn't appear to come from a specific source but, rather bounces off walls, ceilings, and other objects in the scene when a picture is taken.

analog/digital converter The electronics built into a camera that convert the analog information captured by the sensor into digital bits that can be stored as an image bitmap.

angle of view The area of a scene that a lens can capture, determined by the focal length of the lens compared to the size of the sensor (or film.) Lenses with a shorter focal length have a wider angle of view than lenses with a longer focal length.

anti-alias A process that smoothes the look of rough edges in images (called *jaggies* or *staircasing*) by adding partially transparent pixels along the boundaries of diagonal lines, which our eyes then merge into smoother lines. See also *jaggies*.

aperture-priority A camera setting that enables you to specify the lens opening or f-stop that you want to use, while the camera selects the required shutter speed automatically based on its light-meter reading. See also *shutter-priority*.

artifact A type of noise in an image, or an unintentional image component produced in error by a digital camera during processing, usually caused by the JPEG compression process in digital cameras.

aspect ratio The proportions of an image as it would be when printed, displayed on a monitor, or captured by a digital camera.

autofocus A camera setting that enables the D40 and D40x to choose the correct focus distance for you, usually based on the contrast of an image (the image is at maximum contrast when it is in sharp focus). You can set your camera for *Single Autofocus* (the lens is not focused until the shutter release is partially depressed) or *Continuous Autofocus* (the lens refocuses constantly as the camera detects subject movement).

autofocus assist lamp A light source built into a digital or film camera that provides extra illumination that the autofocus system can use to focus dimly lit subjects.

averaging meter A light-measuring device that calculates exposure based on the overall brightness of the entire image area. *Averaging* tends to produce the best exposure when a scene is evenly lit or contains equal amounts of bright and dark areas that contain detail. The D40/D40x uses much more sophisticated exposure measuring systems, which are based on center-weighting, spot-reading, or calculating exposure from a matrix of many different picture areas. See also *center-weighted meter* and *spot meter*.

backlighting A lighting effect produced when the main light source is located behind the subject. You can use backlighting to create a silhouette effect or to illuminate translucent objects. See also *frontlighting* and *sidelighting*.

barrel distortion A lens defect, usually found at wide-angle focal lengths, that causes straight lines at the top or side edges of an image to bow outward into a barrel shape. See also *pincushion distortion*.

blooming An image distortion caused when a pixel in an image sensor has absorbed all the photons it can handle, so that additional photons reaching that pixel overflow to affect surrounding pixels, producing unwanted brightness and overexposure around the edges of objects.

blur To soften an image or part of an image by throwing it out of focus, or by allowing it to become soft due to subject or camera motion. You can also apply blur in an image-editing program.

bokeh A buzzword used to describe the aesthetic qualities of the out-of-focus parts of an image. Some lenses produce "good" bokeh while others produce "bad" bokeh. *Boke* is a Japanese word for "blur," and the *h* was added to keep English speakers from rhyming it with *broke*. Out-of-focus points of light become discs, called the *circle of confusion.* Some lenses produce a uniformly illuminated disc. Others, most notably mirror or catadioptic lenses, produce a disc that has a bright edge and a dark center, creating a "doughnut" effect, which is the worst from a bokeh standpoint. Lenses that generate a bright center that fades to a darker edge are more desirable because their bokeh allows the circle of confusion to blend more smoothly with the surroundings. The bokeh characteristics of a lens are most important when you're using selective focus (for example, when shooting a portrait) to deemphasize the background, or when shallow depth of field is a given because you're working with a macro lens, with a long telephoto, or with a wide-open aperture. See also *circle of confusion*.

bounce lighting The light bounced off a reflector, including ceiling and walls, to provide a soft, natural-looking light.

buffer The digital camera's internal memory, where an image is stored immediately after it is taken until it can be written to the camera's nonvolatile (semipermanent) memory or a memory card.

burst mode The digital camera's equivalent of the film camera's motor drive, the burst mode is used to take multiple shots within a short period of time. The D40 can capture up to 2.5 frames per second, while the D40x is capable of 3 frame-per-second bursts.

calibration A process used to correct for the differences in the output of a printer or monitor when the output is compared to the original image. Once you've calibrated your scanner, monitor, and/or your image editor, the images you see on the screen more closely represent what you'll get from your printer, even though calibration is never perfect.

Camera Raw A plug-in included with Photoshop and Photoshop Elements that can manipulate the unprocessed images captured by digital cameras, such as the D40/D40x's Nikon Electronic Files (NEFs).

camera shake The movement of the camera, aggravated by slower shutter speeds, which produces a blurred image. Nikon offers several Vibration Reduction (VR) lenses that shift lens elements to counter this movement, including the 18-200mm VR and 55-200mm VR lenses.

CCD See *charge-coupled device (CCD)*.

center-weighted meter A light-measuring device that emphasizes the area in the middle of the frame when you're calculating the correct exposure for an image. See also *averaging meter* and *spot meter*.

charge-coupled device (CCD) A type of solid-state sensor that captures the image. It is used in scanners and digital cameras, including the Nikon D40/D40x, but not its pro camera sibling, the D2X, which uses a complementary metal-oxide semiconductor (CMOS) sensor.

chromatic aberration An image defect, often appearing as green or purple fringing around the edges of an object, caused by a lens failing to focus all colors of a light source at the same point. See also *fringing*.

circle of confusion A term applied to the fuzzy discs produced when a point of light is out of focus. The circle of confusion is not a fixed size. The viewing distance and amount of enlargement of the image determine whether you see a particular spot on the image as a point or as a disc. See also *bokeh*.

close-up lens A lens add-on that enables you to take pictures at a distance that is less than the closest focusing distance of the lens alone.

CMOS See *complementary metal-oxide semiconductor (CMOS)*.

CMYK color model A way of defining all possible colors in percentages of cyan, magenta, yellow, and, frequently, black. K represents black, to differentiate it from blue in the RGB color model. Black is added to improve renditions of shadow detail. CMYK is commonly used for printing (both on press and with your inkjet or laser color printer).

color correction Changing the relative amounts of color in an image to produce a desired effect, typically a more accurate representation of those colors. Color correction can fix faulty color balance in the original image, or compensate for the deficiencies of the inks used to reproduce the image.

complementary metal-oxide semiconductor (CMOS) A method for manufacturing a type of solid-state sensor that captures the image that is used in scanners and digital cameras such as the Nikon D2X.

compression Reducing the size of a file by encoding, using fewer bits of information to represent the original. Some compression schemes, such as JPEG, operate by discarding some image information, while others, such as TIFF, preserve all the detail in the original, discarding only redundant data.

Continuous-servo Autofocus An automatic focusing setting (AF-C) in which the camera constantly refocuses the image as you frame the picture. This setting is often the best choice for moving subjects. See also *Single-servo Autofocus*.

contrast The range between the lightest and darkest tones in an image. A high-contrast image is one in which the shades fall at the extremes of the range between white and black. In a low-contrast image, the tones are closer together.

dedicated flash An electronic flash unit, such as the Nikon SB-400, SB-600, or SB-800, designed to work with the automatic exposure features of a specific camera.

depth of field (DOF) A distance range in a photograph in which all included portions of an image are at least acceptably sharp.

diaphragm An adjustable component, similar to the iris in the human eye, which can open and close to provide specific-sized lens openings, or f-stops, to control the amount of light striking the film or sensor.

diffused lighting Soft, low-contrast lighting.

digital processing chip A solid-state device found in digital cameras that's in charge of applying the image algorithms to the raw picture data prior to storage on the memory card.

diopter A value used to represent the magnification power of a lens, calculated as the reciprocal of a lens's focal length (in meters). Diopters are most often used to represent the optical correction used in a viewfinder to adjust for limitations of the photographer's eyesight, and to describe the magnification of a close-up lens attachment.

equivalent focal length A digital camera's focal length, which can be translated into the corresponding values for a 35mm film camera if the sensor is smaller than 24 x 36mm. You can calculate this value for lenses you use with the Nikon D40 or D40x by multiplying by 1.5.

exchangeable image file format (Exif) A format that was developed to standardize the exchange of image data between hardware devices and software. A variation on JPEG, Exif is used by most digital cameras, and includes information such as the date and time a photo was taken, the camera settings, the resolution, the amount of compression, and other data.

exposure The amount of light allowed to reach the film or sensor, determined by the intensity of the light, the amount admitted by the iris of the lens, the sensitivity of the sensor (or film), and the length of time determined by the shutter speed.

exposure lock A camera feature that lets you freeze the automatic exposure at the current value.

Exposure Value (EV) EV settings are a way of adding or decreasing exposure without the need to reference f-stops or shutter speeds. For example, if you tell your camera to add +1EV, it provides twice as much exposure, either by using a larger f-stop, a slower shutter speed, or both.

fill lighting In photography, it is the lighting used to illuminate shadows. You can use reflectors or additional incandescent lighting or electronic flash to brighten shadows. One common technique outdoors is to use the camera's flash as a fill.

filter In photography, it is a device that fits over the lens, changing the light in some way. In image editing, it is a feature that changes the pixels in an image to produce blurring, sharpening, and other special effects. The D40/D40x includes several in-camera filters in its Retouch menu, under the Monochrome and Filter Effects sub-menus. Photoshop also includes several interesting filter effects, including Lens Blur and Photo Filters.

firmware The camera's "operating system," which determines how images are exposed, processed, and stored to the memory card, and what features are available in the menus, as well as how menus are displayed. Camera manufacturers such as Nikon issue firmware updates from time to time that you can use to fix bugs or add new features.

flash sync The timing mechanism that insures an internal or external electronic flash fires at the correct time during the exposure cycle. The flash sync speed for a single lens reflex (SLR) is the highest shutter speed that can be used with flash; with the Nikon D40x, it is 1/200 second; the D40 can sync at up to 1/500 second. See also *front-curtain sync* and *rear-curtain sync*.

focal length The distance between the film and the optical center of the lens when the lens is focused on infinity; usually measured in millimeters.

focal plane A line, perpendicular to the optical axis, which passes through the focal point forming a plane of sharp focus when the lens is set at infinity. A focal plane indicator is etched into the Nikon D40 and D40x at the lower-right corner of the top panel next to the Mode dial.

focus lock A camera feature that lets you freeze the automatic focus of the lens at a certain point, when the subject you want to capture is in sharp focus.

focus servo A digital camera's mechanism that adjusts the focus distance automatically. You can set the focus servo to Single-servo Autofocus (AF-S), which focuses the lens only when the shutter release is partially depressed, and Continuous-servo Autofocus (AF-C), which adjusts focus constantly as the camera is used. The Automatic Autofocus (AF-A) setting switches between the two, depending on whether the subject is moving or not.

fringing A chromatic aberration that produces fringes of color around the edges of subjects, caused by a lens's inability to focus the various wavelengths of light onto the same spot. Purple fringing is especially troublesome with backlit images. See also *chromatic aberration*.

front-curtain sync The default kind of electronic flash synchronization technique, originally associated with focal plane shutters, which consist of a traveling set of curtains, including a *front curtain* (which opens to reveal the film or sensor) and a *rear curtain* (which follows at a distance determined by the shutter speed to conceal the film or sensor at the conclusion of the exposure). For a flash picture to be taken, the entire sensor must be exposed at one time to the brief flash exposure, so the image is exposed after the front curtain has reached the other side of the focal plane, but before the rear curtain begins to move. Front-curtain sync causes the flash to fire at the beginning of this period, when the shutter is completely open, in the instant that the first curtain of the focal plane shutter finishes its movement across the film or sensor plane. With slow shutter speeds, this feature can create a blur effect from the ambient light, which appears as patterns that follow a moving subject with the subject shown sharply frozen at the beginning of the blur trail. See also *rear-curtain sync*.

frontlighting The illumination that comes from the direction of the camera. See also *backlighting* and *sidelighting*.

f-stop The relative size of the lens aperture, which helps determine both exposure and depth of field. The larger the f-stop number, the smaller the aperture itself.

graduated filter A lens attachment with variable density or color from one edge to another. A graduated neutral density filter, for example, can be oriented so the neutral density portion is concentrated at the top of the lens's view with the less dense or clear portion at the bottom, thus reducing the amount of light from a very bright sky while not interfering with the exposure of the landscape in the foreground. Graduated filters can also be split into several color sections to provide a color gradient between portions of the image.

gray card A piece of cardboard or other material with standardized 18-percent reflectance. You can use gray cards as a reference for determining correct exposure or for setting white balance.

high contrast A wide range of density in a print, a negative, or another image.

highlights The brightest parts of an image containing detail.

histogram A kind of chart showing the relationship of tones in an image using a series of 256 vertical bars, one for each brightness level. The horizontal axis represents pixel brightness, with dark pixels on the left and bright pixels on the right, while the vertical axis shows the number of pixels in each brightness range. A *histogram chart*, such as the one the D40 and D40x can display during picture review, typically looks like a curve with one or more slopes and peaks, depending on how many highlight, middle, and shadow tones are present in the image.

hot shoe A mount on top of a camera used to hold an electronic flash that provides an electrical connection between the flash and the camera.

hyperfocal distance A point of focus where everything from half that distance to infinity appears to be acceptably sharp. For example, if your lens has a hyperfocal distance of 4 feet, everything from 2 feet to infinity will appear sharp. The hyperfocal distance varies by the lens and the aperture in use. If you know you'll be making a grab shot without warning, sometimes it's useful to turn off your camera's automatic focus, and set the lens to infinity, or, better yet, set the hyperfocal distance. Then, you can snap off a quick picture without having to wait for the lag that occurs with many digital cameras as their autofocus locks in.

image rotation A feature that senses whether a picture was taken in horizontal or vertical orientation. That information is embedded in the picture file so that the camera and compatible software applications can automatically display the image in the correct orientation.

image stabilization A technology, which Nikon calls *vibration reduction*, that compensates for camera shake, usually by adjusting the position of the camera sensor (in some non-Nikon cameras) or lens elements (in the case of Nikon products) in response to movements of the camera.

incident light Illumination falling on a surface.

International Organization for Standardization (ISO) A governing body that provides standards used to represent film speed, or the equivalent sensitivity of a digital camera's sensor. Digital camera sensitivity is expressed in ISO settings.

interpolation A technique digital cameras, scanners, and image editors use to create new pixels that are required whenever you resize or change the resolution of an image based on the values of surrounding pixels. Devices such as scanners and digital cameras can also use interpolation to create pixels in addition to those actually captured, thereby increasing the apparent resolution or color information in an image.

ISO See *International Organization for Standardization (ISO)*.

jaggies The staircasing effect of lines that are not perfectly horizontal or vertical, caused by pixels that are too large to represent the line accurately. See also *anti-alias*.

JPEG A file in lossy format (short for *Joint Photographic Experts Group*) that supports 24-bit color and reduces file sizes by selectively discarding image data. Digital cameras generally use JPEG compression to pack more images onto memory cards. You can select how much compression is used (and,

therefore, how much information is thrown away) by selecting from among the Standard, Fine, Super Fine, or other quality settings your camera offers. See also *RAW*.

Kelvin (K) A unit of measure based on the absolute temperature scale in which absolute zero is zero. It is used to describe the color of continuous-spectrum light sources, and is applied when you set white balance. For example, daylight has a color temperature of about 5500K, and a tungsten lamp has a temperature of about 3400K.

lag time The interval between when the shutter is pressed and when the picture is actually taken. During that span, the camera may be automatically focusing and calculating exposure. With digital single lens reflex (dSLR) cameras such as the Nikon D40 and D40x, lag time is generally very short; with non-dSLRs, the elapsed time easily can be one second or more.

latitude The range of camera exposures that produces acceptable images with a particular digital sensor or film.

lens flare A feature of conventional photography that is both a bane and a creative outlet. It is an effect produced by the reflection of light internally among elements of an optical lens. Bright light sources within or just outside the field of view cause lens flare. Flare can be reduced by the use of coatings on the lens elements or with the use of lens hoods. Photographers sometimes use the effect as a creative technique, and image editors like Photoshop include a filter that lets you add lens flare at your whim.

lighting ratio The proportional relationship between the amount of light falling on the subject from the main light and other lights, expressed in a ratio; for example, 3:1 indicates that the highlight areas of the subject are three times as bright as the shadow areas.

lossless compression An image-compression scheme, such as TIFF, that preserves all image detail. When the image is decompressed, it is identical to the original version.

lossy compression An image-compression scheme, such as JPEG, that creates smaller files by discarding image information, which can affect image quality.

macro lens A lens that provides continuous focusing from infinity to extreme close-ups, often to a reproduction ratio of 1:2 (half life-size) or 1:1 (life-size).

matrix metering A system of exposure calculation that looks at many different segments of an image to determine the brightest and darkest portions. The 3D Color Matrix system used by the D40 and D40x looks at a wide area of the frame and sets exposure according to the distribution of brightness, color, and distance with consideration for the image composition.

midtones Parts of an image with tones of an intermediate value, usually in the 25- to 75-percent range. Many image-editing features enable you to manipulate midtones independently from the highlights and shadows.

mirror lock-up A feature that gives you the capability to retract the single lens reflex's mirror to reduce vibration prior to taking the photo (with some cameras), or, with the Nikon D40 and D40x, access to the sensor for cleaning.

NEF (Nikon Electronic File) Nikon's name for its proprietary RAW format.

neutral color A color in which red, green, and blue are present in equal amounts, producing a gray.

neutral density filter A gray camera filter reducing the amount of light entering the camera without affecting the colors.

noise Pixels with randomly distributed color values in an image. Noise in digital photographs tends to be the product of low-light conditions and long exposures, particularly when you've set your camera to a higher ISO rating than normal.

noise reduction A technology used to cut down on the amount of random information in a digital picture, usually caused by long exposures at increased sensitivity ratings.

normal lens A lens that makes the image in a photograph appear in a perspective that is like that of the original scene.

overexposure A condition in which too much light reaches the film or sensor, producing a dense negative or a very bright/light print, slide, or digital image.

pincushion distortion A type of lens distortion, most often found at telephoto focal lengths, in which lines at the top and side edges of an image are bent inward, producing an effect that looks like a pincushion. See also *barrel distortion*.

polarizing filter A filter that forces light, which normally vibrates in all directions, to vibrate only in a single plane, reducing or removing the specular reflections from the surface of objects.

RAW An image file format, such as the NEF format in the Nikon D40/D40x, which includes all the unprocessed information the camera captures. RAW files are very large compared to JPEG files and must be processed by a special program such as Nikon Capture, Capture NX, or Adobe's

Camera Raw plug-in after being downloaded from the camera. See also *JPEG*.

rear-curtain sync An optional kind of electronic flash synchronization technique, originally associated with focal plane shutters, which consists of a traveling set of curtains, including a *front curtain* (which opens to reveal the film or sensor) and a *rear curtain* (which follows at a distance determined by shutter speed to conceal the film or sensor at the conclusion of the exposure). For a flash picture to be taken, the entire sensor must be exposed at one time to the brief flash exposure, so the image is exposed after the front curtain has reached the other side of the focal plane, but before the rear curtain begins to move. Rear-curtain sync causes the flash to fire at the end of the exposure, an instant before the second or rear curtain of the focal plane shutter begins to move. With slow shutter speeds, this feature can create a blur effect from the ambient light, appearing as patterns that follow a moving subject with the subject shown sharply frozen at the end of the blur trail. If you were shooting a photo of The Flash, the superhero would appear sharp, with a ghostly trail behind him. See also *front-curtain sync*.

red-eye An effect from flash photography that appears to make a person's eyes glow red, or an animal's glow yellow or green. It's caused by light bouncing from the retina of the eye and is most pronounced in dim illumination (when the irises are wide open), and when the electronic flash is close to the lens and, therefore, prone to reflect directly back. The D40/D40x has two red-eye reduction features: One is a bright lamp that glows, causing the subject's pupils to contract (if they are looking at the camera) and the other is a red-eye reduction feature in the Retouch menu. Image editors can fix red-eye by cloning other pixels over the offending red or orange ones.

RGB color model A color model that represents the three colors — red, green, and blue — used by devices such as digital cameras, scanners, or monitors to reproduce color. Photoshop works in RGB mode by default, and even displays CMYK images by converting them to RGB.

saturation The purity of color; the amount by which a pure color is diluted with white or gray.

selective focus Choosing a lens opening that produces a shallow depth of field. Usually this is used to isolate a subject by causing most other elements in the scene to be blurred.

self-timer A mechanism that delays the opening of the shutter for some seconds after the release has been operated.

sensitivity A measure of the degree of response of a film or sensor to light, measured using the ISO setting.

shadow The darkest part of an image, represented on a digital image by pixels with low numeric values.

sharpening Increasing the apparent sharpness of an image by boosting the contrast between adjacent pixels that form an edge.

shutter In a conventional film camera, the shutter is a mechanism consisting of blades, a curtain, a plate, or some other movable cover that controls the time during which light reaches the film. Some digital cameras use actual mechanical shutters for the slower shutter speeds and an electronic shutter for higher speeds.

shutter-priority An exposure mode in which you set the shutter speed and the camera determines the appropriate f-stop. See also *aperture-priority*.

sidelighting Applying illumination from the left or right sides of the camera. See also *backlighting* and *frontlighting*.

Single-servo Autofocus An automatic focusing setting (AF-S) in which the camera locks in focus when you press the shutter release half way. This setting is usually the best choice for stationary subjects. See also *Continuous-servo Autofocus*.

slave unit An accessory flash unit that supplements the main flash, usually triggered electronically when the slave senses the light output from the main unit or through radio waves.

slow sync An electronic flash synchronizing method that uses a slow shutter speed so that ambient light is recorded by the camera in addition to the electronic flash illumination. This enables the background to receive more exposure for a more realistic effect.

specular highlight Bright spots in an image caused by reflection from light sources or a shiny surface.

spot meter An exposure system that concentrates on a small area in the image. See also *center-weighted meter* and *averaging meter*.

subtractive primary colors Cyan, magenta, and yellow, which are the printing inks that theoretically absorb all color and produce black. In practice, however, they generate a muddy brown, so black is added to preserve detail (especially in shadows). The combination of the three colors and black is referred to as CMYK. (K represents black, to differentiate it from blue in the RGB model.)

TIFF (Tagged Image File Format) A standard lossless graphics file format that can be used to store grayscale and color images, plus selection masks. See also *JPEG* and *RAW*.

time exposure A picture taken by leaving the shutter open for a long period, usually more than one second. The camera is generally locked down with a tripod to prevent blur during the long exposure.

through the lens (TTL) A system of providing viewing and exposure calculation through the actual lens taking the picture.

tungsten light Illumination from ordinary room lamps and ceiling fixtures, as opposed to fluorescent illumination.

underexposure A condition in which too little light reaches the film or sensor, producing a thin negative, dark slide, muddy-looking print, or dark digital image.

unsharp masking The process for increasing the contrast between adjacent pixels in an image, boosting sharpness, especially around edges.

vignetting The dark corners of an image, often produced by using a lens hood that is too small for the field of view, using a lens that does not completely fill the image frame, or generating the effect artificially using image-editing techniques, or by using a special attachment that fits in front of the lens.

white balance The adjustment of a digital camera to the color temperature of the light source. Interior illumination is relatively red; outdoor light is relatively blue. Digital cameras often set correct white balance automatically or let you do it through menus. Image editors can often do some color correction of images that were exposed using the wrong white balance setting.

Index

Continued